THE INVISIBLE BESTSELLER

The Invisible Bestseller

Searching for the Bible in America

KENNETH A. BRIGGS

WILLIAM B. EERDMANS PUBLISHING COMPANY
GRAND RAPIDS, MICHIGAN

Wm. B. Eerdmans Publishing Co.
2140 Oak Industrial Drive N.E., Grand Rapids, Michigan 49505

© 2016 Kenneth A. Briggs
All rights reserved
Published 2016
Printed in the United States of America

22 21 20 19 18 17 16   1 2 3 4 5 6 7

Library of Congress Cataloging-in-Publication Data

Names: Briggs, Kenneth A., author.
Title: The invisible bestseller : searching for the Bible in America / Kenneth A. Briggs.
Description: Grand Rapids, Michigan : Eerdmans Publishing Company, 2016. |
Includes bibliographical references and index.
Identifiers: LCCN 2016008041 | ISBN 9780802869135 (cloth : alk. paper)
Subjects: LCSH: Bible—History. | Bible—Criticism, interpretation, etc.—United States. |
United States—Religion. | United States—Church history.
Classification: LCC BS511.3 .B75 2016 | DDC 220.0973—dc23
LC record available at https://lccn.loc.gov/2016008041

www.eerdmans.com

To Walter A. Briggs (1882–1968)

Grandfather

Bible reader

Contents

Acknowledgments

My deep appreciation extends to everyone who agrees to help fill in the vast gaps in my understanding of what I'm writing about. Agreeing to take time to explain, to explore, to supplement, and to testify is an act of generosity and trust that I hope never to take for granted. In that regard, I'm thankful to everyone who came to my aid in writing about a subject, the Bible, which proved much more elusive than I'd ever imagined. This survey of benefactors doesn't include everyone I was fortunate to engage, but if you are among the unnamed you belong to the circle every bit as much. It would be well-nigh impossible to cite everyone. That doesn't presume that contributors will agree with my conclusions, but I have endeavored to represent everyone justly.

For perspective on the backdrop of the Bible's status, America's religious character, history, and trends, I read widely among the many superb scholars in the field. Among those from whom I gained immeasurably are Robert Bellah, Stephen Prothero, Mark Noll, Chris Smith, and Robert Wuthnow. For discerning the interpretive stages and turns in the Bible's place in Western Christianity I was especially enlightened by Charles Taylor's magnum opus, *A Secular Age,* Michael Legaspi's superb text, *The Decline of Scripture and the Rise of Biblical Studies*, the late Hans Frei's *The Eclipse of Biblical Narrative*, and various writings of Walter Brueggemann and Stanley Hauerwas. Marcus Borg explicated his bold critique of biblical literalism. Gary Anderson of Notre Dame astutely led me through the latter-day debates over canon in the wake of Brevard Child's influence. Many others echoed and enlarged such themes, among them Jacques Berlinerblau of Georgetown University, who raises crucial questions about the Bible's role in secular culture.

Key figures in Bible-related institutions played an indispensable part in lending analysis to causes of striking trends and their impact. The venerable American Bible Society was in the forefront of patient efforts to shape my perspectives. In particular, Philip Towner and Joseph Crockett, principal researchers in the ABS headquarters, spent considerable time and expertise to indulge me in long conversation about where the Bible now belongs in a country where the Bible has been a cornerstone. Colleagues Mark Forshaw, Ellen Strohm, and others from the Global Scripture Impact division similarly welcomed me to discuss solutions to the growing problems of lost readership.

The "what do we do about it?" alarm is spawning a cottage industry of experiment and innovation. Among those who occupy this territory is the creative bundle of energy Bobby Gruenewald, founder of the YouVersion digital Bible, which has led the way in providing an alternative for the cyber generation (and beyond). Talks with him were ventures in thinking disruptively about the survival and future of Bible reading. Likewise, Phil Collins and Steve Bird at Taylor University shared the initial steps of their research into the actual reading habits of evangelical students. Among the increasing number of studies of Bible awareness, none has been more vigorous than at the Barna survey center in California, where David Kinnaman, its magnetic director, passionately made his case for dramatic change in churches in order to win back disaffected millennials. From their vantage point at Huntington University, professors Mark Fairchild, Kent Eilers, and Tom Bergler candidly spelled out the mounting challenges to Bible study at Huntington University, a closely knit Christian college whose struggles have proved typical. Other campus visits with faculty and students indeed amplified and supplemented their experience. Lynn Cohick at Wheaton, Jennifer Knust at Boston University, and Joel Kaminsky at Smith were superb observers of how the subject appeared in their surroundings. Shane Kirkpatrick at Anderson University was unusually instructive in his caring warning about the state of the Bible among those who presume to know it by virtue of their deep immersion in Bible-based churches.

The continuing skirmish over the Bible's origins and meaning streams through this book and required considerable tutoring. For comprehensive oversight of modern critical interpretations, nothing compares to the Society of Biblical Literature, a scholarly association that stems from academia's focus on scientific research. The growing influence of biblical literalists has caused tensions, however, and John Kutsko, the executive director of SBL, was of great assistance in sorting out those and other problems and initiatives in the dynamic organization. Ben Wright, a Hebrew Bible eminence at Lehigh University, was a far-reaching and faithful consultant.

Years ago, an adventurous project called the Jesus Seminar tested the limits to which daring research might go. Over lunch in Chicago, Lynn McGaughy, a distinguished Bible scholar who has been active with the Seminar since its inception, recalled the movement's drama and controversy with fondness and reverie, allowing that the SBL had long since parted company with it.

I'm indebted to many scholars for helping me appraise the strengths and weaknesses of historical-critical approaches to the Bible. While the method continues to be sharply divisive, a growing minority occupies middle ground, neither spurning scientific research nor accepting its results as wholly conclusive without assigning credibility to the claims of faith. Among those who spoke to that complexity most persuasively was Kathleen O'Connor of Columbia Theological Seminary in Georgia.

My travels across the country also placed me among many stout defenders of the Bible's trustworthy accuracy: churches, Bible studies, evangelistic rallies, college conferences, and the like. Invariably the welcome was warm. Hundreds converged at the annual National Religious Broadcasts convention in Nashville. One of those who attended, a lanky, good-natured man named Eric Nichols, hosted radio shows on a Christian station in Lima, Ohio, and depicted with great effect the mission of a radio evangelist whose audience was less and less biblically literate. The number-one watchword among Christian broadcasters: pious music works much better than preaching these days. John Ware, the dynamo founder of the adventurous *268 Film Project* in Burbank, California, acquainted me with an initiative to promote the Bible in the medium of Bible-centered movies, which are experiencing a modest comeback.

I was privileged to talk with scores of random people at some depth about the Bible as they saw it personally and socially. They had so much to say. Their names are found in the text, and I am grateful to them all. I cannot name everyone here, but some include Natan Bourkoff, Bernie Jones, Wayne Turney ("The Gospel of Mark"), Rachel Held Evans, George Guthrie ("Read the Bible for Life"), Gary Swanson ("Tinseltown Ministries"), Ron Storey, Jeremy Myers ("Till He Comes"), Fr. Charles Norman, Bill O'Brian ("The Alternative Seminary"), the Rev. Mark Harder, the Rev. Pat Coughlin, Nadine Pence, Margaret Miles, Heidi Campbell (Texas A&M), Anna Florence (Columbia Theological Seminary), Lawrence Waters,

Emerson Hamsa, Chris Phillips, and Andy and Peggy Brimer and their wonderful Bible-living family.

My good fortune in doing this book owes substantially to the counsel and friendship of my esteemed agent, Bob Markel, a consummate curator of anecdotes. Eerdmans provided an extraordinary setting in which to develop this book. Jon Pott extended the original invitation with his customary graciousness and encouragement before his retirement; Reinder Van Til edited the manuscript with an adroitness of eye and ear that authors dream about; and Jenny Hoffman has calmly guided me and overseen the many gifted contributors to the development of the final product. They have been a joy to work with.

And, lest it go without saying, my affection to Mary P. Beckman, the beloved supporter.

Introduction

My Bible alert sounded when I was a third-grader wrapped in an itchy brown wool suit seated in a pew midway down the aisle of a shoebox-sized Methodist church in East Templeton, Massachusetts — population 300, more or less. Up to that point I hadn't paid it particular attention, but without notice it began showing up in my thoughts like a visitor repeatedly knocking on the door.

Like practically all Americans in the post–World War II religious boom, our family went to church on Sunday mornings — worship combined with social occasions for both grownups and kids. Though the kids were generally out of place as participants, it was hoped they would absorb enough to keep them coming to church beyond the age of consent. Containing their restlessness could tax a parent's powers of attention to the limit.

Overall, I rather liked church, without admitting it, because it offered rewards I found nowhere else. My love of singing found an outlet in the grand, multiversed hymns; the sermon appealed to my appetite for hearing what life was about; and the prayers gave me assurance that I wasn't alone in seeking mercy and peace. Hearing words of encouragement and forgiveness was an inspiration — even for an eight-year-old. My work-in-progress soul was thereby scrub-brushed along with the others, at least for the time being, and the effect was light and refreshing. It wasn't always smooth sailing. One memorable incident featured my brother, then a toddler with a cast on his foot for a broken toe, bursting the solemnity of silent prayer by bellowing out the jingle of a popular radio beer commercial, "Time Out for Dawson's." My parents turned green, but the teetotaling church people were in stitches.

Meanwhile, the centerpiece of the sanctuary, the supersized King James Bible, stood vigil on the pulpit, bound in black leather with gold lettering, opened at the source of the verses selected for this Sunday's reading. It was honored as the wellspring of truth, though few claimed to know more than snippets from its catalog of sixty-six books from Genesis to Revelation. The minister was the Bible's designated handler by dint of his education and his ordination. Laypeople willingly deferred. Our family's unfamiliarity with it was probably more typical than scholars of the nation's revival might have assumed. A copy of Scripture occupied an honored place next to the grocery store encyclopedias on a bookshelf in the living room. It was treated as if it were a holy object that humans were forbidden to touch. At no time in my memory was it ever removed, except when we moved or when we read it out loud. It remained virtually pristine: respected, even venerated, just not picked up and studied.

Looking back, I think the main reason messages from Sunday Scripture readings began sticking in my mind was that they seemed to me just what my *parents* needed to hear. A higher authority was amplifying and upgrading my pointers on how parents and other grownups could better grasp what the Lord actually wanted them to do. It was as if I were a lowly relay station forwarding advice they had somehow missed regarding behavioral and attitude adjustments that would benefit everyone, including God and, not surprisingly, their kids. Later it struck me that those lessons were meant first and foremost for me rather than the older generations, but at the time it seemed to be my role in making things better conform to my wishes.

My alert was most often triggered by Bible passages involving fairness, as I construed it at that time, especially the lack of it. When the Old Testament prophets, the psalmists, Jesus, and Saint Paul put fools and evildoers in their place, I was inwardly cheered and comforted. The situations portrayed often sounded like ones I experienced in everyday life and needed the same remedies that I was happy to silently boost in the spirits of my fellow pew-sitters. A kinder, gentler existence seemed possible if this advice were heard and adopted. In that process I was eager to serve as an errand boy.

The basic terrain on which this juvenile messianic role-playing ensued was family and neighborhood, but there was another, vaguer application of the Bible's passion for justice in the wider community in which I grew up in the 1940s and 1950s. The town wrestled with working-class scarcities of money and opportunity. In the aftermath of World War II, many veterans returned with heavy emotional burdens to jobs mostly in sawdust-clouded furniture factories (and fell ill to related diseases, which the medical profession generally preferred not to discuss). Collectively, given their circumstances (including "battle fatigue," which drove some to suicide), the best many could do was muster a sense of resignation. Scratching out a living meant long hours and scant wages for making top-of-the-line living room suites, dining room tables, and elegant chairs and couches for national distribution. Owners made good profits. It was widely believed that the noticeable inequalities reflected the natural order of merit; claims of injustice were always close to the surface but rarely voiced. My church professed a tradition founded by John Wesley, who ministered to the mineworkers under duress in England and left a legacy of social consciousness. Many men in our congregation made furniture and heard appeals from Methodist social teachings — beyond, I must add, the crusade against drinking, with which it was most identified in the public mind. Without being ideological, the church's basic sympathies were with the poor and neglected as God's special mission, making me particularly susceptible to the denunciations of injustice by Jeremiah, Isaiah, Amos, Ezekiel, and the other giant prophets. Children have an elemental concern for justice, perhaps owing to their disadvantages as small people, so my response could be expected. The outcries of those furious ancient critics left lasting impressions that fueled my later fervor for the civil rights movement and related causes.

Hearing Jesus bless the poor and the peacemakers and raise poor old Lazarus from the dead also stood common sense on its head, making "winners" out of "losers," making the "weak" stronger than the "powerful," and making the "last" come "first." Powerful stuff if it could be believed: the possibility that reality was the opposite of what it appeared to be. The Bible seemed to say, "Now hear this, earthlings, get with the program or else." Some always did listen, of course, and that's what made for hope. Every church I ever attended was inspired by those "saints" who humbly exuded goodness while never calling attention to themselves. As an insignificant messenger of Scripture, I only hoped that everyone around me heard the advice and heeded it.

The dawning of a bigger picture of what life could be and should be was the most influential gift I ever received, and I owed it to the Bible, or at least what I gleaned from it. My ability to see clearly is always distorted by ego and circumstances, but at least I'm more aware when self-serving tendencies go too far. Whatever my foibles and the Bible's enigmas, Scripture remains fundamental to my understanding of life.

That impact has stirred curiosity about the place the Bible occupies in the lives of Americans as individuals and within the nation itself. General observation and social surveys make clear that its place has diminished dramatically in recent decades. My purpose in writing this book is to look for reasons for this decline and to find where and how that disappearance makes a difference. From the Bible's once being widely honored as the source of America's character, it has largely receded from public view, though it endures in every village as a source of rebirth. Meanwhile, has anything replaced it where it no longer prevails?

My grappling with the Bible was slow and fitful. It took many years before I became anything close to a student of it with all its enigmas and complexities. But the cultural trends at the time encouraged me to do so. For Protestants especially, the Bible is touted as essential reading, however much that counsel is ignored, as the fount of structure and meaning for us as individuals and for what we stand for as a society. Clearly, that status has eroded considerably as society's overall enthusiasm for the Bible has waned. As a journalist who has written about religion in America and beyond for decades, I have attempted to understand where the Bible has gone over that span of time. This was an alluring project not just as a relatively untold piece of cultural history but as the prelude to a future where a working knowledge of Scripture has been largely foreign to American Christianity. With that in mind, I gathered evidence of the Bible's status in today's America for two years — beginning in the spring of 2012. My choice of people, settings, and forum was prompted largely by instinct and clue; thus I claim no scientific or comprehensive method. I admire biblical scholars and theologians, but I don't qualify to be a member of either group. To the extent possible, I set aside foregone conclusions and rooting interests for the sake of getting it right. Many of the people and places portrayed in these pages are special in themselves and do not blend easily into generalizations. Yet I hope that the various witnesses and vantage points draw a reasonably accurate picture.

I set out to discover what has become of the holy book that Abe Lincoln called the "greatest gift God has ever given to man," and where it figures into a contemporary America fraught with restlessness and uncertainty. My hope is that it might inspire discussions of where we go from here.

CHAPTER 1

America's Bible:
Loving It and Leaving It

Newspaper reporters, especially before the advent of online editions, had a quixotic way of responding to readers who complained that they had seen no trace of a certain story in that day's paper. The reporter might quip, "You'll have to excuse them, they buried it on page one" — hidden, as it were, in plain sight.

The Bible has had a similar fate. While it is everywhere in America — an average of four or five editions in every US household — and is a standard item in public places from libraries to court houses, it is also famously unlikely to be noticed, let alone picked up and read. It has increasingly become the most revered, invisible feature of our surroundings. It is everywhere and nowhere. As Philip Towner, head of the American Bible Society's research institute, liked to say: "It's not the age of Bible reading anymore; it's the age of Bible buying."

Though that trend has been in the works, it has accelerated at a faster rate in recent years than at any time anyone can remember. The "Mother Book" of the United States is receding from the grip of its children. For more than half the decades since the American Revolution, the Bible dispensed to the fledgling democracy what Dr. Benjamin Spock would later provide for raising American children: sound guidelines for health and moral worthiness in service of higher purposes. The bond between Scripture and citizen survived the torturous test of the Civil War only because North and South found their own ways to decipher key passages to justify their own causes. Lincoln preserved its sanctity in his Second Inaugural and Gettysburg addresses. By the early twentieth century, however, reliance on the Bible was eroding in the face of competing concepts of "success" that were driven by this-worldly yearnings. A further loosening of the bond stemmed from the influx of Catholic immigrants, whose tradition placed little emphasis on personal involvement with the Bible.

The Bible's reputation as a bulwark of unadulterated truth was also weakening. European Bible scholars, especially Germans, have for nearly two hundred years used scientific means to peel away the layers of text to discover its origins and meaning. Its composition was often found to be contrary to what had been assumed: for example, rather than Moses being the sole author of the Pentateuch (the first five books — Genesis, Exodus, Leviticus, Numbers, and Deuteronomy), as tradition had declared, prominent scholars now reported that many hands had been involved in supplying the contents of the Pentateuch over a long stretch of history, and sometimes they contradicted each other. By similar analysis, Isaiah was said not to be written by a single prophet but to be made up of separate sections by different authors. Likewise, the New Testament accounts of Jesus could no longer be assumed to be historically accurate, according to research professors; many of his sayings were added later, they concluded. Most shocking, some of these scholars touched off prolonged debate by questioning whether Jesus had even existed and, if so, how accurate the Bible's portrayal of him was. These conclusions from a rising cohort of Bible researchers were denounced as heretical and the work of the devil by much of the religious establishment and many ordinary people in the pew. But the scholars had raised doubts about the Bible's credibility that would not go away. The belief that Scripture was essentially written by God still held sway, but the new scholarship combined with the growing impact of Darwin's theory of evolution to evoke a strong alternative view as to how the world — and the Bible — had come about.

The debates that raged over the Bible's nature and authority had little noticeable effect on its standing as the Mother Book during the first half of the twentieth century. As much as they may have fought over convictions *about* the Bible's authenticity and its degree of absolute truth, liberals and fundamentalists alike honored it as the keeper of the American soul. A less obvious gap was widening, however, between near universal acclaim and personal use. The "American dream" of achievement, success, and wealth overlapped with the Bible's emphases on virtue, redemption, and justice to some extent; but that dream also promoted values such as individualism and self-gain that arguably clashed with scriptural appeals for the common good and self-giving. In this outlook, piety was one thing, profits were quite another. It was a house divided into competing versions of how the Bible fit into the realm of getting and spending. If the manifestoes issued by Moses in the desert and by Jesus in the Sermon on the Mount are clearly opposed to the economic and social practices of the globe's emerging powerhouse, that might force tough choices for the Bible's most ardent devotees.

In pragmatic terms, that tension could not be allowed to threaten the republic's experiment in free enterprise. The easiest solution was to decide that Scripture had nothing to do with economics and pertained almost exclusively to private rather than public life. The overlapping alternative was to argue that there was no "tension" because the Bible advocated American-style capitalism as part of God's plan. New England Calvinists' linkage between piety and prosperity is often either praised or blamed for helping give rise to this. It was another in a centuries-old series of efforts to rationalize practices of particular societies — from slavery to the divine right of kings. Biblical theology creatively minimized or eliminated obstacles.

No precedent exactly fit the America of unbridled ambition and feverish commerce. It was a new kind of laboratory whose founding documents drew on biblical concepts more consciously than any country ever had. Of course, Scripture was replete with stories directly concerned with economic relations. Several cite employer-worker issues that remain fresh; for example, the unjust steward who cheated his helper was always somewhere in the picture and forever a louse. Meanwhile, the engine of free enterprise rapidly established itself as the unquestioned economic system of the nation. Bless the nation; bless the vigorous economy generating new definitions of success. The rise of corporate behemoths such as US Steel and Ford Motor created a world apart, with Adam Smith's *Wealth of Nations* on its altar. By the mid-nineteenth century, says Mark Noll, noted historian of American Christianity, the churches had essentially "lost" any influence or jurisdiction they might have had over the nation's free-enterprise juggernaut, no matter how its principles and practices might have violated biblical teaching. With few exceptions, the churches ceded the workplace issues and financial welfare of their members to economic forces, with their own systems of right and wrong — virtually independent of biblical review. For some, it was abject surrender; for others, it was a sign of God's plan that blessed the economy as part of that harmonic design, complementing the divine gift of democracy. That bolstered the mythological "American Way of Life" that summoned succeeding generations.

Over the long process of narrowing the Bible's values to the realm of personal life, there was less room for the voices insisting that the fulfillment of Scripture required justice in the social and political spheres. The drive to reform prisons, mental institutions, and family services did inspire profound and heroic efforts in the name of the Bible, the greatest outpouring of those efforts occurring during and after the Civil War. As exemplary as those efforts were, however, they were not common. The main job of Scripture in the nineteenth century was seen as what it had been since Jamestown: the conversion of individuals.

A focused and feisty challenge to the narrowness of the above view had arisen by the turn of the twentieth century in the form of the "Social Gospel" movement, which was inspired by the passion and intellect of Walter Rauschenbusch, a Baptist minister and professor who was at one time the pastor of a church in the Hell's Kitchen section of New York. (He fell ill and went deaf as the result of visiting an ailing church member one freezing Christmas Eve, but kept preaching at the church.) At the heart of the Social Gospel movement was Rauschenbusch's view that biblical salvation involved more than personal redemption: it also meant bringing justice and well-being to society — "saving" it from its evils of greed and abuse — in order to bring about life together in a godly manner of fairness, sufficiency, and decency. The appeal to building a broader biblical vision of a more just society caught on mostly among Protestants from the old pedigreed denominations (Presbyterians, Methodists, Episcopalians, and American Baptists, etc.), a coalition of theological liberalism that used the Bible's texts to assess public policy.

At about the same time, a similar focus was sharpening in the Roman Catholic Church. Pope Leo XIII began what became known as "Catholic social teaching" by instructing Catholics to heed the gospel's call for justice among workers, stoutly defending their right to form unions. The pope's bold initiative, an encyclical letter called *Rerum Novarum* ("Rights and Duties of Capital and Labor"), issued in 1891, also warned that the rights of private property were limited by the need to bolster the common good. Pope Leo and his successors thereby served notice to American Catholics that the Bible's priorities went far beyond concern for the individual soul.

These church-based efforts to reform political, social, and economic conditions became more or less embedded in those traditions, peaking later, during the era of activism for civil rights and against the Vietnam War. Yet they remained distinctly minority lobbies within the dominant conviction of Americans that Bible lessons pretty much endorsed American values without any need for major correction. In the main, Scripture was seen as the blueprint for what policy-makers and industry leaders practiced. Moral crusades were sometimes deemed necessary to bring the country back to its biblical standards, but churchgoers on the whole did not believe that the system itself was seriously out of kilter and were mostly passive in this regard.

Compatibility between the Bible and free enterprise was so accepted in most churches that it hardly needed mentioning. On the other hand, the fervent "gospel of prosperity" drive's success depends on high visibility and dramatic pitches. It has been championed most recently by television preachers such as Joel Osteen and the Copeland couple, Kenneth and Gloria, who assure viewers that the God of the Bible can repay their faith with material "abundance." God wants them to be rich, as astonishing as that may seem, and they have come to the right place for guidance. Of course, it may entail sending a few spare dollars to the TV evangelists as seed money.

Looking back from the millennial year 2000, the Bible's primary use as a means of saving souls and serving as a silent junior partner in the American market enterprise has not changed much over the past century, though Americans are much less familiar with what is actually in it. Otherwise, the Bible's blessings are still widely bestowed, covertly at least, on the country's wars, legislatures, and ever-escalating material hungers. Liberal Christians may cry "foul," but only a few show up with their own biblical reasoning to counter the prevailing conformity. Income inequality has grown, food-stamp programs have been slashed, racial tensions have flared, but no Martin Luther Kings have appeared, Bible in hand, to demand an end to the injustices they perceive. Conservative Christians, on the other hand, campaign for their own version of justice: a cluster of issues such as ending abortion and banning gay marriage, which focus on "personal" rather than "structural" sin, as they consistently emphasize.

For more and more Americans, the Bible has become a museum exhibit, hallowed as a treasure but enigmatic and untouched. Snippets of its language still pop up occasionally in political speeches, as anachronistic as that appears to have become. But overall, the Bible is overridden by consumer appetites and a growing array of lifestyles that, implicitly at least, offer ways of thinking about life, love, and work that have left the Bible behind.

That rapid shrinkage became striking to me as I began researching this book, but by no means does it adequately account for the big picture. Another side of the story is obvious to anyone who sees "Bible" churches popping up across the landscape or watches television revivals, or has noticed, even cursorily, that a profusion of Bible versions styled for everyone from firefighters to teenage girls still sell tens of millions of copies every year. Millions of one's neighbors regularly trot off to Bible study in the middle of the week, strange as that may seem to some. According to CNN Money, though it is read less, the Bible continues to be the most admired book in the nation and the one most often stolen. Fewer Americans evidently delve into it, according to the polls, but for a significant portion of them it is a lifeline. Interviews with a wide variety of them have revealed that they do not neatly fit the common "Bible-thumper" stereotype of rural dwellers whose faith in the Bible has never been "educated" out of them. In fact, the mix includes believers of every class, race, and circumstance who are adjusting themselves to the odd realization that they are religiously out of the mainstream.

Their Bible is not being phased out; it is being repositioned in a culture less willing to pay even lip service to it — or to religion itself — as reflexive tokens of citizenship. Bible lovers accept that their fellow workers and neighbors probably know little to nothing about it. There isn't much illusion that assumes otherwise. Their efforts to spread the Word usually begin with the assumption that they are starting from scratch.

Some imponderables are beyond the scope of this book. Does it matter, for instance, whether America no longer has a Mother Book? Is that anything to be alarmed about? If it has been retired to the archives, do we need a replacement? And has one appeared? (Maybe and no.) If the Bible is allegedly the source of our morality, how seriously has it been emulated, and what kind of life has it produced? If we no longer rely on Scripture for our behavioral ideals, what are we using instead? And is it better or worse than what we have had before? (Pragmatism mostly, individual choices.) For a great deal of our history, after all, we as a society sanctioned slavery, practiced racial discrimination, tolerated child labor, annihilated Native Americans, treated women as second-class citizens and barred them from voting, and criminalized homosexuality. If that was an ethical golden age, perhaps we may do no better, but we could hardly do worse.

Has the Bible shaped our national character so definitively that, if it were passing from the scene, we would be reshaped by forces we don't understand? Is the Bible, in fact, fading away — except for those pockets where it has thrived? Or is it becoming as prominent as it was — but in a new guise? If its privileged place has been lost, does it still influence public affairs to any significant degree?

It would be difficult, probably impossible, to prove that it does. Any resemblance between America and the Bible's prescriptions for the Promised Land seem far-fetched, even delusional. Christians and Jews differ sharply over how the Bible's standards apply to public policy, but agree on what those ethics are and how callously we ignore them. At least a quarter of our children are malnourished, to which the response has been to slash food-stamp allotments. Despite President Obama's health plan, basic, humane coverage remains out of reach for tens of millions. War has been waged for trumped-up reasons and with conscience-numbing weapons. The widening income sinkhole between the well-to-do and poor people, which multiplies the hardship, evokes nothing resembling the psalmists' outrage against inhumanity from self-described "Bible churches." As of May 2013, the National Poverty Center at the University of Michigan reports that more than 600,000 households are extremely poor (living on less than $2 a day); public school segregation is worsening; the class-based, two-track legal system imprisons disproportionate numbers of poor black and Hispanic males. Gun murders continue to wreak havoc, while the most modest of proposed limits to toting guns are undermined by the National Rifle Association. This is to say nothing of attacks on the common good from monstrous banks, corporate lobbies, and tax loopholes. This was not the design proposed by the Sermon on the Mount or Isaiah's prophecy. About the only time the Bible becomes public is when leaders of specific moral causes, such as opposition to abortion and gay rights, cherry-pick Scripture for passages they believe buttress their arguments. Otherwise, the Bible has effectively dropped out of public life.

Perhaps it is not coincidental that the quasi-religious mythology is also under attack. The 1960s critique of the nation's ideals, coupled with the bitterness of Vietnam, has deflated post–World War II confidence; subsequent scandals and racial strife have put further dents in the trophy of exceptionalism that the country has awarded itself. As the Bible's luster has dimmed, so has America's. Was a society created in the Bible's image facing a similar, even related, crisis of authority?

"Individualism," abetted by a long history of support from person-centered religion, provides a catchall term for the engine driving this cultural distancing from the Bible. The primacy of "self" clashes with the Bible's central concern that the "many" build true community. Some Christians contribute to a personal focus by feeding a market that draws on the Bible to foster self-help. It chimes in with increasing euphoria for success through the free-market lure of personal riches.

I undertook this book from a desire to explore where the Bible has moved since the time in my boyhood when it was implanted as a lens that colored my view of life from then on. Does Scripture remain a convincing source of the meaning of life for young people in a digital climate where the Internet itself has become, for many, the talisman (equivalent) of otherworldliness?

Meanwhile, it must have startled most American Bible users to learn that about half of the yearly US sales of paper Bibles (estimated at about 25 million) were printed in China, one of the last bastions of official atheism and a country that has put the clamps on the Bible's dissemination. Bible publishers have joined the rush to outsource for cost-cutting reasons similar to those of shoemakers, tire manufacturers, and other corporations. It started, back in 1987, with an agreement between the umbrella group United Bible Societies and the Amity Bible Company in China (the sole printer that China allows to print Bibles). By 2013, Amity reported printing a whopping 117 million Bibles for Americans, 12.4 million in the past year.

The chapters that follow attempt to sketch some answers to such seeming anomalies and questions that have arisen from my hankering to explore where the Bible has gone and why. To that end, I traveled to several parts of the country and talked to people who saw Scripture from a wide variety of observation platforms: from one-room assisted-living quarters to church pews, from coffee shops to golf courses, anywhere people were willing to share their impressions and insights about Scripture. Within these pages, I have incorporated the generous words and thoughts of scores of witnesses, some bonded with the Bible and others ignorant or dismissive of it, an assortment of Bible-study participants, university classrooms and scholars, a pile of surveys, hours of sermons on deciphering Bible texts, books on key aspects of the "crisis," and analyses by experts on the culture's impact on Scripture. In cases where subjects expressed qualms about being identified, I have substituted pseudonyms for their real names. Where personal reflections overlapped, I have compressed them for the sake of readability.

I would like each chapter to mirror one or more of several themes that I culled from the sources and that became working hypotheses. Among them:

- The Bible speaks a language of otherworldliness and transcendence that fewer people still speak. A colossal change has evidently taken place that makes it less possible for contemporary people to believe in anything that doesn't pertain to the world of our immediate senses of taste, touch, sight, smell, and feel. The Bible has become a tough sell.
- The Bible's impact depends on what readers believe about its origins — divine, human, or a mix of the two. Those who contend that God alone wrote it — and that it is thus without errors — face mounting

opposition from Christians who have accepted scientific analyses of that development, including most leading Bible scholars.

- Bible reading has declined precipitously across virtually all Christian groups, even among those, such as evangelicals, who put great emphasis on it.
- Bible promoters responsible for blanketing the country with Scripture have sounded alarms at the recognition that fewer and fewer of those who receive Bibles ever read them — and the shock of that is leading to joint strategies to reverse the threat.
- Young people, even evangelicals, have triggered the biggest worry as they have shunned both the church and the Bible in numbers that are unnerving to church elders. Reaching them has become the feverish mission of such new media as Bible Apps, which has made the entire Bible instantly available by a click on a smart phone.
- Cultural motives for learning Scripture have existed side by side with religious incentives. Educators and civic leaders, arguing that knowledge of the Bible is essential for people to have in order to grasp the Western tradition, are stepping up efforts to teach students biblical references in literature and history books. The learning is meant to enhance an understanding of the Western tradition while remaining impartial toward religion itself.
- As biblical literacy has decreased, churches have reduced the Bible's place in worship and congregational life. A growing tendency has been to minimize Scripture and to go straight to Jesus, though the only near contemporary information about his person and mission comes from the New Testament.
- Fundamentalist certainty that the Bible contains no errors is suffering not only defections but also divisions within its own ranks; meanwhile, the defenders of a literal reading of Genesis as the true account of creation have continued to fend off traditional Christian "modernists," who accept scientific explanations for the universe's origins.
- Movies and television are once again featuring biblical subjects after a long hiatus. *America's Bible Challenge* on the Game Show Network and the major film production of *Noah* are among the most notable. Their impact was largely to rally believers rather than attract converts.

However its place has shifted, the Bible has remained a prize collectors' item. On September 8, 2012, applause erupted in London's Omega

Auction House when one of Elvis Presley's autographed, household King James Bibles sold for $94,600, nearly twice the estimated top bid. That Bible, a gift to Presley from an uncle in 1957 and one of dozens distributed throughout the house, contained hand-jotted notes. Among them: "To judge a man by his weakest link or deed is like judging the power of the ocean by one wave." Less than a year later, on June 25, 2013, Einstein's Bible, signed by him in 1932, brought $68,500 at Bonham's in New York. The anticipated price was pegged at $2,500 at best. The master physicist, who claimed no religious beliefs, once said that the Bible was "a great source of wisdom and consolation, and should be read frequently."

CHAPTER 2

The Story Told by Numbers

If you'd snooped around the homes of Americans in early 2014, you would have found that 88 percent of them had at least one Bible; more than a third contained two or three; 22 percent owned at least half a dozen. A cascade of other vital signs were to tumble from the yearly "State of the Bible" report, a bellwether statement in the vast enterprise of Bible publication, consumption, and evangelism, the redoubtable American Bible Society's version of the Index of Leading Economic Indicators.

Prepared by the Barna Group, a California polling firm for the nation's oldest Bible promoter (dating back to 1812), the report cast an eye on religious groups — eager to see which way the spiritual weathervanes were pointing — and on the broader society, whose curiosity about recent reversals in religion's fortunes had been piqued. Whether or not Americans actually read it, most people still hold the Bible in the highest esteem and believe that they have picked up its main points along the way. Eight of ten Americans (79 percent) regard it as a sacred book, far outdistancing their regard for the Qur'an (13 percent), the Torah (7 percent), and the Book of Mormon (5 percent); even so, that is 10 percent lower than it was just a few years ago. Reflecting the stronger readership on the part of conservatives, the King James Version, celebrating its four hundredth anniversary in 2011, tops the list of favored editions (34 percent), followed by the similarly oriented New International Version and the somewhat modified "New" King James Version. Whatever version they choose — or don't choose — 50 percent say that the Bible has all the answers to life's important questions. Clearly, the Bible is still cherished, but fewer Americans are very familiar with it or reflexively venerate it. Its significance has always differed among the various confessional groups: from Protestant (inspirational) to Catholic (distant), from liberal Protestant (heady) to evangelical (reverential), from older people (habitual) to younger ones (incidental), from the South (incessant) to the West (marginal) — those distinctions have been widening, according to the surveys, and there are more people outside the circle of those for whom the Bible matters at all.

Though several other surveys have produced sensational headlines showing that Americans have a dismal grasp of Bible facts, seven in ten people (69 percent) consider themselves "moderately knowledgeable." Unsurprisingly, Bible readers remain most prevalent in the South (63 percent) and the Midwest (53 percent); those percentages drop to 46 percent in the Northeast and 48 percent in the West.

Several findings emphasize a continuing slide. The latest shows that nearly half (47 percent) say they never read the Bible (26 percent) or at most read it once or twice a year (21 percent) (which classifies them effectively as nonreaders); 53 percent are considered "readers" — somewhere between those who say they read it every day (15 percent) or "several times a week" (13 percent), and the remainder, most of whom say they sample it three or four times a year. Daily readers and total nonreaders are now at equal strength — a quarter of the adult population each — representing a notable rise in noninvolvement.

Cynics could further indulge their habit by noting how little Americans actually know about the Bible. Asked to name the first five books of the Bible (the Jewish Torah, the Christian Pentateuch), about half (46 percent) succeeded (the older-age cohort being a few scant points ahead of the youngest ones). This is a decline, to be sure, but, like so many results, compared to what? Public awareness of other major areas of learning is likewise lamentable and grist for "shocking" one-liners. To take a hypothetical example: What percentage of Americans would know whether Abe Lincoln used a microphone to deliver the Gettysburg Address? Similar questions about such things as the Bill of Rights or the periodic table or the causes of the Great Recession produce batches of humorous/disturbing responses.

Gallup Polls have provided such statistical fodder on Bible knowledge for more than two decades. Among the commonly cited findings: just half of the adult respondents can name even one of the four Gospels; slightly more than a third can identify all four. Seven in ten are sure that Jesus was born in Bethlehem, but only four in ten know that he delivered the Sermon on the Mount, and two-thirds cannot produce a quote from that sermon. Every one of these bloopers is a variation on the same theme: the Bible has become an unknown quantity even among the many who have spent time learning it. The "tut-tutting" has grown louder, especially among the formerly religious and nonreligious. But again, is it worse than other kinds of ignorance? The answer is yes among believers, because the Bible is the pathway to salvation for them. Nonbelievers aren't about to put it on their required reading list — barring, perhaps, a threat to their survival.

For the time being, at least, poll findings like the above are still widely used to entertain, alarm, and spark student interest. In his introductory Hebrew Bible class at Smith College, for example, Prof. Joel Kaminsky drolly uses some startling, even counterintuitive, facts to break the ice. Do his students realize that a whopping two-thirds of Gallup's surveyed adults cannot name half of the Ten Commandments? That a majority of graduating high-school seniors believe that Sodom and Gomorrah were husband and wife (while Barna found that 12 percent of adults thought Joan of Arc was Noah's wife)? Funny and/or meaningful? There is more. As a professor of Bible, Kaminsky can expect to encounter stereotypes, mostly unstated, that sometimes have kept students from signing up for his course: that the study of Scripture assumes that one is being indoctrinated; that it is a repeat of Sunday school or evangelism; that the same rigorous scholarship is not applied to it as to other historical or literary documents. Kaminsky adeptly dissolves those bugaboos with humor and enticing nuggets. The Bible is "the single most significant text in Western history," he casually offers. "Most people are not aware of its rich resources, so [the students] would be among the privileged few to delve into its storehouse of stories and wisdom. The material isn't simple or always transparent; texts are crafted in a bunch of languages; the ancient Hebrew style of shorthand poses puzzles (its alphabet uses only consonants), and translation is often mind-bending. Having arisen in fragments over centuries of tangled, often enigmatic history, the Bible is hard to understand."

The thirty-five students taking Kaminsky's class at this historic women's college drink it in pensively and with pin-drop attentiveness. Among them are many former — and some active — religious adherents: Catholics, mainline Protestants, Unitarians, agnostics, an avowed atheist, and those, such as a Chinese student, who have no religious background. Most have had at least a smattering of Old Testament (Hebrew Bible) education, mostly in religious institutions; but only a handful have gone far or retained much. But many of them have downloaded the complete Bible onto their smartphones or iPads. For millions of actual or would-be readers, digital is becoming the wave of the future: an Omni Poll shows that from 2010 to 2012, the use of e-Bibles among pastors alone more than tripled, from 14 to 44 percent. As each student gives a reason for being in the class, the responses cohere largely around a willingness to give the subject another try, on another level, for the sake of better understanding the philosophy and literature of Western culture.

Shakespeare's thirty-seven plays, for example, are stuffed with biblical references, many of them cryptic allusions, such as the title of one, *Measure for Measure,* which comes from the seventh chapter of the Gospel of Matthew. *Hamlet* and *Othello* have at least fifty-nine biblical allusions each. The total in all the plays is estimated to be anywhere from 1,200 to double that figure, depending on the criteria for selecting references. Some scholars extrapolate the barest hints of scriptural origins into valid illustrations, while others are not convinced. Meanwhile, literary detectives keep looking for more instances that have been overlooked because of subtleties of language or context.

Kaminsky's popularity on campus has helped win students over. He sports a trimmed gray beard, and his face glows with a pinkish complexion, exuding enthusiasm and good cheer. Though he has raised the curtain on many courses over the years, he says that the first day still makes him nervous. But he springs into the cozy classroom full of unknowns and immediately chatters with the students, seeming to immediately connect with their concerns. Of all the required assignments, he instructs them, the regular Bible readings are mandatory. Reminding them that this is no child's play but can offer rewards if pursued with diligence and effort, he emphasizes that the selections "have to be read more than once. It's not like adding two plus two. You have to puzzle over it."

*   *   *

It has generally been imagined that Americans of yesteryear weren't in need of an orientation like Kaminsky's because they were naturally neck-deep in Bible lore and that the nosedive in comprehension has come about only rather recently. Visual and anecdotal evidence are offered as circumstantial proof that the Bible suffused civic and religious life in centuries gone by, whereas mathematical polling has charted these markers more exactly for just the last sixty years. Within that limited range, the surveys have certainly supported the view that Bible reading has tailed off. One poll, for instance, reports that the percentage of people reading it at least weekly has sunk dramatically over twenty years, from 73 to 59 percent. But it cannot be known whether either figure is higher or lower than it has been in our earlier history, when there were no polls and a lot fewer people were literate. (Did hearing it read in church count?) Was it higher after the Revolutionary War, a time when historians estimate that only 15 percent of the colonists belonged to churches? And was public and private morality any indication? The Civil War took place during a period of relative Bible saturation, yet more than half a million "brothers' keepers" killed each other.

Despite the impossibility of making comparisons, Gallup nonetheless felt confident in concluding in 1994 that "basic Bible knowledge is at a record low," and nothing has changed that conviction over the past two decades. One of the country's most seasoned preachers and evangelists, Woodrow Kroll of the Back to the Bible radio ministry, exhorted churches to use survey results to put first things first, and that might entail switching priorities. "Today," he says in one of his nearly fifty books, *Taking Back the Good Book: How America Forgot the Bible and Why It Matters to You,* "the great battle isn't over Biblical infallibility [fundamentalism's non-negotiable conviction]; it's over Biblical illiteracy."

In the temples of religious trends, Numbers isn't just a book of the Bible; it is a metaphor for considering the significance of the whole Bible in this land. The inexorable march of social science has taken aim at the attitudes and behavior *toward the object,* in this case the Bible, rather than the effects it might have on the subjects: How do people regard it and how do they use it compared to the way it was used in earlier times? The contents of the Bible itself — its origins, its ingredients, and its effect on those who use it — are left to theologians and scholars. Meanwhile, the sociologists, historians, and psychologists use polls and surveys seeking to grasp where the Bible stands *objectively* with certain populations in certain locations. Archaeologists, paleontologists, and geologists add another layer of hard science to this picture.

The results from both "social" and "hard" science camps yield both fascinating discoveries and hyped-up common sense. An example of the former involves the lordly camel: two Israeli archaeologists have concluded that the animal could not have been used by humans before 900 BC, a thousand years later than the Bible claims that they were ridden and used as beasts of burden by the patriarchs. This throws yet another dart at biblical literalism (and was hence hotly refuted by some Christian writers). On the "true but obvious" side, a study finds that ninety-one of ninety-six major US cities are not "Bible-minded."

The Gallup poll was for decades the pacesetter in sizing up the nation's religious character. Its surveys have been invaluable in calling attention to religion as a primary field of scientific study. For the media, its annual findings still become a Rorschach test for sizing up America's religious character. George Gallup Sr., a genial, creative Iowan, wasn't religious himself, but he recognized the importance of religion to American culture. How often people prayed, read the Bible, and went to church became fixtures in Gallup polling from the 1950s onward. His son, George Gallup Jr., who took a central role in the leadership after his father's death, shared his father's curiosity and was also religious — fervently and affectively so. Whether the junior Gallup's deep faith inclined him toward outcomes that were favorable to religion is open to question. As a person who knew him, worked with him, and admired him, I believe Gallup intended his polling to be as rigorous in pursuit of religion facts as it was in charting any other area of life; but it could be soft on religion.

The summary line for Gallup's religion surveys and those that followed its lead was that the country's faith was robust and that Americans stood apart from the widespread European loss of faith by fending off secular challenges. For decades the takeaway finding that confirmed this state of affairs was that 40 to 45 percent of American citizens went to church every Sunday. The data were collected by phone and relied on "self-reporting" — implicit belief that respondents were answering truthfully rather than giving answers they thought others would find pleasing. As the twentieth century wore on, many people scratched their heads over that one: *they* didn't see any such thing happening in their neighborhoods or among people they knew. But they assumed that it might be the case in other places.

By the early 1990s, skepticism was being justified by on-site studies of churchgoing. A team of academic researchers — Kirk Hadaway, Penny Long Marler, and Mark Chaves — used advanced demographic analysis and ground-level head counts of worshipers to measure actual attendance. Their results showed that only half as many Americans went to church weekly (about 20 percent) as Gallup had reported (about 40 percent). Their first report, "What the Polls Don't Show: A Closer Look at U.S. Church Attendance," published in *American Sociological Review* in 1993, helped mount a powerful challenge to Gallup and other pollsters who still rely on self-reported information (and thus maintain the much higher percentages) rather than shifting to more empirical methods. Typical of the gathering strength of the counterevidence claims was a 1998 article in the church-grounded *Christian Century* by members of the same team, entitled "Did You Really Go to Church This Week? Behind the Polling Data."

But the higher figure that Gallup repeated more or less infused a glowing religious trait into the psyche of American mythology that would prove hard to dislodge. In countless media reports, academic studies, and religious literature, America is regularly hailed as an extraordinary, counterintuitive example of religiosity among advanced nations, whether or not it is true. Like all attempts to place religion under the scientific microscope, church attendance has proven elusive. Reliable information on the country's religious habits and beliefs has been famously scarce, even nonexistent. Nobody knows how many people belong to what churches, or whether respondents answer sincerely or understand the issue when asked if they believe in the divinity of Christ. (Do they, for example, feel pressured to give answers that they "should" give?) Most religion studies of this kind, useful as they are in defining megashifts, are limited by the "external" approach they understandably use. The "inner" life is not their job, but an information-hungry culture eager for assurance readily conflates the inner with the outer, so that a churchgoer who says she believes in an afterlife can be assumed to be a deeply spiritual person who is certain she will be rewarded in heaven. Two different perspectives meld together as if they were one. A person who reads the Bible five times a week is, ipso facto, a devoted disciple of Jesus.

Gallup's initiatives in religion-surveying coincide with the exceptional post–World War II religious boom, when belonging to houses of worship was a witness to patriotism and an American expression of gratitude for our victory over "satanic" forces in Asia and Europe. In the decades that followed, Gallup's annual religion reports reflected that upbeat note, affirming in a straightforward way that faith traditions are inextricably bound to America's special calling and success. Subsequent sharp losses in mainline church membership and "me-generation" lack of interest in matters of spirit dimmed that patina of hopefulness and confidence, though a surge in evangelical "born-again" movements captured the news and strengthened the impression that the "old" staid Protestants were giving way to a new wave of Christians who would not only make up for mainline drops but would create an even larger constituency. It took a while for opinion-makers to see the evangelical bonanza for what it was: a vibrant response to modernity and liberal Christianity that was limited by its exuberant style, and a theology that required the rejection of science-based theories such as evolution.

As the decline of mainline Protestantism persisted, and evangelical growth slowed, even stagnated, George Gallup Jr. saw that the premise under which his polling had operated — the aura of religion's indispensable role in the American enterprise — was fading. The paradigm of religion's function was shifting. It seemed clearer to Gallup, as it did to other observers, that authentic religion would exist as a counterculture, a set of values and beliefs that didn't necessarily rubber-stamp societal values but, as a minority, might resist them. In Max Weber's terms, believers' mindset turned further from religion as coterminous with society to seeing themselves as sectarian. Religious practices and beliefs that had appeared to meld so easily into the country's ideals were increasingly at odds with popular ambitions. With regard to the Bible, Gallup the younger lamented that the public's knowledge of it had become "a mile wide and an inch deep."

Evangelicals are a special case. As political conservatives, they ardently stand for traditional patriotism (particularly when it comes to military defense buildups), unlike the wariness shown by liberal religionists. But they are also in open protest against sexual, social, and political policies, such as a woman's right to choose an abortion and the legitimacy of same-sex marriages, which are supported by a majority of citizens — thereby defining themselves as nonconformists.

Though the religious landscape is a patchwork of ups and downs, by the dawn of the twenty-first century the "American way" bullishness that had buoyed religion was largely gone. This shift in attitude was evident in the reporting of poll results. During the upbeat period, a good news/bad news language was unspoken but real. The more fannies in the pews, the greater attesting of daily prayer, the stronger percentages believing in the Trinity — the better it was for both religion and the country. Atheism and agnosticism were scourges, a tiny fraction of the population that posed no immediate threat, but needed to be watched lest they catch on, threatening the very founding and purpose of the nation. For more than a decade, however, polling could no longer guarantee good results. The naysayers and nonjoiners were growing in numbers, and established religion was — at least compared to earlier times — on the ropes.

Monitoring the changing situation required sensibilities and "street cred" that Gallup lacked. The coordinates for measuring the religious climate needed a different kind of approach toward an unfolding scene of disarray and uncertainty. Whoever was to take up the baton had to understand the times, not only the inner dynamics of religious institutions but also the outside forces that were reshaping them, principally the quasi-religious realm of technology.

*   *   *

As I researched this book, the religion surveys of the Pew Charitable Trusts packed the biggest punch. Its vast funds, expertise, and reputation placed Pew in a class above the rest of religion pollsters, and its big-box clout could change the media narrative of where religion existed on the national map. But David Kinnaman seemed most likely to inherit the charisma Gallup had had: Pew's facelessness stood in contrast to Kinnaman's bring-him-home-to-mama visage. Kinnaman had learned survey research from George Barna, the respected founder of a polling company well known for serving conservative Christian clients. Starting as an intern in 1995, Kinnaman was a prize pupil: he quickly learned the ropes while publishing books of his own on the church's problems with young people. By 2009 he had become principal owner of the Barna Group, its fresh-faced president by the time he was in his mid-thirties. Known for candidly addressing issues of religious decline rather than explaining them away, Kinnaman steered Barna in a more "truth squad" direction, hoping that servings of honesty would dispel illusions and foster better approaches. It would be difficult to imagine anyone better equipped to design new and bolder purposes for what had been a rather staid operation. His writing and demanding schedule of talks to academic, religious, and civic audiences amply displayed his talents as an engaging, articulate thinker, adept at plumbing depths and, rather than being distracted by surface whimsy, modulating between somber counsel and warm encouragement. His heritage also won him trust in churches: his father was an evangelical pastor of distinction, and he followed his father to a Christian stronghold, Biola College, where he caught the survey research bug. He speaks the language and beliefs of conservative Christians, but he also mingles easily with nonconservatives. He is no less an apostle for Christianity than George Gallup Jr. has been, nor is he any more willing to compromise the scientific method in polling; but his explicit use of polling data to further religious ends has set him apart and stirred some controversy.

Like Gallup before him, Kinnaman is subject to the criticism that Barna's polling sometimes seems too disposed toward results that favor his goals as an evangelical activist and that he too readily switches hats from pollster to church reformer. Such complaints — usually private rather than public — are endemic to the polling business, of course, as it strives to maintain statistical integrity while drawing fair conclusions from the data. Despite some skepticism about how well Barna has held the line, Kinnaman's standing as a trusted source of information remains solid. Nearly everyone welcomes his fresh entry into the field and the valid issues he is seeking to evoke.

No matter how the data is spun, Kinnaman is, after all, a "numbers man" first. His flight into books and articles is finally dependent on the validity of the data from which it takes off: percentages and ratios and trend lines make up the runway. His principal research — on which much of his reputation is based — used survey findings to probe the mysteries of the "Millennials," those young people between eighteen and twenty-nine who have been designated "game-changers" by many social commentators for their allegedly pivotal impact on cultural change. Rightly or wrongly, there is a buzz about this generation: they are seen, by turns, as insulated, visionary, self-centered, and tolerant — among other things. Their chief calling card is immersion in the digital world, where they appear to their elders to conduct most of their lives — in a sequestered state of cyberspace without much need for external connection. This makes them utterly enigmatic and/or annoying to older generations. While not notably alien to their surroundings, Millennials are often not at home in it. Curiosity about them springs from a popular impression that they have been, in effect, raised by technology and thus they preview a distinctly different way of being human, which, in turn, reinforces the view that they are harbingers of a gargantuan revolution in human consciousness.

If that were to turn out to be true, churches have plenty to worry about, for the Millennials are that age group whose membership will be crucial in deciding the future of most congregations — analogous to a "swing vote." And recent evidence shows that large portions of these adolescents/young adults are voting no on the church. As a cusp Millennial himself, Kinnaman has taken it upon himself to find out why these young people are bolting from the church. His venture has led him into the religious Dark Matter of adolescents and young adults, where he has asked hundreds of them what turned them off about the church and what might get them back. Like a missionary returning from a faraway land with exotic tales to tell, he has gathered facts and observations for a book whose title pretty well sums up his conclusion: *You Lost Me.* It is the springboard for his spreading the alarm on leading radio and television outlets and speakers' platforms. His verdict is tough on the churches.

One sparkling southern California spring morning in 2012, Kinnaman brought his wake-up call concerning Millennials to 250 Christian educators, youth workers, preachers, and church-growth specialists, each of whom had a program folder with the words "Joy in Investing" on the cover. They were assembled in the auditorium of a church financial office, Ministry Partners Investment, which made loans to mostly evangelical church ventures that had money troubles.

The audience greeted Kinnaman warmly. Most knew of his work even if they hadn't read it; they had come here to hear more about his work, and they thought he would be a valuable guide to the realities with which they wrestled. Kinnaman stood in the tradition of prophets whose youthful clarity alerted complacent minds to the urgency at hand. A lanky man with a long face and an expression that never defaulted to less than a smile, his appearance was both impish and nerdy. Like the different generations he straddles as a pollster, his dress was a miscellany of eras: jeans, a tie-less buttoned-down shirt, a light gray suit jacket, and spit-polished brown leather shoes. He was the picture of a relaxed, understated Westerner.

"I'm thirty-nine," he said calmly. "I care a lot for Millennials." His report from the front would "challenge and provoke" the audience, he continued, because "we are on the precipice of enormous cultural change." He quoted 1 Chronicles 12:32, where the Issachar supporters of King David, no young slouch himself, are praised for their gift of "understanding of the times, to know what Israel ought to do." The implication was that Millennials could offer churches special insights toward creating a fruitful future — if they would stick around. But that was a dubious prospect. Barna studies show that six of ten Millennials (59 percent) "lose their faith" and that of their parents, resulting in a drop-out rate that is higher than in any previous generation.

"Why do they leave?" Kinnaman ticked off the research-based reasons: they find the church "overprotective, shallow, anti-science, repressive, exclusive, and doubtless" — just for starters. Too closed-minded, especially toward sex, and too sure they had all the answers. "The church doesn't seem to answer questions raised by a more complicated culture," Kinnaman said. "It doesn't help that they live in a complicated world." The Millennials do not feel that their concerns are taken seriously or that everyday church theology has enough depth to engage those concerns. Yet 72 percent report that Jesus is an important figure in their lives. "The biggest problem isn't aggressive atheism," Kinnaman declares, "but [a] superficial Christianity" that can't handle contemporary issues. "Most" Millennials feel that they have been presented with a "simplistic Gospel" that can't handle the complexities they encounter in the modern world.

Kinnaman splits his survey subjects into three groups based on his findings; the "nomads" have wandered away and are searching; the "prodigals" left and came back, at least tentatively; the "exiles" are the most disaffected, some because they reject the claim that it is impossible to "be Christian and believe in science."

If absence does make the heart grow fonder, church affection for Millennials should be rising; yet Kinnaman's research leads him to believe that older adults find it difficult to connect with a generation that keeps to itself so much. But to Kinnaman, they are the ones who feel the pulse of the world to come. He sees the opportunity for "reverse mentoring," whereby Millennials can enable their elders to grasp the monumental changes embedded in current culture and preview what the church needs to adapt to in the decades ahead. Millennials, he contends, are the scouting party that is scoping out the future, the vanguard of a webbed consciousness capable of ushering in the next stage of biblical understanding for ages to come. In Kinnaman's estimation, learning to follow their pioneering lead could rejuvenate the church. Or they could become the first wave of a devastating succession of indifference and exile.

At this meeting in southern California he received the inevitable pushback. Scoffers claimed that young people have always strayed from the church, but most return when life settles down to marriage and children. The Millennials would follow suit, they predicted. In response, Kinnaman argues that most Millennials — who are, of course, a moving procession rather than a static cohort — are "not conventional" because their slower completion of steps toward adulthood has been unlike that of any previous generation. The "conventional" process typically means attaining five major goals before the age of thirty: education, marriage, job, home, and children. Millennials have broken that pattern by bypassing such rites of passage, or by experiencing some or all of those rites idiosyncratically and at an older age. That's what Kinnaman's surveys show, and he is convinced that the delayed timetable, such as it is, acts in conjunction with new modes of digital language and engagement to produce a radically different mentality. Unfortunately, Kinnaman tells his audience, "we don't have institutions [churches] that can catch those who don't fit the mold."

A group ministry from a Presbyterian church in San Diego felt Kinnaman's gauntlet drop at their feet. They have sought to win young people to Christ and have heard the statistically loaded obstacles. Lots of alienation to overcome — with too few skills. They heard Kinnaman caution that Millennials "can tell when you're paid to be their friend," which could have described them by reversing means and ends. And they admit that there are no easy strategies to get through their likely objections. Among them, a somber man named Bob said the talk had awakened him to a contradiction: members of the conventional church think that they are "open to Millennials"; they are willing to hear their religious doubts, but not their "answers," that is, their views of "sex, the life of the mind, and lifestyle," including acceptance of homosexuality. Believers like Bob hamstring themselves by thinking that the church has "all the answers" and by trying to "put clamps on religious belief." By being more "amenable," the church might show a kind of humility that perhaps could open channels of communication. To Bob and the others, the Millennials' closed-circle digitalese makes it impossible for them to bond with ministers in the one-to-one manner that ministers are used to. It has dawned on him that he needs to ground himself more thoroughly in the digital world in order to relate to them on their own terms. A line from Kinnaman's talk flashes back: "The Christian community needs exiles [for instance, Millennials] to help us navigate faithfulness in a changing culture."

*   *   *

Bible polling has caught on as attention to its evolving effect on culture has spread, and the results can be surprising. Baylor University, for example, shook stereotypes by showing that frequent Bible-reading has had a liberalizing effect on religious conservatives. A third or more of them joined liberals in opposing the death penalty and the military Patriot Act and, at the same time, favoring science and believing that being a good person entails seeking "social and economic justice." The same trend does not affect conservatives' rejection of abortion and homosexual unions. Reporting on the Baylor survey for *Christianity Today,* Aaron B. Franzen notes that those who read the Bible most "see it as authoritative, written by an author who had a special context and intent, and they want to conform to its message. After all, why read the Bible with no desire to embrace it?" The highly respected Willow Creek megachurch in suburban Chicago looked closely at what happened when members embraced the Bible. An in-depth study of its members shows direct correlation between Bible-reading and spiritual growth, a much stronger effect than generated by a raft of specialized and costly programs that were newly created to foster such maturity.

The prevalence and assumed authority of polling has increased in Bible studies as it has in other areas of everyday life. Is its value akin to an x-ray's clues to the realities within, or is it closer to the tenuous tie between astrology and the cosmos? The steady barrage of "bad news" polls is replacing the hallowed picture of Americans as sturdy Pilgrims braving snowdrifts on their way to church with a collage in which Sunday morning is a worldly playground for a multitude of leisure pursuits. But how accurate are these charts and graphs?

"Highly questionable" is the answer, according to a fresh analysis by Princeton University's Robert Wuthnow, a highly respected sociologist and specialist in religious trends in America. In his book *Inventing American Religion,* Wuthnow warns that big-name polling is fast losing its ability to reflect whatever reality it is capable of presenting. From the biggest purveyors, such as Gallup and Pew, to smaller operations that flourish during election campaigns, the industry is in deep trouble, Wuthnow argues, because the ground that supplies the key ingredients, that is, enough people available to answer pollsters' questions in accord with the scientific requirements, is drying up at a scary pace. A drastic drop in the percentage of people willing to answer pollsters' questions (under 50 percent and sinking) has shrunk the base and sent pollsters scrambling to fill gaps. The fundamental calculus is threatened. The possibility of increases in procedural errors and false conclusions adds to existing criticism of how the wording of questions affects outcomes and the truthfulness of respondents' answers. The goal of scientific objectivity has thus become more elusive and has further undermined confidence in polling's ability to mediate a trustworthy portrait of American opinions and attitudes.

Wuthnow's dismay derives largely from his conviction that hired pollsters' demand for quick results and their implicit pressure for certain outcomes has increasingly alienated commercial polling from scholarly, disinterested research that explores social phenomena in depth. To put it another way, polling "heavies" dig deep; polling "lites" skim the surface. Researchers like Wuthnow use what they see as solid polling data — without depending solely on those data — in conjunction with other research tools. He sees the rift growing between scholarship and private enterprise, to the detriment of truth. He wonders whether commercial polling may even become impossible.

Wuthnow's astute look at polling's broad impact includes the widely shared assumption that surveys freeze the public into categories that might be partially or totally wrong ("Americans are a 'religious people'" being the broadest one). For those who fret over the Bible's apparent retreat, such claims could be good or bad news. Perhaps they and their fellow citizens have become wrongly persuaded that things are much worse for the Bible's standing than they actually are. Or, of course, that secularism has become even worse than they'd imagined.

CHAPTER 3

Does It Make Any Difference?

For nearly two centuries, the *Farmer's Almanac* has been one of the few staples that has appeared alongside the Bible in many American households. Like Scripture, the *Almanac* — like *Poor Richard's Almanac* before it — delivered prophecy and wisdom, though of a more pedestrian variety. Its stock-in-trade included sure-minded, long-range weather forecasts and folksy advice on everyday affairs. Instead of divine lessons, it delivered practical solutions to common problems, predictions of favorable and unfavorable crop conditions, and good-natured wheedling on self-improvement. From its start in 1818, the *Almanac* has gained a sizable and loyal following, and it has occupied a special niche, with the Bible, as an unparalleled reference book — with annual sales still in the millions of copies.

The credibility of these two mainstays — the *Almanac* and the Bible — has plummeted in the past four decades, as their prescientific views have failed the modern truth test. Declining numbers of Americans have confidence in them: they are still cherished, but they have become items of nostalgia rather than reliable guideposts. The *Almanac*'s bold forecasts of blizzards and hot spells still draw wry comments from newscasters and meteorologists in the twenty-first century, especially when anxious viewers worry about the upcoming winter, even though its prognostications prove to be as reliable as flipping a coin. For greater accuracy, moderns these days look to empirically based meteorology, though its conspicuous imperfections have also drawn a load of acerbic remarks. The fact is that forecasting has taken great strides from the *Almanac*'s beginnings at the end of America's first significant "cooling" in the early nineteenth century, when the pattern of weather fronts was anybody's guess.

The Bible's contents have likewise lost the aura of sacredness that once left little doubt that Jesus actually walked on water and that Moses parted the Red Sea. References to such supernatural feats are nowadays much more likely to be given as tongue-in-cheek asides or colorful metaphors rather than offered as real-life accounts. Listeners are still entranced by miracle stories, but fewer, especially the better educated, take them at face value any longer.

Does this redefinition of what kinds of truth the Bible can be counted on to supply imply that Americans are also losing confidence in a supernatural source behind it all? Are scientists putting otherworldliness out of business by providing answers to mysteries, such as disease, that had previously been explained by religion? Are the new solutions, along with their trial-and-error proofs, crowding out the possibility of a world beyond? Or has nothing basically changed except our ability to research such things? The Bible is a passionate campaign brief for that other world that has been believed to be as necessary to us as the power plant is to our microwave. The prior question, therefore, is whether secularized Americans are any longer certain that there is another world.

If not, the Bible melts into the bookcase as nothing more or less than human beings relating their history, struggle, and wisdom. Nothing wrong with that, perhaps, but it wouldn't pack the same clout as when it arrived at the dawn of the Enlightenment in the eighteenth century with Word of God immediacy that penetrated daily consciousness.

The Enlightenment galloped into the shrine, brandishing reason and science as arbiters of truth, knocking otherworldliness off stride but only gradually and partially displacing it. The planets came into view, heliocentrism made its debut, Newton named gravity as the reason why heavenly bodies moved, and linguistics scholars exposed biblical irregularities. Transcendence still held sway, but its wings were getting clipped.

Centuries later, opinion polls trumpeted the fact that Americans remained solidly in the God camp. In seven decades of yearly religion surveys, Gallup has consistently found that nearly everyone surveyed (more than nine out of ten) says that God is real. It is the data centerpiece in the oft-cited brag that the United States is the most religious country in the world, except for India. Preeminence in the economy, the military, and belief in God has been an advertisement for claiming divine sanction for democratic capitalism.

The robust polling endorsement of the Almighty was offset by impressions culled from my random talks with a cross section of Americans, which turned up an expansive list of acceptable alternatives to traditional concepts of "deity." Clearly, transcendence has survived in one form or another, from unwavering trust in the definitions of God in the early Christian creeds to deity-free Asian hybrids to New Age forms of god-within-the-self spirituality. The yearning to transcend the world has leaped way beyond conventional Western theism in a matter of decades. While such newly revived practices as Buddhist sitting, hypnotic trance, or past-life regression do not normally qualify as achieving transcendence under the old Christian standards, many of the followers of these practices testify to uplifting or self-transcending experiences that sound similar. Whatever the differences among them, it seems logical to assume that the practitioners of the newer modes would readily include themselves in the "yes, transcendence" category, though a closer look will locate significant apples-and-oranges distinctions.

The range of in-person responses I heard to the question of whether God exists sorted themselves into roughly four options: (1) the idea of God has been ingrained from childhood and remains there as a nonpersonal fail-safe position; (2) God is a live personal presence with whom there is regular contact; (3) God is a spirit rather than a person, understood through symbols and metaphors like "cloud of unknowing" or "mother"; (4) there is no God.

It seems to me, therefore, that polling results cluster a variety of answers under a single category — "believes in God" — which cannot be easily blended. A "spirit" is obviously not the same as a personal, interactive God, nor is it necessarily outside this world. Likewise, God as a mental conception is at a far remove from personal bonding with a "friend" deity. Though such differences could be supposed to have always existed, it is reasonable to assume that they were much narrower even a century ago when Christianity instilled a nearly universal view of transcendence. As the climate thickens with competing worldviews, it is easy to envision more nontraditional hybrids, such as Joe, a seventy-six-year-old former restaurant owner, who says that he has always believed in God because it affirms something he identifies with the "soul of America"; but he dismisses the idea of a personal God as "pure fantasy" and disavows any previous affiliation he had with Christianity. He has explored Taoism for some time and tried (without much luck) to promote his own brand of meditative practice on the Internet. At this point he visits a Buddhist temple every so often and prays to nobody in particular.

People I canvassed in stores, schools, parking lots, synagogues, and a multitude of other settings generally vouched for a supreme being; notably, though, many paused to think it over before doing so. Transcendence strikes many respondents as an elusive or unrecognized experience that doesn't easily yield to yes-or-no definitions. When in doubt, the tendency is to choose the comfort of the "yes" majority. It is an instinctive token of citizenship insofar as the American myth is widely believed to be grounded in transcendent blessings.

The striking number of pro-God votes cast under duress denote deep uncertainties, calling to mind the "good bet" escape hatch known as "Pascal's wager." It was posed by Blaise Pascal, the seventeenth-century polymath, as a reasonable alternative to the similar "do you believe?" dilemma. "Belief is a wise wager," the mathematics genius reasoned. "Granted that faith cannot be proved, what harm will come to you if you gamble on the truth and it proves false? If you gain, you gain all; if you lose, you lose nothing. Wager, then, without hesitation, that He exists." It is perhaps not surprising that in a secular age this option, with its element of whimsy, might be an attractive choice.

A sharp rise in Pascalian bettors, or "God-neutrals," could account for both the sky-high percentage of God-believers and the increasing ambivalence. Perhaps the greatest growth has been among those who operated on a wing and a wager. The surveys show that on the surface, at least, supernaturalism is very much alive in America: believing in God is for most the entry point. Conscious awareness that something supernatural and quickening permeates day-to-day existence has dramatically dimmed, however, since the early decades of America, according to Sidney Ahlstrom, the late eminent historian of American religion in his book *A Religious History of the American People.* From all appearances, the modern, secular world is heading in its own direction without help from a higher one. Contact with transcendence still has a distinct place in one's private devotions or meditations, but it has become further distant from the routines of home, work, and leisure. Those activities are generally thought to entail the autonomy of the self apart from any involvement by higher spirits or beings. The secular surge is effectively detaching the unseen realms from the seen. To "believe" increasingly implies sidelining transcendence rather than expecting it to be ever-present. Countless practically minded, self-described religious Americans go through their everyday paces without a hint that a higher power has any part in it. There are exceptions, of course, but in the main, people exude a sense of self-sufficiency that bears no relationship to a supreme being or dependence on the Bible. Religion isn't scorned; on the contrary, it is generally applauded. Its acceptance, however, is like a private resource. Rationality and the demand for provable outcomes have taken their toll on premedieval connections with the "other world." The undisputed source of the Bible itself has become disputed.

Regular synagogue- and churchgoers haven't thought much about this or any other religious upheavals since evolution drove a wedge between its modernist proponents and its Christian fundamentalist adversaries, and the Second Vatican Council refashioned the Catholic Church. They were thus only dimly aware that leading scholars of religious trends saw a revolution of religious orientation: from reimagining traditional belief to exploring the moveable feast of proliferating "spiritualities" emerging from a variety of sources, including those claiming supernatural origins. Religion's decline is being attributed largely to a weakening of its supporting otherworldly authority. The sudden explosion of the "new atheism," with Richard Dawkins as its brazen "bad boy," has bluntly provoked that awareness with a no-compromise attack on everything otherworldly. Its arguments are scoffed at by a wide variety of opponents — religious and nonreligious alike — but my canvassing indicates that for some it has also struck a chord. Damning the atheists as a lunatic fringe (though Dawkins, a Nobel Prize–winner, has given it substantial standing) sometimes, ironically, has awakened some denouncers to their own doubts about God — even in the midst of their ironclad faith. Unlike previous eruptions of atheism, perhaps this one isn't so easily squelched because its categorical message has a broader appeal at some level than ever before. The huge amount of media attention has promoted and sustained it, but I believe that the public has also fastened onto it because it has touched a nerve. At least it has among an informal sampling I spoke with about what they found hard to believe. (Some are referred to or quoted here.)

Though none went so far as Dawkins does in abolishing the supernatural entirely, as citizens of a secular, "prove it" society, they have breathed a common air of skepticism that has caused some doubt in even the most stalwart believers. Some of those who attacked Darwinism most scathingly also confessed that they would be hard pressed logically to convince nonbelievers that God was real. Monty, a thirty-two-year-old bicycle racer, put it this way: "Those who are against faith often seem to have the best arguments, and sometimes I admit that I agree with them." As fiercely as Monty and others like him resist the atheists' assaults, they have as moderns been exposed to enough secular and scientific reasoning to cultivate some subconscious or subliminal sympathy for the atheists' side. Against their best intentions, perhaps, believers can find themselves attracted to aspects of the atheists' polemic that are appealing precisely because they inadvertently highlight believers' "unacceptable" dilemmas. This quandary helps keep the atheists' bandwagon rolling.

*   *   *

None of this means that the market for otherworldliness is drying up. On the contrary, preachers, teachers, missionaries, and countless devoted Christians of every occupation and stripe are proclaiming the supernatural wonders of Father, Son, and Holy Spirit in sanctuaries, living rooms, workplaces, and revivals all over the country. Apart from otherworldly conversion, there is no promise of salvation or spiritual renewal. The Christian realm has depended on the Word from on high from the start. My soundings in far-flung churches suggest, however, declining confidence in winning souls to that transcendent vision. The message seems as impassioned and sincere as ever, but it is delivered in a greater awareness that the odds of success get tougher. An undertow of unbelief and rootlessness is evoked as a more awesome obstacle from pulpits and television evangelists. Whereas fostering awareness of providence has long played directly into the American ideal, a competing orientation has appeared on the scene. To hear preachers refer to it, the new wave is harder to reach because it is indifferent rather than defiant. The absence of belief in higher powers is more a process of osmosis than some kind of conspiratorial atheistic plot. The culture seems suddenly to encourage nonbelief in ways that are scary to believers. Trend-watchers agree that more Americans just aren't interested in what believers have to offer and consequently are decreasingly alarmed about the fate of their souls — which they are less inclined to associate with an afterlife. Believers are more apt to see their mission as countercultural rather than any longer consonant with the nation's history. To them, faith in "things unseen" is being discarded in favor of worldly, material, egoistic purposes that have engulfed the culture, including believers themselves.

Spotlighting the reported rise in "Nones," those who identify themselves with no religion at all (15-20 percent of the public, according to the latest Pew survey), has become big news. It has caused more religious jitters than anything has for a long time. In some forecasts, this bump presages an expanding secular hegemony paralleled by further withering of organized religion and evaporation of the supernatural in human consciousness. But another aspect of that survey puts those assumptions at least partially on hold. While the "Nones" are increasing, a hefty percentage of the nonjoiners also say that they believe in some kind of higher being. Whether or not their beliefs comport with old-fashioned supernaturalism, they apparently continue expressing the God gene one way or another — while finding no need to join congregations. While the specter of unbelief ostensibly raises the bar for evangelism, it also fans the flames of revival. Church growth has most certainly gotten tougher, but for the most ardent messengers of the Lord nothing less than the future of the supernatural is on the line. The crisis recalls the fragile status of the earliest Christians, who had to rely on trust alone in the absence of governmental or general societal support to boost their fortunes. The alert was still in its early stages: vitality and success would depend on fashioning a message to win over those who didn't find urgency or relevance in the old language of redemption from above.

But wait a minute! While religious futurists moped about marketing the "other world" as they knew it, something like supernaturalism — on a popular level — has been thriving. How else can one explain the wild enthusiasm for surrealistic and magical movies, books, and television shows — such as the *Harry Potter* series and *Game of Thrones*? Hundreds of entries now fill the bin labeled "Supernatural," and they saturate a market heavily populated by many of the same young people who never darkened the door of a church. The genre isn't offering exactly the equivalent of Christian mysticism or Buddhist oneness. In fact, the fascination of this entertainment camp following appears to spring from areas of the brain that have more to do with imagination itself than religious vision; yet the emergence of this video appeal to the "extraterrestrial," as it were, is at least an intriguing coincidence. Real-life practices presupposing supernatural causes are also prevalent: faith-healing, ghost-hunting, returning from near death, and communicating with the dead — to cite just some of those that likewise bypass standards of scientific proof.

At any one time, many people allude in a variety of ways to being in touch with something beyond. Has this supernatural longing appeared even as conventional ideas about transcendence are being discarded? Are the movie portrayals responding to the same thing or something different, even contrived? Whatever it is, it suggests that otherworldliness can be alive and well quite apart from science or an amalgam of supernaturalism and science. Or is it simply an attempt to recapture an illusion?

That puzzle suggests a transition of thought so powerful as to be unmatched in Western history. At its heart is how we define reality: what we consider true and false. On the conceptual side, it inaugurates a scholarly, pointy-headed exploration, like those that reconceived psychology (Sigmund Freud), history (Edward Gibbon), and science (Albert Einstein), which could reorient our understanding but could also prove to be a blind alley. Most people pay little or no attention; they go about their business largely unaware of the signs of religious upheaval that occupy the scholars. Large sectors of the population stay where they are. They belong to religious groups that celebrate a joyful, articulate witness to the only transcendence their forebears ever knew. Secular analysts sometimes view them as quaint, dying embers of an ebbing civilization; but to be among these worshipers is to feel alive. They are increasingly aware, however, that their view of things is under siege from both within and without.

Researchers and writers rooted in both religion and academia have taken turns over the past half century to construct narratives to account for the unmistakable revolution reshaping perceptions of transcendence. Among the markers along the way:

- *Time* magazine's 1966 cover story, "Is God Dead?" emblazoned in red lettering on a black background, triggered an excited shudder across a nation already shaken by social and political upheaval. The trio of scattered theologians behind it — Thomas J. J. Altizer of Emory University, William Hamilton of Colgate Rochester Divinity School, and Paul van Buren of Temple University — loosely coalesced around a "God is Dead" banner, though their views weren't easily harmonized into that slogan. The headline was nonetheless widely viewed as a shocking assault on public piety that was presumed to be broad and deep, standing at counterpoint to the menace of atheistic communism. To suggest that the enemy had triumphed by toppling God sparked outrage. It was like a clay pigeon launched into the air awaiting a fusillade of shotguns. The counterattack was vehement, denouncing the fledgling movement on radio and television, and in publications of all kinds. Bumper stickers reading "My God's Not Dead, Sorry about Yours" cropped up quickly to rally the troops. The "God is dead" theologians were buried in cries of heresy and devil worship before being able to respond. The budding initiative was ostensibly snuffed out almost before it could begin, but, like the bulbs beneath plucked tulips, the concept stayed alive underground — only to flower once again. The premise was that the mental terrain of modern Westerners didn't ordinarily include a living God. Rather, they lived in relative self-sufficiency as if there were no God, true or not. The God-is-dead theologians were describing an "atheistic" situation in which they saw growing numbers of Americans carrying on their lives without a nod to any kind of deity. However large the uproar it caused, that claim seemed hard to argue with.

- Harvard University theologian Harvey Cox touched a similar nerve a year before with his book *The Secular City,* in which he argues that citizens of economically advanced societies act without an acknowledged need of a transcendent enabler. The modern age needs ancient wisdom, he observed, but he didn't feel as if it were supervised by or needed counsel from agencies beyond human resources. Cox was also caught in the sharp pincers of controversy, but whereas *Time*'s shot across the bow reached the general public, the reaction to Cox was more confined to academic circles, where he faced rebuttals from formidable figures such as Peter Berger. The critics pooh-poohed the idea that God had disappeared or that humans had outgrown the need for transcendence. Despite Cox's depiction of a closed system, they retorted that people regularly sang and danced to the harmonies of heaven and found salvation in the Lord. The ensuing debate kept the book and its thesis in the discussion.

- Twenty years later, in 1985, Robert Bellah, a sociologist from the University of California–Berkeley, chimed in with his enormously influential *Habits of the Heart,* an exploration of how American individualism has relegated religion and its biblical undergirding to the private sphere, where its convictions about truth are not subject to scientific testing or objective standards that are ordinarily applied to hypotheses. Religion as subjective experience (my religion has its own validity simply on the grounds that it is my sincere belief) has been largely separated from public exposure, where claims such as biblical literalism would ordinarily be formally scrutinized. The book vividly depicts the drift toward individual religious identity, which is starkly contrary to the concept that the person gains a religious "self" by belonging to the collective body of believers. For thousands of years of recorded history, the person had been taken into the group and expected to adopt its beliefs; now the person created the terms and content of faith, and might or might not seek a group to expand that experience. Bellah's book became the touchstone for previous and future considerations of what the secular age had wrought.

* * *

33

These contributions awaited a magnum opus on the subject, and in 2007 it appeared. The job required a mind that could grasp the weaving together of vast philosophical, theological, sociological, and historical strands. Providence, as it were, found that figure in the person of Charles Taylor, whose woven tapestry is a book with a prosaic title, *A Secular Age,* but with sweeping insights. In the book Taylor wraps his mind around more facets of the human story than I can fathom, creating "a work of staggering genius," to borrow a phrase. Where it will eventually rank in status and impact among seminal writings naturally depends on how it weathers a gathering swarm of comment and criticism; but it has already become a required frame of reference — a touchstone for response — for subsequent analysts and theorists. At its very outset, Taylor casts the die:

> So what I want to do is examine our society as secular ... which I could perhaps encapsulate in this way: the change I want to define and trace is one which takes us from a society in which it was virtually impossible not to believe in God, to one in which faith, even for the staunchest believer, is one human possibility among others. ... [There are those] whose way of living I cannot honestly just dismiss as depraved, or blind, or unworthy, who have no faith. ... Belief in God is no longer axiomatic. There are alternatives. And this will also likely mean that at least in a certain milieu, it may be hard to sustain one's faith.

He framed the paradox in a nutshell: Why was it virtually impossible not to believe in God in, say, AD 1500 in our Western society, while in 2000 many of us find this not only easy, but even inescapable? A corollary inference drawn from Taylor's thesis includes the Bible: as transcendence wanes, so wanes the power of the Bible. The Taylor exploration, laid out in nine hundred pages by the esteemed philosopher at McGill University, details the rise of the secular mind as an adjunct to godliness rather than its negation. It isn't a stark all-or-nothing choice, but a nuanced gradation of sufficient meaning systems that have sprung from Enlightenment sources and whose autonomy from higher powers appeals to a growing number of modern people. Taylor's rich text methodically treats the intellectual, psychological, civic, and spiritual dimensions of what he calls "a titanic change" in our Western civilization. That change, he continues, makes traditional belief one of many valid options rather than the truth standard against which everything else is inferior.

The complexity and scholarly depth of Taylor's groundbreaking framework is beyond my ability to sum up succinctly, nor would it suit the purposes of this book. That task and the longer expositions belong to the scholarly journals that occupy an invaluable niche apart from the highways and byways where I looked for evidence of the Bible's presence in everyday circumstances. *A Secular Age* is already gaining seminal stature in periodicals, think tanks, and church colloquies. Within some leadership circles, it is helping to revamp thinking. But it isn't the stuff of coffee-shop talk or church Bible studies, at least not in its full-blown expression. For that to happen, it will need apostles who can act as its troubadours and translators, those who render Taylor's scholarship into points of light that may help dissipate the spiritual fog that has enveloped belief itself.

And that is happening as Taylor's magnum opus gets chewed and crunched into more bite-size portions for wider public consumption. The apostles are explicating Taylor for an audience that is eager, but one that nonetheless needs explication of Taylor's points. One of those apostles is James K. A. Smith, who has written — in addition to a half dozen other books, all to impressive reviews — a book on Charles Taylor entitled *How (Not) to Be Secular: Reading Charles Taylor*. Smith's blend of updated, reinvigorated Calvinism and critiqued evangelicalism are stimulating to a remarkable range of audiences — from left to right on the theological scale.

On a damp spring evening in 2014, Smith shared the fruits of his study of Charles Taylor at a public lecture at Lehigh University in Pennsylvania, centering on why Charles Taylor believes that the straight gospel of religious orthodoxy has fallen on so many deaf twenty-first-century ears and why the secular world does not need to be feared. Though the fortunes of the Bible were not the primary focus of Smith's talk, they were presupposed. Regard for the Bible, after all, depends precisely on how well the spiritual superstructure keeps it alive. This lecture was a testing ground for doing so: it was attended by a mix of professors with and without predigested debating points; students fulfilling class requirements; PhD candidates; random undergraduates; and a smattering of townspeople dispersed throughout a darkened amphitheater. Not a thorough cross section of America, perhaps, but a fair sounding board.

The way secularists explain it, the view that has gained the most press is that the secular state is what is left after the "extraneous appendages" of religion, such as "superstition" and "myth," have been "subtracted" or "lopped off." As the Western mind has drifted in that direction — that is, away from otherworldliness — it has been "left with human rationality" as the basis for determining truth. Without transcendence, consciousness is reduced to this-worldliness, or immanence, devaluing religious belief as a reliable choice. The secular realm is not a "leftover," says Smith, but an "accomplishment," a comfortable place within an "immanent frame where appeals to transcendence are not needed." Astounding as it may seem, Taylor's concept of the secularist's "exclusive humanism" means that "human society has forged 'full-life' meaning without reference to transcendence or eternity" and thus does not "require belief in God." The causes of this colossal switch in gears were a host of mostly Enlightenment factors, among which Taylor specifies the following: (1) the exaltation of reason; (2) the rising confidence in proof-based science as the arbiter of what is real; (3) fustian humanism nourished by Renaissance classicism; and (4) the relativism of post-Reformation Christianity, which has broken the assumed dependence of people on heavenly beings. Human autonomy is in the offing, existence that is secular insofar as it doesn't feel it needs supernatural connections.

Conventional wisdom concerning this subject has leaned heavily toward a polemical judgment: either/or. That is, the triumph of the secular means the defeat of the religious. If higher powers are no longer recognized, what can be left of belief? And if secularist claims of autonomy from spirits are delusions springing from hubris and arrogance, as some believers see it, isn't otherworldliness like a bound-up Gulliver awaiting liberation by a humbler humanity?

Taylor introduces a "third way": given the reality that we live in a secular world, that does not mean that religious consciousness has gone away. Does it mean that "we live in disbelief"? asks Smith. Can a religious deciphering, a cornerstone of Taylor's thesis, "be a better account of this secular age"? The advantage of the religious account, Smith claims, is that it fills in exactly what the secularists ignore: evidence that extrasecular or spiritual longings emerge in this age in a variety of settings, even among people who claim no religious identity — often unexpectedly or without the prompting of wishful thinking. Not full-fledged confessions of faith, but momentary glimpses.

Smith offers two examples from ostensibly nonreligious subjects. One is the decidedly secular British writer Julian Barnes, who asks in his memoirs, "What if [spiritual claims] were true?" And he testifies to the mystery he finds in Mozart's *Requiem*. The other example comes from the late Apple genius, Steve Jobs, who, during his widely viewed interview with Walter Isaacson in his dying days, allowed that he "liked to think something survives" after death and — more specifically — "maybe your consciousness endures." For good measure, Smith adds the novelists Jonathan Franzen and David Foster Wallace as examples of secularist writers who nonetheless have experienced mystery that eludes pure reason.

These are mere scraps of testimony, to be sure, but perhaps they are indicative of a pervasive dimension of human experience that seems rooted in a world apart from the senses. Taylor's third way does not make such an experience a prerequisite for a meaningful life, nor does it banish religious piety as something that intelligent humanity has outgrown. Rather, honesty requires that the continuing testimony of encounters with something akin to transcendence become part of the cultural analysis. In Smith's formatting: "There is something unsatisfying about the secularist account because it doesn't do justice to certain [transcendence-oriented] data." Those data will not fit neatly into premodern religious molds. Much of it cannot be called theology by those standards, nor is it couched in anything close to traditional Christian or Jewish traditions. But if you listen closely, you can hear intimations of immortality, broadly speaking, as well as in the Taylor outline that breaks the either/or stranglehold and retains a place, theoretically at least, for religion among the possible sources of abundant living.

The astonishing result of the secular age, according to Taylor (via Smith), is that it has *multiplied* religious expression rather than choking it to death. Given broader definitions of a higher being, more religion — rather than less — dots the landscape. Taylor calls this the "nova effect": like an exploding star, it has expanded "modes of believing." Take that, hardcore religion exterminators!

For born-again, rosary-practicing, creed-confessing, Bible-centered Christians, this is a stretch, to say the least. Even those with no religious ax to grind wonder whether Taylor is simply trying to make the best of a bad situation — that is, where organized religion is faltering. Don't traditional believers, including Taylor, a reform-minded Catholic, and Smith, a Reformed Protestant, have strong incentives to justify the continuation of supernaturalist Christianity, with its miracles and revelations? Certainly. But that motive, by itself, does not disprove the "third way," nor is it a defensive attack on other truth claims. It places Christianity in a precarious position: as one choice among many, rather than cock of the walk and undisputed champion.

The more typical response to secularist advances and latter-day agnosticism is to reassert the supremacy of the church while denouncing unbelievers. Rather than defend the old against the new, Taylor has found reason to celebrate the chief cause of the revolution, the rise of the secular, as an "achievement" of the human spirit with its own self-sufficient purposes apart from religious belief. If his exhaustive analysis were merely a means of preserving Christian prerogatives, its conciliatory approach seems oddly defeatist. Criticism of Taylor's thesis, including what bubbled up at the Lehigh lecture by Smith, has fastened itself in part onto that hypothesis, without much evidence, however, to sustain it against Taylor's brilliance. Better critiques will certainly come. For his part, Smith is helping to spur the most compelling debate in decades concerning the circumstances in which the Bible is attempting a comeback.

Yoram Hazony, a dazzling Israeli philosopher/political theorist, thinks the ancient culture clash between Greek rationalism and Hebrew revelation has exiled the Bible from common understanding in the West. While Western learning has grounded itself in reason as the "natural endowment," the arbiter of life's mysteries, Hazony told a session of the Society of Biblical Literature, the Bible claims otherworldly "revelation" that "bypasses that natural endowment" in providing direct, otherworldly access to truth. Universities have long since banked primarily on reason, consigning revelation to the realm of the alien and outmoded. As much as it might be desirable for students to accept "God speaking in the [biblical] text," Hazony continued, the concept "doesn't have a place in the curriculum. The purpose is to help students think for themselves." Platonic reasoning in one form or another replaces the "miracle" and students lose their ability to comprehend what hearers knew among those for whom the Bible was written. Before 400 BC or so, he suggests, it appears that there may have been no clear distinction between reason and revelation to confuse the issue.

*   *   *

Related to that intrigue is the specter of "relativism," a term that has been used to describe the alleged replacement of absolute, objective truths with ephemeral "truths" that arise out of highly subjective angles on the world from very particular circumstances. Relatively speaking, for example, there is no universal principle of child-rearing that spans cultures and ages, only the myriad concepts that respond to special cultural needs, perhaps overlapping in certain respects, but nothing near uniform. The flow of constant change makes it virtually impossible to compare what societies across time have meant by initiating a child into adulthood — even if that concept *were* applicable from place to place. The broad, deeply conflicted contours of this argument acutely grip the humanities. Can anything be said to be true for all people in all places? Conversely, are such things as eternal verities so far out of reach that no common principles could guide our future into stable peace and well-being? Is truth, as it has been understood, ever achievable, or are we locked into severely limited, highly flawed cubicles of self-interest? Is there a universal God of varying designs, or no god, or gods of any consequence beyond those fashioned within our minds and purposes?

In literature, the name used by those who insist that there is no such thing as bottom-line truth, only layers of distortion, is "deconstruction": infinite regression. So far as I can tell, Taylor isn't a deconstructionist because he does not see inquiry as having to yield to a bottomless pit. His reach does not end in futility or despair of finding verities. Instead, he finds plural expressions of a more or less single entity rather than an essence of that entity. It's a life-giving pluralism, not a fragmenting kind that flattens significance into slivers of insignificance.

The blossoming of racial and gender identity has evoked different kinds of reaction: to conservatives, it is a hopeless, confusing splintering; to progressives, it is a freeing of human variety that has been suppressed by sexual/racial/ethnic dominance. Using relativism in its creative, liberating sense implies that different "takes" on divinity are not by definition averse to the "one God" focus, though it sometimes puts powerful constraints on it. Stretching the boundaries of difference sometimes does break any common bonds and undermines the possibility of a shared spirituality, but it isn't inevitable.

Relativism of the "good" kind gives rise to reinterpretations of once-settled lessons, injecting new life where it has been dormant. Take the Tower of Babel story, for instance: for most of us, it is a fabulist tale wrapped in bold, symbolic imagery with a no-nonsense lesson in "bad" pluralism. The people talk the same language, and this only renders them more full of themselves as they hatch a scheme to promote solidarity and pride. They will build a brand-spanking-new city with a tower designed to land in "the heavens" — in God's living room, as it were — thus playing as equals on God's turf and exercising a kind of shared authority.

According to the standard Sunday school telling of that story, God catches wind of these shenanigans and is alarmed by how pesky these invaders would become if they were to gain access to his living room. So he (the Bible says "we," a pluralism in itself that crops up every so often as a form of God's self-reference) takes charge by chasing them from the tower into the far-flung world, cutting them off from each other by assigning every group a different language. The moral of the story: we must rein in our pride. The practical use: explaining why we have different languages. The broader point: the Bible's message is rarely, if ever, self-evident.

Kathleen O'Connor, in her 2009 presidential address to the Catholic Biblical Association, likened the hubris-driven tower to "an empire, a city and tower of settled thinking, of uniform planning and acting, that seeks to *control* languages of praise, that *negates* women's lives and voices, that *prohibits* speech about the subjects it designates as taboo, and that *cuts off* words of anyone who disagrees on matters affecting their own most intimate lives" (the emphasis is mine). God's wrath is more accurately aimed at the city/tower's overriding "desire to control and, from fear of the world's multiple tongues of faith," most heinously "to impose one language on 'all the people,' squelching the Spirit."

What's a Creator God to do? Through O'Connor's lenses, the Almighty did indeed send the tower establishment packing — but for a reason totally opposite to the conventional view. God busted up the monolithic command of the project and sent people to distant lands, where they would be freed from coerced conformity and could learn to speak in languages of their own. It represented a new start, a multiplying of voices that were kept under oppression. "This text," O'Connor declared, "anticipates the Pentecost scene in Acts 2, where the Spirit comes in tongues of fire."

The breaking of the chains of imposed uniformity — by church, by patriarchy, by racism — has fed a healthy pluralism and has recognized the legitimacy of many voices in testifying to their experiences of transcendence. It seems probable that Charles Taylor and James Smith were in the cheering section. Transcendence may be on its way out, or may be expressing itself via different names. As it is with transcendence, so is it with the Bible, from which it draws its lifeblood.

For all the vigorous debate, the single most enticing question remained open: Could a line be drawn between scientific and spiritual "truth"? Could the authority of history be reconciled with the claims of faith?

CHAPTER 4

Bibles Galore

From the beginning, Christianity has been about marketing. Big time. "Go therefore and make disciples of all nations," the risen Christ declares in the final passage of Saint Matthew's Gospel, "baptizing them in the name of the Father and of the Son and of the Holy Spirit, teaching them everything that I have commanded you." A tall order, but one that early Christians embraced and ran with, spreading the Word and gaining converts with abandon. Winning souls through preaching, teaching, and jawboning thereby became a hallmark of Christian mission from then until now. Without that expansionist template, the rise of modern free-market enterprise seems inconceivable. America, in fact, is a nation where nearly everyone is trying to convert someone else to something else.

The Bible would eventually become the missionary's primary prop, but for the first 1,500 years — 75 percent of church history — common people hardly ever laid hands on a volume of Scripture. The few volumes hand-copied by monks (at what cost of carpal tunnel? we might ask) were mostly for liturgical use in parishes. Though portions were read to churchgoers, the Latin rendering made the lessons inscrutable to nearly everyone. Equally indecipherable Scripture verses were woven into the Latin mass. The homily offered the best chance of hearing Bible references in one's own tongue, however briefly. Sometimes visual depictions of sacred history filled part of the gap. Statues of heroic figures in the Old and New Testaments often occupied prominent places in the sanctuary; frescoes and paintings of pivotal Bible stories, martyrs, and scenes from the Gospel narratives of Jesus could be "read" on walls and ceilings.

The drive to claim the world for Christ thus raced ahead for a millennium and a half virtually without Bibles. Nor was the Bible an ordinary subject of reference or study by the vast majority of parishioners. The priests were presumed to be schooled in it, but in general their knowledge was scant and geared toward its use to undergird church doctrine (scripturally based or not) rather than studied on its own to discover nuances or fresh insights. At the parish level, church life was conducted basically without Bible-reading or study. The governing assumption was that the Bible's meaning could only be determined by the clerical order; laypeople were not believed to be equipped to understand it or interpret it for themselves. Priests and bishops, therefore, would selectively decide what it said and then tell parishioners what they needed to hear. Until the Second Vatican Council (1962–65), Catholics were discouraged from reading the Bible on their own.

At no time was the Bible's formative impact on Christianity doubted, but it was in effect ushered off center stage to serve scholarly or pastoral purposes behind the scenes. Its relative recession into ecclesiastical obscurity allowed other factors to fill the vacuum by shaping the church's objectives toward nonbiblical ends. The Bible's absence as a lodestone permitted the church more leeway to work its own designs. This issue looms larger these days as the Bible's role in the lives of Christians has shrunk: Bibleless Christianity has become thinkable.

The Protestant Reformers of the sixteenth century zeroed in on the subject. To a great degree, their revolt against the Roman Catholic Church was a wholesale indictment that Catholicism had forsaken the Bible for worldly pursuits. In their eyes, the flagrant selling of indulgences only typified the corruption. They would take no chances. The Reformation's catchphrase *sola Scriptura* ("Scripture alone") captured their position unequivocally: the Bible would be for them the sole source and judge of Christian truth, subject to no human authority. Whereas Catholicism had given weight to both gleanings from tradition and the Bible, Protestant luminaries pledged to place full confidence in Scripture, and thus they translated it for the common folk. Letting the full Bible loose on the rank and file was liberating but risky. It could both deepen faith and create divisions, since readers would differ over what passages meant. But though the Reformers backed the total availability of the Bible, they weren't so ready to surrender their place as its rightful interpreters. Balancing freedom and compliance, fragmentation and order, would always prove difficult.

The Reformation, followed by the Catholic Counter-Reformation — combined with Gutenberg's marvel of moveable type — stood Bible history on its head. The nasty repressions that had kept Scripture from surfacing in native languages gave way to a rush to produce translations for ordinary people. The Bible quickly became accessible and mind-bending. In Hilary Mantel's acclaimed novel *Wolf Hall,* set in those raucous 1500s, the redoubtable Cardinal Wolsey reflects on the resulting explosion of intelligence as readers discovered powerful Scriptures unknown to them.

> There is an obdurate winter ahead. But he feels a force ready to break, as spring breaks from the dead tree. As the Word of God spreads, the people's eyes are opened to new truths. Until now . . . they knew Noah and the Flood, but not so St. Paul. They could count over the sorrows of the Blessed Mother, and say how the damned are carried down to Hell. But they did not know the manifold miracles and sayings of Christ, nor the words and deeds of the apostles, simple men who, like the poor of London, pursued simple wordless trades. The story is much bigger than they even thought it was. He says to his nephew Richard, you cannot tell people just part of the tale and then stop, or just tell them the parts you choose. They have seen their religion painted on the walls of churches, or carved in stone, but now God's pen is poised, and he is ready to write his words in the books of their hearts.

The late Robert Farrar Capon (1925-2013), a wry Episcopal priest whose popular writings wittily weave theology with commentary on the passing scene and gourmet cooking, describes it this way in his book *Between Noon and Three: Romance, Law and the Outreach of Grace:*

> The Reformation was a time when men went blind, staggering drunk because they had discovered, in the dusty basement of late medievalism, a whole cellar full of fifteen-hundred-year-old, two-hundred-proof Grace — bottle after bottle of pure distillate of Scripture, one sip of which would convince anyone that God saves us single-handedly. The Word of the Gospel — after all those centuries of trying to lift yourself into heaven by worrying about the perfection of your bootstraps — suddenly turned out to be a flat announcement that the saved were home before they started.

The first major Protestant delivery vehicle was the Geneva Bible (1556), a highly readable translation that was the collaboration of English exiles in Switzerland. Copies of it were soon flying around England and parts of the Continent, causing the kinds of sensation Mantel and Capon allude to. It was the Geneva version the Pilgrims brought with them on the

Mayflower. The celebrated King James Version, which the king sought as a monarchy-friendly alternative to the Geneva version's egalitarian leanings, made its debut fifty-five years later and gradually became the top translation in circulation, and it has remained so for four hundred years — against increasingly stiff competition.

America's predominantly Protestant, Bible-centered beginnings, along with its utopian, evangelistic fervor, planted the Bible at the very center of the emerging nation. Its emblematic figure was the intrepid preacher in full shout, clutching a dog-eared Bible in his hand, which he raised in exhortation toward the sky, imploring the presumed spiritually deprived burghers to heed the gospel and be saved. The great cause of leaving no soul untouched allowed no pause and no palaver. The market was endless. Revival was a fitting metaphor for a growing faith and for an ambitious young nation.

Historians Mark Noll and Nathan Hatch capture the extraordinary blend of Bible and community that prevailed during the early decades of Puritan New England in their illuminating book *The Bible in America.* These early colonists inhabited a world that "was entirely suffused with the Word of God. It furnished the terms and vocabulary with which they instinctively confronted life's meaning and interpreted the significance of their collective presence in the New World."

As the country evolved and the demand rose following the Revolution, the business side of Bible distribution rapidly became the main engine for supplying missionaries, preachers, and a wide variety of believers with the Word. The Scriptures still helped facilitate hands-on conversion, but the burgeoning of Bible publishing as a profitable enterprise increasingly separated Bible purchasing and reading from religious involvement. You could have your Bible and treat it as you wanted to.

*   *   *

The cascade of Bibles flowing through the market, however, hasn't let up. Worldwide, as many as 80,000 versions have appeared in more than five hundred languages, though no exact count is available. US sales on a yearly basis are generally agreed to be at least twenty-five million copies. As many as two hundred million more, in whole or in part (individual Gospels such as Mark, Old Testament prophets such as Isaiah and Ezekiel, and particular letters of Paul such as Romans), are disseminated around the world, keeping the Bible atop the bestseller rankings. The numbers always vastly outstrip the nearest book competitor on the list of the year's top ten. Because of the Bible's distance from most people's daily existence, however, the mammoth sales figures might initially startle those who have never heard them before; it would strike these folks as peripheral to the ordinary circle of "getting and spending." It is like repeating the annual total of turkeys consumed on Thanksgiving in comparison to duck or meat loaf; that is, it's a big number, but its predictability and lack of consequence make it rather meaningless. But for the record, during the half century from 1962 to 2012, the Bible left Chairman Mao's *Little Red Book of Quotations* in the dust, with nearly four billion alleged Bible readers, compared to the Chinese leader's relatively meager 820 million, according to Squidoo Communications; the *Harry Potter* series reached half of Mao's total (400 million); *The Da Vinci Code* registered 57 million; and *The Diary of Anne Frank* garnered 27 million, to capture the tenth spot.

The assortment of versions that have rolled off the presses over the past sixty years has been staggering, estimated to total about nine hundred. King James's original edition, released in 1611 by a daunting team of scholars, still led the field after World War II; but translators with new linguistic and historical tools have kept busy for more than a century on updating that has improved its sources and accuracy, with strikingly different results. The question has been to what extent teams from differing theological camps would allow modern scientific techniques to determine accuracy and authenticity. Liberals are clearly more receptive than conservatives are. At Yale, a decidedly receptive committee of leading scholars from mainstream Protestantism produced the Revised Standard Version (RSV) in 1946; the umbrella group American Bible Society sponsored a text in language that was closer to that of the daily newspaper, entitled *Good News for Modern Man* (1966), which proved enormously readable and popular; and evangelicals welcomed an alternative to the Revised Standard Version called the New International Version (NIV), which became a top seller.

By the first decade of the twenty-first century, the market was scrambling to design Scriptures for different slices of the population. Publishers aimed at niche audiences by wrapping bundles of materials pitched to special-interest, age, gender, and professional categories (from celebrity features to advice columns) around whole Bibles or portions of the Bible, such as the Gospel of Matthew or the Psalms. The Bible publisher Thomas Nelson created them as BibleZines initially to attract teens, later for audiences as diverse as firefighters, military personnel, bikers, single men, and young mothers. Similarly, the *God Guy Bible,* published by Crossway in 2014, promised to help boys thirteen and older to "grow into the men God made them to be," while the NIV's *Revolution* was pegged to "today's teenage guy going toe-to-toe with a hard-hitting world." The *Grandmother's Bible* was one of a half dozen offerings for that cohort, and another NIV spinoff was aimed at fathers: *Dad's Bible: Daily Inspiration Even If You Only Have One Minute.* Tweens, couples, and beginning readers could also have their own Bibles, as could single men and football fans.

*   *   *

The short list of customer favorites were sold by major trade publishers in remote sections of mostly dwindling Christian bookstores. A full run of the more specialized versions were available on their Internet sites in a wide variety of sizes, colors, snazzy covers, and extra features (such as marital advice). Though the Bible's customer appeal is limited, the big purveyors continue to snag a reasonably predictable slice of that estimated $25 million-per-year dispersion. For purposes of Christianity's defining goal of marketing and evangelism, however, Christian bookstores represent the front lines. There the Bible never takes a back seat to nonreligious books, and all the other lines of merchandise, from potholders to wall hangings, bear witness to its lessons. They function as supply depots in the cause of winning souls and embodiments of the message itself, beckoning seekers to fulfill their lives by entering. Thirty years ago, four thousand of them dotted the map, bunched thickly in the Midwest and South but plentifully in the Mid-Atlantic, New England, and California as well — so that nearly every sizable city and town had one within easy reach. The vast majority were aimed at conservative Christian tastes. That proved to be the high point of this particular evangelistic strategy. Christian shopkeepers soon saw their fortunes decline along with the rest of the print media, as customers increasingly turned to digital and video means of reading religious texts. Many believers used both, and the demand for print Bibles remained relatively strong; but Christian stores, like their secular counterparts, were stung by slumping book sales even as they rushed to fill the gap with CDs and videos. Many failed. At the start of the twenty-first century, the total number of Christian stores had plunged by nearly one-third, to 2,800, and by 2013 only 954 were still active.

Of the survivors, Family Christian Stores was the largest franchise: in 2012 it still had 281 stores in 261 cities, according to *Publisher's Weekly.*

Founded in 1931 by the brothers Pat and Bernie Zondervan, religious enthusiasts from rural Michigan who went on to build a lasting Christian publishing business (Zondervan Publishing now belongs to HarperCollins), the Family Christian chain's history mirrors the ups and downs of American church vitality. By 1975, in the early stages of an evangelical revival, the company owned a respectable group of forty stores; but as the revival took off, the total zoomed beyond four hundred before settling back to 356 in thirty-six states as the revivalist fires cooled by the turn of the century. Nearly one hundred of the Family Christian stores have closed since then, though the chain still represents nearly a third of all Christian stores in America.

Visiting one of them in the Midwest provides a look at where the Bible belongs these days in a presumably intensely religious region, where it would supposedly receive much greater reverence and attention than it would in an overtly secular setting. The Bible may be ignored elsewhere, but here it would surely be the top priority. Well, yes and no. It's there in a handful of translations and colors, treated reverently as the Book of Books and the wellspring of faith, the designated lifeline to God. But that isn't the whole story. For all the dignity and piety with which it is held, it is confined mostly to a corner of this store — to the left of the entrance — while a flood of impressions draws the customer to other attractions in the store. Those alternatives offer psychological healing, advice on how to deal with teenagers, dating, and coping with work and home life. Then there are Christian-styled music videos, story DVDs and CDs, a solid wall of novels and nonfiction books pegged to Christian readers — and much, much more. It is an attempt to re-create the panoply of products in the secular world, and to some extent it offers that parallel universe, though it often seems contrived and artificial (for example, the Christian comedy CDs).

*   *   *

Whatever value those adaptations have in retaining or expanding faith commitments, the spinoffs simply dwarf the presence of the Bible that is believed to underlie it all. The Bible *is* extolled and sanctified, but more like a grandparent with whom family members seldom actually interact but who exists as a symbol of vaguely familiar wisdom and truth. "Bible" is synonymous with such bookstores, yet the Bible itself seems secondary, like an unwelcome homework assignment. The more urgent goal for publishers seems to be to meet the growing demand for products that weave old-time Bible stories through modern modes of entertainment, primarily fiction and film. One plausible reason for the success of merging the two elements is that it brings the ancient world into the present, making it more accessible to many believers for whom it seems forbiddingly remote and largely irrelevant. Scriptural teachings, as interpreted by the creators of these products, permeate novels such as Cindy Woodsmall's *A Love Undone* or Christian self-help books such as Neil Anderson's *The Bondage Breaker* or DVD videos like *Heaven Is For Real.* The risk is that the interpretation of the original texts is in the hands of writers and film producers who can distort their meanings and implications.

As these hybrid alternatives become more prevalent, readers and viewers may experience more brushes with Bible material that is once re-moved, that is, in forms of entertainment whose purpose is also — some-times primarily — secular. The mixture of ingredients isn't necessarily det-rimental to either major component, but it does perhaps dilute the biblical elements by simultaneously indulging the more worldly tastes of those who mostly patronize these options, the ranks of evangelicals. Love of and dedication to Scripture remain fervent, but the changed framework also reinforces those worldly values, including individualism and materialism. The Bible itself has been to some extent subordinated to worldliness in the course of establishing that parallel evangelical universe of entertainment and lifestyle. On the other hand, a seeker might find the plain-talking *Lies Women Believe,* by Nancy Leigh DeMoss, or a probe of the modern psyche by Joyce Meyer, *Battlefield of the Mind: Winning the Battle in Your Mind,* to be more direct entrees into the Christian fold than tackling the obscurities in the Gospel according to Saint John. Modernity is a gain and a loss.

The thorniest problem for spreaders of the Word is that marketing implies self-interest, the urge not to dispense the Bible's gospel in a fair, generic form but rather to push translations favored by certain groups. Lit-eralists gobble up the King James Version for its presumed loyalty to the "original" text, while nonliteralists, moderates, and liberals hue to the Re-vised Standard Version and others that represent changes that have come about on the basis of scholarly inquiry (claiming, for example, that the end of Mark's Gospel had been tacked on to the original). Conservatives shun and denounce the revamped versions; the liberal scholars who did the re-vamping often regard the original texts as quaint but cobbled together from different sources. Obviously, those tensions make Christianity look bad. How can any biblical sales pitch be believed if they can't even agree among themselves? The Christian bookstore I visited exemplifies the conservative brand of certainty that God wrote the Scriptures without error. Accordingly, two renditions dominate their shelf space: the venerable King James Version, and the New International Version, which was deemed "safe" by evangelicals in search of a modern translation that was shaped by a conservative cast of editors and translators. Those looking for modernist versions are out of luck. The single exception is the English Standard Version, which manages to appeal to elements of both sides with a translation that sticks to original wording but updates its usage. Otherwise, the shelves are devoid of any works that invite thought or questioning outside the evangelical box that the store represents. The clear objective is to buttress approved ideas rather than debate them.

Some evangelicals themselves find this approach too narrow. Jayson D. Bradley, a former pastor, complains in his "Church" blog that Christian bookstores feed the problem rather than offering a solution. For one thing, he says, they "marginalize" those Christians who aren't evangelical by offering them very little that they can relate to (with notable exceptions: I found a Catholic section in the store I visited, complete with a picture of Pope Francis). Bradley was also upset at the amount of Christian-style patriotism and nationalism, as well as the prevalence of "celebrity worship" that attaches faith to wealth and success. His strongest charge is that the stores are anti-intellectual, echoing a charge that has been leveled at evangelicals at every step of their history. "You'll find less than a handful of academic works in most Christian bookstores," he writes. Instead, they stock "a cul-de-sac of homogenized teaching." Such theological pabulum, he argues, shows disrespect for the "educated, committed believers who recognize the complexities in biblical translation and interpretation . . . including biblical inerrancy." At the same time, he faults the Christian store culture for compulsively copying secular commodities instead of creating inspiring, enriching resources of their own. Critics allow that, whatever evangelicals' other foibles, at least they still believe in bookstores as a means of promoting Holy Scripture. Nearly all others in various denominations and theological inclinations have given up. The evangelicals are like youngsters who keep their lemonade stands open as sidewalk refreshments are disappearing.

One great leap awaited me: the digital Bible. I'd heard about it, but the reality hit me one Sunday morning in an uplifting "River of Life" shout-out "service of praise" in a Midwestern city. The few dozen worshipers came mostly from a once-stately neighborhood now bordering on disrepair, and they met during the week at each other's homes for Bible study.

The bishop/preacher directed his people to a passage in Ezekiel, which they immediately looked up in their personal Bibles. Though it had crossed my mind, I'd forgotten to bring one along this Sunday morning. Not to worry. A cheerful, attentive woman wearing a soft yellow hat with a delicate brown feather turned around from the next pew and handed me her smartphone displaying chapter and verse. I was momentarily flummoxed. Astonished, I even wondered if using it could somehow be sacrilegious. But that had to be sheer nonsense — as if that kind woman, who later introduced herself as Marsha, would have violated the etiquette of her church home. I thanked her and took it.

Digital Bibles have been stealthily competing with print Bibles since the final decade of the last century. It was the nerve center of a small corps of technology nerds, and publishers and promoters generally did not notice — or pretended not to notice. In the beginning, it was a flake in the blizzard of byproducts of the dizzying electronics whirlwind, a tiny offshoot of that revolution that keepers of the print tradition weren't openly worried about. Some pooh-poohed it with an air of disapproval that resembled my initial response to the computer Bible from the woman at the "River of Life" church. Isn't there something improper about reading holy text on a phone? The idea seems silly. The American Bible Society assures the world that its surveys show that nearly nine in ten Bible readers prefer paper. The survey is undoubtedly right, but the larger point is missed: the digital alternatives are catching up, especially among young people, and the future seems irrevocably digital.

The inevitable has announced itself in the staggering totals of Bible apps downloaded in the United States and the rest of the world. The pace is breathtaking. The biggest and most ambitious player is YouVersion, a plucky, sophisticated entry by LifeChurch in Edmund, Oklahoma. By mid–2013, YouVersion had registered one hundred million downloads worldwide and was aiming for five hundred million. Its chief organizer and innovator is a far-sighted, soft-spoken slip of a man named Bobby Gruenewald, who has become a Bible app wunderkind after once having managed a website for pro wrestlers. The meteoric rise of his and other apps — and the hopes raised by the momentum and scope of this snazzy venture — has left Gruenewald nonplused. He is a professed evangelical Christian who waves off any interest in selling the app for the estimated $300 million it is worth. He repeatedly says his goal is to spread the Word. Though the array of print Bibles and accessories keep finding their way into homes in time-honored fashion, the prospects of the printed Bible are fading. The rise of Bible apps is the latest and perhaps final stage in the push to distribute the Bible throughout the whole world.

Meanwhile, a signature method of peddling Bibles, the door-to-door evangelist and/or sales representative, has effectively vanished in favor of new media promotions. In a thickening secular climate, religion has become an ever more private matter, and the public's tolerance for personal proselytizers has shrunk considerably, though Americans continue to promote nearly everything else to each other. They are madly trying to sell mousetraps to anyone in sight, but have become testier about doing so with religion — for good or ill. History is, of course, replete with abuses of religious freedom, so caution was warranted. Less clear is the damage to religious believers from hyperprivate extremism that denies religion its rights.

The traveling Bible sales routines were depicted compellingly in a 1968 documentary entitled *Salesman,* directed by Albert and David Maysles and Charlotte Zwerin. The film features a team of four Mid-American Bible Company salesmen from New England plying their trade in the Deep South. They target the financially strapped members of a Catholic parish who have supplied their names to the company. The team salesmen specialize in a variety of ornate Catholic Bibles ($50), but they also carry the Catholic encyclopedia and the post–Vatican II missal — payable in three installments.

"The money is out there," their supervisor assures them. "Go out and get it." Don't think of it as "Bible peddling," he tells them. They are doing their "Father's business," he says, which means that they will "never be held in higher esteem in the eyes of the world. . . . When you realize what you're doing for others, you'll hold your head high. God grant you abundant harvest." One salesman wants to make $35,000; another is shooting for $50,000. But it's a hard sell and a dreary path, ending in frustration and defeat. The film comes to focus on a salesman named Paul Brennan, an Irish-American Catholic from Jamaica Plains, Boston, who struggles to maintain his sales. Even "success" seems tainted by the monetary burden that a sale places on the struggling customers. One elderly woman testifies to how sales pressure can matter more than attraction to the product itself. "I just hope I'll get around to reading it," she sighs.

Heightened opposition to "pushy" religion has led to stricter protection of potential customers from those practicing the pressures of proselytizing. Those measures have, predictably, triggered controversies over basic freedoms and personal boundaries. Case in point: Walter J. Tutka, a former substitute teacher in the middle school of Phillipsburg, New Jersey, who was fired for giving a Bible to a student. On its face, it looks like an incidental occurrence; still unanswered is whether it might have been a conscious challenge to the school board.

Depending on the division of opinion on the matter, either the devil or the angels were in the details. Tutka, a middle-aged, solid man with a stolid expression and thinning hair, was accused of breaking the school district's ban on handing out religious materials to students on school property. Facing his accusers at a crowded school board hearing, Tutka did not deny the charge; rather, he contended that he had acted properly. By his account, he was overseeing students filing into school one day. A boy who was running late rushed to catch up with the end of the line. Whereupon, Tutka says, he told the boy, "Don't worry. The last shall come first . . ." (the words of Jesus from the Gospel of Matthew). He testified that the boy later asked him more than once where those words came from; one of those occasions was during a break when Tutka says he was reading his pocket-sized New Testament. At that point, he says, he gave the Bible to the student, and that was that. The student didn't provide testimony, so Tutka's testimony was unchallenged. The school board fired him after taking time to deliberate. His complaint to the Equal Employment Opportunity Commission against the school board was denied, but he vowed to press his cause.

One factor that played significantly against Tutka's defense was that he belonged to the local unit of Gideon's International, the famous supplier of free Bibles to hotel rooms and Bibleless people around the world (distributing 84.6 million in 2012 alone, nearly two billion worldwide since 1908). Only five months earlier, on May 29, Tutka's group of Gideons had stood on the sidewalk outside the high school to hand out orange, pocket-sized Bibles to students leaving school for the day. Though his signature was on the original petition, Tutka said he had refrained from that handout because it would have conflicted with his teaching status. The Gideons were on public property, thus within their rights, but the incident ruffled feathers in the district and the community. Legally, the action counted for less than the extent to which Tutka's association stirred doubts that his motives were entirely educational. His lawyer claimed Tutka had been fired precisely *because* he was a Gideon. His supporters, including fellow Gideons, his pastor, and fellow congregants from the Abundant Life Community Church and Liberty Institute, a conservative advocacy group from Texas, saw him as a victim of religious persecution. They argued Tutka wasn't "handing out religious literature" but honorably responding as an educator to the boy's question. Even the many who thought Tutka had broken the rule thought the punishment outweighed the crime. Prior to the board's firing, the school superintendent issued a lesser penalty of a ninety-day suspension.

Debate flared over the case during the nearly nine months in which it was covered by local, then national, news sources — sometimes provocatively. The closest newspaper to the scene, the *Express-Times* of Easton, Pennsylvania, received record levels of responses as the weeks wore on (a headline in its December 11, 2012, edition read: "Bible-wielding Teacher Facing Suspension"). It became a remarkable window into the public's views of church-state relations and the concept of freedom *of* or freedom *from* religion. Backers of the school board's action emphasized that the board had no choice: Tutka had violated the rule, whatever his motive. Others wondered whether Tutka's supporters, for their part, would also approve of the action of a teacher who gave a student a copy of the Qur'an. The educational merits of providing the boy with a Bible won advocates, though they favored changing the rule rather than condoning Tutka's actions: "Whether or not a person believes the Bible is truth, the stories and quotes are frequently used in life," wrote one. "Unless a teacher was trying to preach religion to the young person, the Bible is just a book to be read." The other conclusion by strong Christian partisans was that Tutka's firing was the latest attempt to banish God from the schools. In the opposing camp, a reader thought it reinforced the need for vigilance against proselytizing, claiming that Tutka had "openly pontificated and distributed religious materials."

Navigating church-state waters has continued to raise new challenges. A south Florida school district settled a similar dispute by allowing every religious group (including Buddhists, Muslims, and Hindus) to display and distribute their sacred and educational texts during one day of the school year. Though getting nowhere so far with his cause, Tutka believes, he said in an interview, that he will be vindicated — "because God is in control."

The Gideons continue to go full steam ahead, undeterred by countless jokes at their expense. A British hotel-owner self-consciously provided one in 2012 when he announced that he was replacing Gideon Bibles in all forty of his Damson Dene Hotel rooms with copies of *50 Shades of Grey*, which, he said, "everyone wants to read," as opposed to the Bible, which "no-one reads." A local vicar, the Reverend Michael Woodcock, begged to differ, insisting that the Bible continues to be a "source of comfort and inspiration that many do find helpful."

CHAPTER 5

What If Nobody Read It?

By the time the "300 Ministry Powerhouses," as they were dubbed by the American Bible Society, had found their way to Orlando in November 2011, the proverbial bloom was off the rose-colored glasses. Bibles were still being dispersed at an impressive pace, but they rarely became users' manuals, and that spelled trouble. In marketing terms, it was as though crockpots were still selling well enough, but suppliers had become aware that almost nobody used them. Without a greater use of the Bible by people, demand would gradually dry up. For the "Powerhouses," the cost would be nothing less than the loss of faith.

Teachers in high schools and colleges struggle with a similar gap. By their testimony, the books, stories, and articles they assign students to read go largely unread, that is, to a much greater degree than was true in the past. Put anything you like on the reading list, they say ruefully, but don't expect students to pass their eyes over it. Which is to say, of course, that the whole country is less interested in reading much of anything that is not Facebook entries and text messages. Contemporary authors can identify with Leo Tolstoy (*War and Peace*) and Marcel Proust (*Remembrance of Things Past*) — that is, widely circulated, seldom read. The Bible people are far from alone, but the most passionate among them believe that their cause is different, because God has virtually written Scripture and has the power to nudge readers toward it.

Therefore, the Orlando participants saw their summons to face particularly glum facts and dispel any illusions that the masses were gravitating toward the Word on the prompting of the Spirit. Evidence has added up: the chasm between distributing Bibles and reading them yawns wider than ever. Nearly two-thirds of Bible purchases are gifts to other people who, according to statistical likelihood, add it to a couple of versions/translations/ editions they already have. Hard as it is for some leaders to accept, fewer and fewer of these Bibles ever get read. Lingering notions that, if publishers simply get them out there, people will gobble up their contents (like the *Field of Dreams* expectation that "if you build it [the baseball diamond] they will come") were vanishing like the morning haze. Of course, even when the Bible was much more squarely at the center of American life, it was never read to the extent that some might have imagined. A dynamic Bible culture always depended on the existence of enough thinking, curious, soulful minds to keep its seemingly limitless mysteries alive against the ever-present danger of its collapse into sheer doctrinal or moral indoctrination. Questioning, reflecting Christians have been a scarce breed even at the peaks of Bible enthusiasm — much scarcer now. Typically, the cognitive-imaginative approach searches Scripture for clues regarding its formation and its meaning then and now, exploring mysteries that are far from settled either by themselves or by other searchers in communities and universities. (Among professors of Bible, for example, some are believers while others are not, creating tensions within the flagship conference of biblical scholars, the Society of Biblical Literature — to be discussed in chapter 8 below.) While this minority of Bible eggheads places a priority on cognitive struggles, most churchgoers don't. Most of them draw faith from deeply emotional "experiences" of palpable spiritual awakening: for evangelical Protestants, an uplifting, life-changing presence of divine visitation while singing, praying, and responding to the pastor's urgings; for Catholics, renewal and liberating grace in the Mass as the culmination of being ushered into holiness by the liturgy.

For "saved and redeemed" Christians, then, the Bible serves as a kind of Wikipedia collection of answers and proofs for reinforcing ironclad convictions rather than an instigator of nettlesome or intriguing questions. Protestant fundamentalists favor the former, steel-trap approach: that is, settling questions rather than opening them up. Moderate/liberal Protestants generally prefer open discussion. Despite the Vatican's new openness to honest probing, few Catholics venture in that direction, having been cautioned that the Bible's true meaning is the business of the clergy and will be relayed to them when necessary. However, they do receive helpings of it in the Mass — from the Psalms, the Old Testament, the Epistles, the Apocrypha, and the Gospels — according to the order of the liturgy.

Meanwhile, the historic mainline denominations (Presbyterians, Lutherans, Methodists, Episcopalians, Disciples, etc.) struggle to meld reason and faith by examining the Bible via rigorous scholarly standards that cast serious doubts on long-held beliefs about its origins (they were innumerable, not dictated seamlessly by God) and accuracy (there are two "creation" accounts in Genesis, and presumably one is right, the other mistaken). Though the mainliners still hold the Bible in high regard, its vaunted reputation as the final authority has eroded to an astonishing degree among them, especially among the better educated. Meanwhile, though the defenders of an errorless Scripture still regard that as unassailable truth, they gain access to it increasingly by way of a maze of technology from overhead screens and sound systems rather than by privately absorbing a written text. The Bible has thus become more *virtual* than actual in many of the sanctuaries where the Reformation motto "Bible alone" still prevails. Has that reshaped its message in some ways?

Bible reading is admittedly down across all church denominations and types, but people from churches with the most traditional liturgies — Catholic, Episcopal, and Lutheran — sometimes claim that their traditional worship formats, which weave Scripture throughout, provide a hedge against losing touch with the Bible's lessons.

"I'm an Episcopalian," says Philip Turner of the American Bible Society, "and I have the Bible presented through the lectionary [the daily diet of readings] and liturgy. We're immersed in a liturgical world where the Book of Common Prayer is a rich source of Scripture." Other aspects of the worship service, such as vestments, also bear biblical references, he says, to keep congregants further aware of the Bible's presence. "This is the kind of knowledge that doesn't show up when the American Bible Society measures biblical impact."

The one function that the Bible has continued to offer to all Christian groups is providing a handy source from which to pluck quotable verses, usually out of context, with which to justify personal opinions or causes. However, overshadowing all the factors contributing to Christians' current estrangement from the Bible is the unsettling trend that shows young people, and increasingly their elders, reading scarcely any books at all. That matters because, as the Orlando alarm signifies, the Bible is the mother's milk of the faith, and, in theory at least, it has kept the church from running amok — without traditional checks and balances. Scripture has provided content and parameters. Now it has increasingly become one more item — like the complete recordings of Bach's piano works or a Swiss army knife — whose owners value it as a possession to one degree or another, but rarely if ever seek it out. To the Bible seller or promoter, it has not necessarily mattered that the purchaser does no more than slide it into a bookshelf, just as long as the product keeps moving. As soon as the Hula-Hoop transaction is completed and the payment clears the bank, each end of the bargain is on its own. But with the Bible it is different.

Widespread ignorance and neglect of it is a recipe for further distortion and abandonment of basic beliefs and practices that, as Charles Taylor attests, have been acutely strained since the Reformation. Independent go-alone churches, with few or no ties to a historic worship and piety, crop up every week, predominantly of the evangelical and Pentecostal persuasion — groups that have in the past clung most tightly to the Bible. Now it is do-it-yourself Christianity that compensates for the cutback by quietly lowering expectations. Members of these typically small, tight-knit churches are not eager to talk about it, but the change has been unfolding. Preachers feel less able to trust that the biblical references they sprinkle in their sermons will be understood. The details of Jesus' life and ministry are deemphasized in favor of urging a personal bond of salvation with an ahistorical Jesus only sketchily traced to New Testament documentation from the likes of Saint Paul and Saint Luke. A dis-em-Bibled Jesus, a Jesus without many Gospel trappings (obligations), more often occupies the center of high-energy worship.

That, along with the litany of family values, seems to round out messages that are often projected using the latest video monitors and digital audio boxes, hinting at substance and delivered in the computer-screen style to which members are habituated. So the future of Christianity seems dependent in no small measure on whether that biblical storehouse of creation accounts, history, law, prophecy, morality, poetry, story, witness, and miracle is the soil in which churches will be built — or not. But wait. Hadn't Paul and Peter and their friends won scores of converts and planted the very first network of churches from Rome to Jerusalem without possessing a single New Testament as we know it? Maybe it's possible.

The leading reason people say they don't read Scripture is that they can't understand it. Language, style, and references to a lost world have made it unapproachable, they testify, despite hundreds of new translations that have turned the obscurities of King James–era English ("And I was afraid, and went and hid thy talent in the earth: lo, there thou hast that is thine" [Matthew 25:25, KJV]) into language for the twenty-first-century ear ("So I was afraid, and went and hid your talent in the ground. Here you have what is yours" [NRSV]). On that point, Mark Twain quipped: "Most people are bothered by those passages of Scripture they don't understand, but the passages that bother me most are those I *do* understand."

*　　*　　*

After centuries of highlighting the printed Word, the specter of Bibleless Christianity, or something close to it, looms on the horizon. Not only is it possible; it is already happening — yet only dimly recognized in those very churches where it has been evaporating for some time. Preachers read from it and base sermons on its passages, but they often add privately that they can no longer count on congregants to understand the larger settings from which the words come. The *sola Scriptura* is turning into a kind of "nola Scriptura."

In the squeaky-clean sanctuary of a yellow stucco charismatic church outside Spokane, Washington, Bibles once occupied every pew rack. But they were so seldom used, explains the worship leader, a wiry man named Norris, that the church is no longer replacing the missing ones. A Presbyterian minister in Florida says ruefully that he feels the need to choose uncomplicated and straightforward Bible citations to avoid losing those who aren't familiar with the words or the differences among its literary forms. Churches at various points on the theological spectrum are simply making do with the unnerving fact that, most commonly, familiarity and knowledge are quietly fading away.

A piquant example is First Churches in Northampton, Massachusetts. The Reverend Jonathan Edwards, an intellectual giant in pre-Revolutionary America, presided as pastor at this location, but he was also a renowned biblical scholar and theologian in the Puritan community from 1729 to 1751. Edwards, one of the first graduates of Yale University, wrote some of the most eloquent, erudite commentaries on Scripture, philosophy, and science ever produced in America. His sermons were legendary, studded with fearsome calls to repentance that forever nullified any suspicion that he might have been soft on sin. One of those sermons frames him in a wrongful caricature to this day: "Sinners in the Hands of an Angry God," a graphic depiction of the eternal horrors that await those who do not turn aside God's wrath by confessing their sins and begging for mercy. Though soft-spoken and kindly in temperament, Edwards had a hard-line approach to salvation that finally led to his dismissal from the Northampton church (gratitude for what he'd done for the church was suddenly in short supply, to the eternal regret of later generations of members). At the same time, it was the fire-and-brimstone side of Edwards that helped spark America's First Great Awakening revival, which, in turn, fostered revolutionary, anti-British fervor. Unfortunately, the retrospective image of Edwards as the overwrought agent of divine fury, a fire-eating crusader consigning souls to hell, has too often overshadowed his rarefied standing among the youthful of America's best and brightest. His death from an experimental vaccine against smallpox shortly after being chosen president of Princeton cut short a life that represented a remarkable blending of Scripture, theology, and the natural world.

Edwards's First Congregational parish (now the United Church of Christ), founded in 1661, recently merged with the local American Baptist congregation, which was organized in 1826, to become First Churches, housed in an elegant stone edifice on the spot where Edwards once preached. By the time Rev. Todd Weir, a United Church of Christ minister, became the new pastor in 2012, the torrent of biblical passages that once enveloped the membership had slowed to a trickle. The church is recognized today as a citadel of progressive Protestantism, at the forefront of social-justice causes such as same-sex equality; but it is not known for its involvement with the Bible — privately or under church auspices.

Pastor Weir, a slim, easy-going Iowa native with a head of blond hair and a studious mien, mingles easily among his parishioners. He has decided to do something about his parish's involvement with the Bible — if he can. He arrived at the historic church from a pastorate in Poughkeepsie, New York, where the congregation's blend of Vassar College personnel and area residents is similar to that of his new parish in Northampton, which is a mixture of members from the community and from Smith College, just up the street. "When you preach to this congregation," he says, "you have to speak to many different levels of understanding. There are professors, up to a dozen ordained clergy members, and people from a wide variety of occupations and interests. You have to be on your toes." He hopes to heighten enthusiasm for Scripture by introducing a regular Bible-study class before Sunday morning worship.

In his short time with the parish, Pastor Weir has found some people who place the Bible at the center of their religious lives but who "don't have that devotional relationship to it" that he'd nurtured since boyhood, when it was the central focus of his Baptist church and family. "At church gatherings, they'd offer prizes to those who'd read the whole Old Testament and New Testament, and thirty people would stand up," he recalled. Young people earned their own prizes for memorizing Scripture. The relative scarcity of such commitment in Northampton is a common trait among mainline Protestants, he notes, and while he understands its causes, he believes something essential needs to be restored. "This is not a congregation that generally participates in reading the Bible daily, or even weekly," he says. "What's lost is a sense of intimacy with Scripture and with God, a grounding in a wider perspective."

*　　*　　*

A widespread network of religious people share Weir's conviction that everything worthwhile emanates from a prayerful reading and contemplating of those sacred pages, that true spiritual vitality emerges from its lessons when they are absorbed by mind and heart. That is the dimension beyond marketing, the willingness by possessors to look for a deeper wisdom and truth in its verses. Bible agencies, susceptible to our national obsessions with "growth" as the sign of success, have continued to pump hundreds of millions of Bibles into the country and the world on the wishful thinking that the Bible will naturally inculcate itself into the consciousness of recipients. But a correction is in the works, due in large measure to a recognition of the new reality by the flagship American Bible Society. Switching gears, the society says it has overemphasized distribution and will now shine a national spotlight on why so many people are not cracking the Bible open — and how they could be induced to do so. As noted earlier, simply passing out Bibles will not satisfy the society's chief purpose. It is a puzzling disconnect.

As Harold Hill is to River City, Iowa, in *Music Man,* the American Bible Society is to the campaign to change the narrative from distribution to "reception": rejuvenation has required letting go of old assumptions of inevitable progress and daring to do something new and brassy. Among the first signs of the society's serious intentions was the decision to sponsor the Orlando Summit, where a cross section of mostly evangelical leaders would pledge their hearts, minds, and souls to restoring a fallen Bible to its rightful stature. That is, getting people to read it, which is both a formidable goal and the new commandment.

Having digested the bad news for some time, most of the major players who arrived in Orlando had wrestled with its dire implications and come up with at least tentative strategies for getting noses back into Bibles. They are sparkplugs in this effort — smart, resourceful, and serious. It is no exaggeration to say that collectively they are entering unknown territory. They have been occupied almost exclusively with *supplying* the goods; circumstances now force them to grapple with the more elusive challenge of *inculcating* them. But as Americans they share a congenital optimism and confidence that — separately and together — they can, as the American Bible Society vowed on a similar occasion, "fight against ever-declining Bible comprehension and engagement."

They met under the tent of the ABS's "Forum of Bible Agencies," an association of Bible missionaries. The attendees were diverse: individuals such as Facebook evangelist Mark Brown, who had won 8.5 million "friends," and Rick Warren, author of *The Purpose Driven Life;* veteran promoters such as the Scripture Union and the "Back to the Bible" radio show; researchers such as David Kinnaman of Barna and Allen Reesor of Metrix Research; and ethnic church advocate Sam Rodriguez, president of the National Hispanic Christian Leadership Conference. The drive to win converts naturally fosters rivalries and loyalties to particular ways of going about the mission. Competition is inherently American and potentially damaging. To forestall any possibility of that in Orlando, the conference leadership advised participants to "leave behind their logos and egos" for the greater good.

Lamar Vest, the ABS's president and CEO, promptly laid down the conference's markers. He cited Barna polls that purportedly showed Americans to be "pro-Bible" — in that 86 percent thought it was "sacred or holy." The question is: "What are Americans doing" with all the Bibles they own? If they're not reading those Bibles, he asked, "what difference does it make in our society?" He suggested that, "if people were reading the Bible on a consistent basis, wouldn't the world look a little better?" Vest offered as proof the widespread violations in American life of the "Bible's highest standards," such as telling the truth, keeping marriages intact, "loving our neighbors," and "turning the other cheek." Toward correcting the decline, a "good start is to move from being a Bible owner to a Bible reader."

Sam Rodriguez had a much bigger turnaround in mind. "The Bible has long stood as the centerpiece for the moral ethos in this country," he declared. "We have lost that. This movement [represented at the conference] will reaffirm biblical orthodoxy among us. It will be a prophetic, truth-telling movement. We will re-engage the culture with this story."

This vision of a sweeping transformation, like Vest's charge, contains both the promise and the pitfalls. The zest for renewal is there, and the analysis sounds right; but both have fallen prey to the temptation to sell the Bible primarily as a moral catalog. Over the centuries, this is what it had tended to boil down to for countless Christians: a handbook for instilling approved behavior and a measure of personal integrity. There is merit in that: that is, the Bible is full of moral standards and divine judgments against violators. However, morality is the outcome of having entered a sphere of spiritual consciousness that totally redefines one's outlook on God, on oneself, and on the surrounding world. It is this enveloping re-orientation to an enlivening faith that plays out in behavior. In this understanding, behavior is the outgrowth of a life that has taken on new meaning.

As helpful as Vest and Rodriguez might have been in highlighting the moral dimension in the Bible, they were signaling trouble for the cause. Equating morality with Scripture has proven to be a deadly turnoff when it is interpreted as rules without rationale or as weapons of rejection. By-passing the salvation core of the gospel — the forgiveness, acceptance, and peace — means being left with dry, even arbitrary, discipline. That has sent many fleeing from the church and has erected a barrier to those who might have entered. If Americans are to be drawn into the Bible, this potential roadblock will need to be altered or redefined.

Yet, if this and other misconceptions can be set aside, it seems entirely possible that a concerted effort that evolved from the Orlando conference and similar think tanks could answer a pressing and perilous emergency. Practically every study of the current state of the American psyche reports deep wells of loneliness and shallow stores of purpose and meaning. From my own survey for this book, the Bible seems to be a vastly underappreciated antidote to this emptiness. (Is it just coincidence, for example, that a move away from the Bible, a sharp foe of self-centeredness, has coincided with the alleged rise of narcissism?) It is an extraordinary exploration of human nature in all its gore and glory. The fact that it is unflattering to the human race is a supreme testimony to its underlying authenticity. From the invitation to think about the creation of everything in Genesis to the introspections of the prophets, the teachings of Jesus, and the dazzling commentary of Paul, the Bible lays out reasons for living and causes for which to die, with stacks of proverbs with which to conjure everyday ironies. It can be enormously helpful to the self, but it is not designed as a self-help book, nor is it meant to be one. It is concerned about ultimate reality and unearned gifts of spiritual awareness of the other rather than proposing pragmatic steps to inflate a self-defeating ego. There is a reason Abraham Lincoln and Harry Truman, among throngs of others, considered it the greatest composite of wisdom and knowledge ever written.

Having been basically shunted aside as an irrelevant artifact or an outdated moral manual, the Bible is poised within the cycle of return to become ripe for rediscovery, an option more enticing as a means of making sense of life than the ever-mounting heap of self-help books. In contrast to the narrow aims of every five-step road to success in fashioning a more attractive "you" or finding shortcuts to wealth, the Bible proposes a multidimensional, panoramic, time-tested view to generations whose unfamiliarity with it makes possible fresh discoveries, offering seekers an opportunity to gain a new foothold. If seekers can look beyond the stereotypes — that the Bible is inscrutable or that its inerrancy offers the only valid interpretation — and permit themselves to question aspects of its history, language, authorship, and culture (for instance, slavery), they will find in it an adventure to explore.

Whether resurgence could get this far, or Scripture could make a comeback along the entire spectrum of churches, is questionable, given the momentum of secularizing. But at least the problem is out in the open, and a challenge has been laid down. In Orlando enterprising leaders trotted out plans for jump-starting the process. The common goal of the institutions and their logos featured "engagement": for example, "Don't just get the Bible in the door" (as the Catholic Bible salesmen did in the documentary) but "get people to read it and 'engage' with it." Groundbreaking methods were being rolled out in pursuit of that goal, some by the Orlando launchers, others by related interests. They bore names like the "Center for Bible Engagement" (Back to the Bible), "Uncover the Word" (the American Bible Society), the "Center for Scripture Engagement" (Taylor University), "Read the Bible for Life" (Southern Baptist Convention), the "Big Bible Project" (a British equivalent based at the University of Durham), and the Barna project on Millennials.

Most of these ventures were still in the initial, experimental stages of conducting research to better understand why the Bible isn't read or understood much anymore. Evangelism is, by its very nature, an urgent matter and thus is impatient with any more delays or planning than is absolutely necessary. The Orlando participants left the meeting with enthusiasm and resolve, but the challenge of reversing the powerful current, even within their own churches, that is carrying the public away from the Bible — with little from the past to guide them — is a challenge of biblical proportions.

CHAPTER 6

The Perfect Is the Enemy of the Good

It's okay with some people in Dayton, Tennessee, that their town is barely noticeable from its approach on U.S. Highway 27. Attracting attention has been at best a mixed blessing since the fateful Scopes trial on the teaching of evolution created an uproar there in 1925. For ten days, more than 3,000 reporters, educators, street vendors, and curiosity seekers crashed the quiet town of 7,191 residents to view what had been billed as a national spectacle. It wasn't by accident, nor were the citizens victims of an outside invasion. Go-getters in town had angled for the right to land the trial in Dayton as a means of attracting new business. Jobs had disappeared with the loss of coal and steel operations, and commerce was suffering accordingly. The boosters who took it upon themselves to reverse these fortunes succeeded in bringing the trial to Dayton, but, perhaps inevitably, they got more than they had bargained for.

The worst consequence was that the town got branded as "backward," which for all intents and purposes was another word for "fundamentalist," which in turn implied "ignoramus." Reports of the trial in newspapers and magazines across the country depicted those who lived in the compact, hardscrabble community as mean-spirited rubes who were intolerant of anyone outside their reactionary churches. Simply put, John Scopes's being on trial for teaching evolution was evidence enough to many of those covering the event (including the *Chicago Tribune, The New York Times,* and *The Baltimore Evening Sun)* that Dayton was full of religious and mental primitives. The most famous and polemical of them, H. L. Mencken, said after the trial: "Two months ago the town was obscure and happy. Today it is a universal joke" (*Baltimore Evening Sun,* July 9, 1925). Mencken, like other self-appointed sophisticates, blamed the Bible for this state of depravity;

the Bible was thus "über-backward," a blow against its sanctity that has endured. On all counts, the stigma was frightfully undeserved.

Such tarring hasn't been easy to wash off. Though it resulted from a scheme that was dreamed up by Dayton's own civic and business leaders, it hasn't faded, along with the false hopes for town betterment that set the event in motion. The lasting image has put a damper on town spirits and instilled a protective reluctance to be too conspicuous to travelers passing over the county highway. Walking and talking with Daytonites is an exercise in the ambivalence toward Scopes history: some are willing to address the painful legacy, yet are simultaneously wary that outsiders might be trying to reinforce the old stereotypes rather than honestly seeking the truth.

Many townsfolk, like Edwin, an electrical worker who says he doesn't always tell people where he lives so as to avoid awakening old ghosts, insists that the badmouthing has been the result of a total misreading of the trial as a crusade by religious zealots against science. "There's no arguing that this is where it happened," he said, cracking a smile and returning his iPhone to his shirt pocket. "But other than some bigwigs in town, the people here had nothing to do with it. They were just bystanders when and where the politicians decided to put on a show. It was political. Did people here like evolution? No, but they weren't about to pin anyone against the wall for telling school kids about it. Were they religious crackpots? No way you can generalize about that."

In fact, John Scopes, the high school teacher who agreed to bring the case for the American Civil Liberties Union against Tennessee's ban on teaching Darwin, had only briefly taught biology as a fill-in for the regular science teacher. His regular job was coaching football, basketball, and baseball. He was an amiable young man who appeared unruffled and detached through the furor — and he remained popular afterward. Scopes told handlers before the trial that he wasn't sure he'd ever mentioned evolution to the class (some still claim that it had been taught previously in the school without complaint). Scopes, whose role as an accused innocent bore a surface likeness to Melville's Billy Budd, did admit that he had taught it, but he was so unschooled in evolution that he had to be tutored in the basics of it as preparation for his trial. He apparently had no animus toward the Bible or religion and was never called to witness. He was found guilty by a jury made up mostly of Baptists and Methodists, who had little reason to decide otherwise; he was fined $100, which was ponied up by Mencken's paper, *The Baltimore Evening Sun;* and he never spent a day in jail. The law against teaching evolution remained on the Tennessee books until 1967.

Thirty-five years later, the melodrama and the sordid reputation it superimposed onto Dayton was fading into history's murk when it was smashingly revived and falsified in the hit 1960 movie *Inherit the Wind*. Frederic March loomed large on the screen as William Jennings Bryan, Scopes's chief accuser and a famous public figure; Spencer Tracy brilliantly played Scopes's lead defender, the renowned Clarence Darrow. The two legal titans literally sweated it out in blistering July heat in the stately East Tennessee courtroom (and once on the court grounds when the inside temperature had become insufferable) for ten days. In the film, Darrow's persona as the defender of free inquiry reaches its apex when he places Bryan on the stand and logically demolishes his opponent's literal reading of the Bible. Bryan thus became the ridiculed stand-in for millions of Christians who held similar opinions: that Scripture is errorless because the Almighty has written it exactly as it appears in the King James Version, including every detail of how the universe came about; that Genesis contains the blueprint and the record of the accomplishment of creation in six days of twenty-four hours each; and, just as Genesis says, every species was formed on its own — not one species starting as one thing and "evolving" into something else. The bottom line is that human beings are not newer, refashioned models of apes, but a breed apart from the beginning — as were all other species. To think that one did grow or adapt from the other would, by literalist standards, imply that humans lack the full dignity, the "likeness to God," that Genesis says they have. Given the film's implicit confidence in modern science as the path to progress, the arguments of the Bible believers, articulated by Bryan on their behalf, were the shattered remnants of a backward, less-evolved mentality.

Bryan cloaked himself in old-time religion, but he wasn't that much of a literalist. For instance, he believed that a Genesis "day" could be millions of years rather than twenty-four hours; he did not object to the teaching of evolution in schools so long as it was clearly labeled "theory" rather than "fact" (a point generally conceded by scientists); and he allowed time for the creationist viewpoint (evolutionists argued that this amounted to apples and oranges inasmuch as scientific evidence backed their explanation, whereas fundamentalism's "creationism" was purely a matter of faith). Nonetheless, the movie's tacit favoring of Darrow's scientific orientation consigned Bryan's Bible analysis to nincompoopery. That was no wonder, given the moviemakers' wider target. They saw the Scopes scenario as a vehicle by which to pillory Senator Joseph McCarthy for endangering individual rights by crusading against the alleged communist threat to American democracy. McCarthy's infamous congressional hearings exposed witnesses to ruinous personal and political attacks in a climate of hysteria that often indulged in ad hominem diatribes and unsubstantiated charges. Because he used tactics that fanned the flames of the fear of communism in the general public, McCarthy was condemned on legal and ethical grounds and was eventually censured by Congress. The filmmakers saw the Scopes trial as a precursor to the McCarthy assault on free thought, requiring a sharp "good guy/bad guy" confrontation, pitting champions of truth against doctrinaire closed-mindedness. Accordingly, *Inherit the Wind,* which began as a play, superimposed the vindictiveness and narrow-mindedness of the McCarthy witch hunt onto the Scopes trial, casting the Bryan character as the villain.

Finbarr Curtis, a scholar of American religion at Georgia State University, plumbed the Scopes legacy exhaustively, particularly Bryan's role, in his research for his PhD dissertation. He concludes that Bryan's reputation was tarnished to suit the movie's goal of creating a "secular myth" of progress and enlightenment that was free of the shackles of religious intolerance. By implication, the imagery foresaw the new paradigm of truth-through-empiricism, replacing an outmoded and ignorant fundamentalism stuck in irrational superstition that venerated an ancient, irrelevant book.

Prof. Curtis told a college audience in 2012, drawing from his extensive research, that *Inherit the Wind,* in order to feed the myth, painted Bryan as "a right-wing reactionary" who flipped out under Darrow's grilling. The movie tried to "maximize the conflict," Curtis continued, by showing Bryan as vouching for the fundamentalist claim that the earth was (against geological findings of the time) just 6,000 years old. But the facts proved otherwise. Bryan accepted geology's dating of the earth in eons and multiple millions of years, and he "didn't go crazy, despite the play's image." The drama "makes Bryan seem less tolerant than he was: Darrow *had* to be the tolerant one" to fit the myth, Curtis contended. The script "eliminated Darrow baiting Bryan — he calls the latter an ignoramus" — and leaves the impression that "people in the court were convinced by Darrow" through pure reason. "It never happened," Curtis asserted. "Bryan held the room."

Feelings of hurt pride are just below the surface in Dayton, though they have naturally lost intensity and power over the passing generations. As the affront has moderated, younger people often have only sketchy details of its origins and intensity. Since the late 1980s, a yearly festival commemorating the events has been the aim of a group that is concerned with making an opportunity out of whatever degree of misfortune still remains. They did so by turning the story into a drama, with local citizens playing the parts of the original participants. But enthusiasm for staging it has waxed and waned until finally, in 2012, the play was canceled for lack of interest.

The shutdown raises the question of whether it is worth continuing efforts to keep the trial a tourist attraction in a revised form that could more closely reflect the town's memory and the court transcripts, or to give it up as a lost cause. The answer has come in the form of a new play, entitled *Front Page News,* by Deborah de George, a nearby writer with close ties to the town (her husband teaches at Bryan College). The play is a strikingly fresh approach, incorporating original music by Nashville songwriter Bobby Taylor, the exuberance of Southern gospel harmonies, and the coziness of familiar Tennessee folk tunes, a blend that unabashedly appeals to the area's sensibilities. The musical has domesticated the story more than any previous staging had. It was performed in the venerable old courthouse itself, which stood virtually unchanged from those days when eight hundred trial observers crammed into a space designed to hold four hundred. (The county's trials are still held in the same ornate wooden courtroom.) Unlike the older dramas, which relied on the town's limited resources, the new production is a partnership between the Dayton Scopes Trial Festival and the nearby Cumberland City Playhouse, which is well regarded for its professional standards and ambitious production schedule. On its list of upcoming plays is *Inherit the Wind,* perhaps out of fairness to the other side of the story.

Those who attended the debut weekend performances of *Front Page News* in July 2012 were so enraptured by it that a second round was hastily arranged for the following weekend. Theatergoers especially raved about the joyous and spiritually uplifting music, which sounded more like them than anything did in the movie's dour portrait. The play's portrait of the town residents more closely matches their own, or at least the one they prefer to have of themselves. It does tell their side of the story in a manner that includes interludes of standing and singing hymns extolling the Bible's message to the high heavens.

*   *   *

The Scopes trial was indeed about politics, freethinking, tolerance, and wound-tight religion, but nothing approached the impact it had on the Bible. Since the early decades of the 1800s, scholars with increasing objectivity had dissected Scripture like geologists inspecting layers of rock to discover the earth's record. The new enterprise, drawing on early-modern laboratory methods, was called historical-critical scholarship, probing beneath the surface of Scripture to learn about its complex process of composition, wording, and style. The premise is that the Bible was not published by God in perfect form, but that it was put together rather haphazardly, written and rewritten piecemeal, blending varying strands of text, mixing history with "faith" and mythology, elements from surrounding cultures with a diversity of voices that sometimes sound similar and sometimes treat the same or similar subjects very differently. Mounting discoveries of texts, such as the Gnostic Gospels, and archaeological ruins, such as Jericho, among others, increasingly verify biblical accounts or challenge their accuracy. The historical-critical scholars — first in Europe, then in the United States — have pursued solutions to mysteries and greater truths about the Bible's composition, even though their findings may shake the faith of those who believe in its unadulterated perfection.

The scholars have overturned core assumptions, at least for those willing to accept the research. Among their conclusions are these: the Bible isn't a unified volume but a collection of books with a multitude of authors and versions assembled over centuries; the vast distances in time and culture since the composition of those books make the language and references obscure to modern readers, their meaning sometimes all but impossible to grasp. Sections written by different authors were found to be pieced together over time by astute editors and talented blenders. One of the most notable scholarly findings is that some of the hallmark Epistles attributed to Saint Paul were almost certainly written by close associates rather than by the apostle himself. These claims, made by a host of experts in language, history, and literary form, cast great and lasting doubts on the Bible's authority as a seamless transmission of divine will. Genesis, for example, long believed to be a univocal report of creation, was recast by the historical-critical scholars as the product of at least three major streams that had been finally folded into a single narrative. A scholar named Julius Wellhausen demonstrated to the satisfaction of those open to such research that Moses did not write the Pentateuch (the Hebrew Torah) — the books of Genesis, Exodus, Leviticus, Deuteronomy, and Numbers — as tradition held; instead, those books were assembled out of countless components that had been written and rewritten over and over. Interpretation of any portion was widely held by scholars to be largely in the eye of the beholder.

The scholarly claims not only divided scholars but flew directly in the face of the common belief that the Bible is exactly what Christian teachers have more or less always said it is — the undefiled transcript of God's direct testimony. Any apparent errors are solely due to human translators: the original copies — or "autographs," as they are called — contain the directly inspired transmissions from God. No originals have ever been found, but their alleged existence somewhere is a standard default argument in the face of obvious snags in available texts.

It is impossible to tell how many Christians still base their faith on that assurance; but the numbers are most likely falling because of the inroads of secularism and science. And it is not only the results of the historical-critical process that has placed them in a defensive position: the legacy of Scopes — that biblical literalism is "irrational" — greets them at nearly every turn in their dealings with the wider world, and it poses a problem in getting ahead. The crunch could come under unexpected circumstances. For Becca, a thirty-two-year-old driver for a cross-country truck line, the problem arose during a job interview. She had driven for nearly seven years and had a spotless performance record. As one of few women in the field, she'd expected male resistance ("You're taking a job away from some guy with wife and kids" was the gist of a lot of it, she said), but she coped with that, and with the come-ons, and with the objections from some family members and friends that it wasn't "ladylike." However, it was when she applied for better-paying jobs that she thinks she bumped into the religious factor. She had been a lifelong member of the Church of Christ, wore on her collar a silver cross framed by the words "God So Loved the World," and carried a pint-sized Bible in her vest pocket. She'd passed the urine test.

"I went into the trailer for the interview," she said. "I'd thought I checked out on everything, and then he wanted to know how religious I was. You're not supposed to ask questions like that, but I didn't feel I could complain. Rather than not answering, or making light of it, I thought it couldn't hurt. This was Oklahoma, after all, where religion's a pretty good thing. So I said I was a born-again Christian, saved by Jesus, and that I trusted the Bible as the total truth. He just asked one other question: 'Don't you think people use fairy stories from the Bible to try telling other people what to do?' I didn't say anything. I didn't get the job. Maybe it didn't have anything to do with the Bible thing, but it was the only thing that made sense at the time."

By the time of the Scopes trial, battle lines had already hardened considerably between those who accepted a Bible as redefined by critical scholarship — that is, built of materials of uneven quality and credibility —

and those who staunchly rejected the scholarly revisions as undermining their trust in Holy Scripture.

Scopes had by no means triggered the conflict over evolution. But the trial came to stand for it, etching it into the cultural memory of America more than any other such skirmish. In the popular mind, the first trial ever broadcast nationally held up a figurative neon sign in the shape of a Bible pointing in two directions: one toward the PRIMITIVE PAST, for those "locked into Biblical creationism, opposed to reason and science"; the other toward the SMART FUTURE, for those who "regarded the Bible highly as spiritual advice and irrelevant to matters of history or the physical world." It became a marker with which supporters and foes of biblical literalism could point fingers at each other. The "smart" set claimed the high ground in literary and university circles, especially among the college-educated, affluent populations of the North and to a somewhat lesser extent the Midwest. Long before the trial, the keepers of inerrancy were largely Protestant country-dwellers in the South who lived low off the hog. The trial raised their visibility and intensified their image in much of the country as living in a religious dark age. By implying that this old-fashioned viewpoint stood in the way of a better life offered by science, Curtis noted, the teaching of evolution as advocated by the "secular myth" led Bryan to fear further condescension toward fundamentalists, imposing an even deeper stigma that feasted on regional, ethnic, and religious biases — and has lasted to this day. The Scopes trial was decisive in fixing those images into the consciousness of the country.

Curtis further deduced that the inerrantists had good reason to worry that the trial could "reduce the Bible to a scrap of paper." What could mean more than losing the debate over the creation of everything? Undermining the Bible's stature as ultimate truth-teller allowed philosophies of materialism to gain a stronger foothold. Evolution essentially left transcendence totally out of the picture. Bryan spoke not only as a defender of inerrancy but as a famous Progressive Party's champion of the rights of ordinary masses (he ran twice as the Democratic candidate for President). His view of the Bible spilled over to politics and economics. Like many other Bible followers, for example, Bryan warned that evolution's central doctrine, survival of the fittest, when applied to human behavior, would spur selfishness, oppression, and greed (predatory capitalism), the antitheses of the Christian virtues of love, forgiveness, and self-sacrifice.

*   *   *

The parlor sport of bashing fundamentalism (then and now) has inexorably chipped away at the Bible's stature, steadily edging its stature downward through the twentieth century. The slide has been inseparable from the coincident rise in science's prestige and the diminishing status of the humanities, the academic category in which the Bible belongs. Astonishing breakthroughs from the beginning of the twentieth century in physics, medicine, archaeology, chemistry, paleontology, geology, and astronomy radically altered the understanding of the natural world and boosted science's standing as a source of truth — either in concert with religion or in opposition to it. The debate continues: Are the two compatible or at odds? Which one should be accorded greater commonsense credibility in determining the reality that surrounds us? Are certain topics, such as the meaning and purpose of life, the special province of religion, or does science challenge that as well? Can Christianity and/or Judaism any longer depend on a Bible whose reliability has been questioned by empirical methods of slicing and dicing? Is it mostly metaphor? Does a science-adulating society such as America, for whom Albert Einstein, Madame Curie, and Thomas Edison are the new demigods, have room any longer for the Bible? Will such a society (which has found it difficult to believe in transcendence, as Charles Taylor has observed) devote less and less time to looking for answers outside empiricism or accept as its primary dogma that empiricism will eventually explain everything? These questions trouble all churches, especially those trying to hold the line against the secular wave that they regard as demonic.

By their own testimony, evangelicals clearly make up the subculture that cares most about the answers to the above questions. To them falls the burden of sustaining a belief in a pure, heavenly Bible that is increasingly thought impossible by growing numbers of people who have no particular stake in the issue or for whom a Bible flawed by human authorship makes more sense, disappointing as that may be. As a whole, evangelicals are the last line of defense for the notion of the Bible as divinely dictated, an article of faith they believe has existed from the earliest days of the church. This "high view" of Scripture is now in jeopardy, and evangelicals are Horatios at the bridge, protecting this sacred vessel even at the cost of contradicting their confidence in scientific disciplines in other areas of their professional and personal lives as engineers and airline pilots.

Moderate and liberal Protestants have rather passively absorbed the implications of the slicing and dicing that has knocked the Bible off that pedestal, and they have recataloged it more or less as they would any other book. Bible research fits the scholarly model of the universities most of them have attended — and thus they accept it as such. By and large, these progressive Americans honor the new Bible knowledge as much as they marvel at discoveries of links between humans and primates and the possibilities of parallel universes. Accepting the Bible as a limited source of history, biology, and cosmology, subject to correction and different orders of knowledge, reinforces their perception of it as a document fashioned by human minds and hands, a rich storehouse of witness *to* God, but no longer assumed to be *by* God.

* * *

From Scopes onward, there have been constant tensions among Christians between the inerrancy backers and the so-called modernist supporters of the historical-critical approach. But the most bitter and passionate struggles have been among evangelicals themselves about whether any concessions can be made to the scholarly challenges. Like Cuba, whose communist ideology was under constant threat by the lure of its democratic superpower neighbor, evangelicals are under mounting pressure to give up their struggle to keep inerrancy as a viable option in the face of growing scientific hegemony. Their resolve to stay the course means keeping watch over their scattered coalitions for signs that their bond is being violated. Meanwhile, a steady stream of defectors, some of them with high profiles, have abandoned inerrancy. Some have simply joined a church more agreeable to their revised views, quietly leaving literalism behind, while others have issued parting shots. Books and articles by former members of inerrancy churches and institutions of higher learning who are now intent on debunking that line of thought have become a cottage industry. Their motives seemed fueled by a need to vent frustration at the mistaken precepts they once embraced and to validate their conversion to nonliteralism.

Evangelicals are the lone stakeholders in a seemingly untenable struggle in which their collective ego is heavily invested. Whatever their rigidities — in their problems with putting Luther's *sola Scriptura* in sensible context and in their stubborn refusal to give an inch to the clearest counterclaims — they see the implications of ending up with a toothless Bible that has only fragmentary, relative authority. And they are willing to go overboard to defend against that demise. Their methods and tactics often overshoot their goal so much that their purpose is defeated; but they press their case, lest the whole cause be lost. They will not be lectured like schoolchildren by their cultural "betters"; it is, among other things, a religious, cultural, and — up the line — political point of pride. The inerrancy cause has already been lost among moderate and liberal churches; sustaining it requires running against the expanding hegemony of scientific assumptions.

A qualification of that state of affairs seems appropriate here. Though the division over literalism generally obtains, practically everyone has chosen to be a literalist at one time or another. While conservative Christians are more consistent and thorough about it, liberals and moderates — in whose company I count myself — could be just as sure that certain passages are ironclad true. While liberals may consider Moses's parting of the Red Sea a metaphor, for example, and will deny the validity of verses used to condemn homosexuality, they can insist that Jesus's warnings against the dangers of wealth and the neglect of the needy are nothing short of direct quotes from the Lord, regardless of the scholarly debates about how and when these verses found their way into the one or the other of the Gospels. Liberals are just as capable as conservatives are of imputing eternal truth to a piece of Scripture to claim victory in a heated debate. It is tempting because the Bible's words and cadences lend themselves to ultimate profundity. Nonbelievers have indulged in it, too, tossing off bits and pieces of biblical testimony partly in sardonic fashion to mock it, though one suspects some affection and respect for its mysteries.

In 1975, the noted evangelical writer Harold Lindsell sounded a pungent alarm about what he saw as a serious drift away from inerrancy, at least as he defined it. His stinging critique was found in a book entitled *The Battle for the Bible,* which became a bestseller and immediately ignited controversy. Lindsell, a former editor of the influential magazine *Christianity Today* and a professor who had taught at two theological schools and had been the vice president of leading-edge evangelical Fuller Seminary in Pasadena, California, brooked no compromise with anything less than total commitment to the Bible as infallible. It was bad enough that Christian modernists had forsaken that belief; evangelicals were increasingly prone to do it themselves.

"I will contend that embracing a doctrine of an errant Scripture will lead to disaster down the road," Lindsell declares in *The Battle for the Bible.* "It will result in the loss of missionary outreach; it will quench missionary passion; it will lull congregations to sleep and undermine their belief in the full-orbed truth of the Bible; it will produce spiritual sloth and decay; and it will finally lead to apostasy."

The slope that Lindsell wished to describe was indeed slippery. One misstep in admitting error in the biblical text could ruin the faith (though he made it clear elsewhere that such waywardness didn't necessarily stand in the way of salvation). Few doubted his premise: if key elements of Scripture were proved by scholars to be self-contradictory and fallible patchwork, the effect would be an unraveling of the garment by higher critics' pulling the strands of yarn. But the measures he used to define infallibility, and his hard-nosed judgments against alleged apostates, rankled a broad range of evangelicals. Most toxically, he blasted Fuller Seminary for permitting the very kind of creeping apostasy he was warning against.

Lindsell obviously aimed his manifesto at fellow evangelicals in hopes of overcoming deepening strains among them. The fact that he wasn't a biblical scholar limited his impact among church educators and leaders, but his high-pitched indictment rattled many evangelicals and highlighted the issue of whether biblical infallibility *was* a necessary or sufficient doctrine. And if so, how could it be defended?

The strains have not only remained, but have deepened. One factor is that more evangelical professors have gone to prestigious secular universities for graduate work. Those settings, with their inherent confidence in the scientific method and its Darwinian applications, have moderated or transformed the confidence in infallibility. The center hasn't held the way it could when the doctrine was encased in cultural isolation. There is no such thing as settled biblical interpretation among evangelicals — only volatility and tenuous peace. Added to that is the effect of the Gallup, Barna, and Pew surveys that have dispelled illusions of unanimity of perspective.

An upshot has been the defection of some evangelical "stars" from the churches and movements that nurtured them. Some have gone voluntarily; others have been shown the door. Though a few have drawn the attention of major media, most have taken place with little notice. Though depictions of conservative evangelicals marching in lockstep to defend the walls of fundamentals such as inerrancy have become commonplace caricatures, my travels among this subculture are striking for a contrasting image of widening cracks in those walls of certainty. Not only are evangelicals reading the Bible less, but more of them either respond indifferently to infallibility or, when pressed, hedge their answers. This is not meant to discredit evangelicals, only to witness that how evangelicals respond to the cultural norms around them understandably alters their views. As this segment of the population rises educationally and economically, they are more likely to be influenced by mainstream American suppositions about things like belief in science.

Peter Enns is among the brainy, widely admired biblical scholars who was fired from his job on charges that he promoted false teachings — namely, nonfundamentalist ones. With a solid evangelical background and a PhD from Harvard, Enns had been sought after by conservative seminaries. In 1994, he chose Westminster Theological Seminary in Philadelphia, a stronghold of inerrancy. His rise was rapid: he gained tenure six years later and full professor status in 2005. During that peak year, however, the publication of his book *Inspiration and Incarnation* began the conflict that led to his ouster. The book struck two nerves in particular: first, it declares that the Old Testament contains many lines of thought rather than a single harmonious voice; a second point, following from the first, insists that the Bible isn't solely the flawless inspiration of God but that mortals have also had a hand in it, thus lending it to human error. Those claims and others put him at odds with that Presbyterian/Reformed seminary's generally accepted interpretation of its statement of faith — which professors are required to sign. As controversy swirled, Westminster's new president, Peter Lillback, who had that same year been picked to replace a president suspected of being too soft on inerrancy, called for a faculty-wide discussion to determine whether Enns had run afoul of the seminary's principles. The faculty met periodically for two years, eventually clearing Enns of any wrongdoing in December 2007 by a vote of twelve to eight. Lillback then forwarded the case to the trustees of the seminary, who reversed the faculty's decision by an eighteen-to-nine vote the following March, thereby ousting Enns. From that point onward, Enns's reputation grew as a formidable critic of inerrancy whose tenured status had not protected him from being expelled from a citadel of evangelicalism for exercising academic freedom. In trumping free speech, the trustees cited Enns's alleged breaking of his pledge to uphold the vaunted 1636 Westminster Confession of Faith. The degree to which Enns might have consciously provoked the confrontation wasn't clear.

The firing caused a media splash because of both the painful faculty-trustee rupture that lay in its wake and the addition of another disenchanted evangelical to a growing list. It placed Enns in the virtual Greek chorus of influential former and borderline evangelicals who had broken ranks and openly bewailed biblical perfectionism. He later wrote a book, *The Bible Tells Me So,* that effectively ruled out any thought of mending fences with literalists and signaled the gathering strength of the dissidents.

Another catalytic figure was Bart Ehrman, a religion professor at the University of North Carolina who earned his undergraduate degree at evangelical Wheaton College. Like Enns, Ehrman is a specialist in ancient languages who similarly came to see the Bible as a patchwork of myriad, even conflated, origins rather than an otherworldly monolith. Ehrman makes that point emphatically in two of his books: *Forged: Writing in the Name of God — Why the Bible's Authors Are Not Who We Think They Are* and *Misquoting Jesus: The Story Behind Who Changed the Bible and Why.*

Christian Smith, a widely respected Notre Dame sociologist, also left evangelicalism to become a Roman Catholic largely because he objected to what he called "Biblicism," which wrongly idolizes the Bible as infallible, ultimate truth. Smith sees this as a deifying of Scripture that displaces Jesus Christ at the center of the Christian life, worshiping the witness to the teacher rather than the teacher himself. He delivers his assault on biblical literalism in a best-selling book entitled *The Bible Made Impossible: Why Biblicism Is Not a Truly Evangelical Reading of Scripture.*

The Bible is a thicket of lost meanings and obscure perspectives by a vast assortment of writers, Smith argues, and it becomes even harder to comprehend by readers with limitless personal and cultural lenses of their own. Its lessons are thus neither transparent nor self-evident. "Short of a divine miracle," he writes, "the Bible cannot function as an authority today, whether or not the Holy Spirit is involved, until it is interpreted and made sense of by readers. Every scriptural teaching is mediated through human reading and interpretation, which involve choosing one among a larger number of readings. . . . The truth of the Word of God is not self-evident even in the Bible." Five readers might come up with five different interpretations. Smith's view is a far cry from the uncluttered certainties of Harold Lindsell's legacy.

An alternative approach, called *lectio divina* (the "divine reading" of Scripture), is an ancient Christian practice that has been revived and is gaining popularity in a variety of churches. It springs from an inner, silent, and meditative method of attaining deeper meaning rather than a striving for textual precision. Its four stages — reading, meditation, prayer, and contemplation of Bible passages — presupposes that the practice will reveal God's purposes as contained in those verses. Prosaic interpretation takes a back seat to the awareness of God's presence.

Cracks in inerrancy's solidity have also been showing up in the pages of *Christianity Today,* the flagship evangelical publication that has an enviable reputation for reporting both the good and bad news about evangelicals. The cover story of its July-August 2012 issue compares the struggles of two scientists to reconcile their devotion to conventional science with their faith in the account of creation found in Genesis. The fight to preserve Genesis as a reliable record has produced a series of mental and linguistic gymnastics to keep the mounting evidence of evolution from crushing literalist holdouts. "Creationism," as it was first known, denounces evolution as a godless substitute for the "truth" of Genesis. Among creationists, "young-earth" believers continue to insist that creation took place only about 6,000 years ago despite geologists' mounting pile of fossils dating back millions of years in the past, along with the rock formations and minerals in which they were embedded. The next stage, called "intelligent design," makes concessions to science, while it is reluctant to admit that. It allows that there can be development in species within basic forms, but that God, rather than Darwin's theory of randomness, shapes those changes.

Neither creationism nor intelligent design offers scientific proof, though advocates of both alternatives have campaigned to have them taught as equivalent theories in the schools. The courts have decisively found that the faith-based alternatives were just that — matters of faith, but not scientifically credible. Meanwhile, sincere and decent keepers of the anti-evolution flame have expended huge amounts of time and creativity to keep science's wolf from the inerrantists' door, resorting to a succession of awkward formulations and contortions. Their effort to cast out evolution or achieve some compatibility with it is a herculean task, without a scrap of evidence to support it. Their passionate commitment to refuting or compromising with science is in many ways an admirable defense of the age of faith; but it has the unmistakable marks of a lost cause, a refusal to come to grips with reality, as if devotees of Philadelphia cheese steaks were on a mission to prove health experts wrong about the arterial risks of eating their meal of choice.

On one level, the *Christianity Today* article could be read as confirming that stark reality by exposing the price of evading it. The profiled scientists had endured trials both within themselves and in the professional challenges they faced. They typified an increasing number of evangelicals trying to match old-time religion with modern science, often with one intellectual hand tied behind their backs. Thus, neither scientist in the article is the cookie-cutter upholder of fundamentalist convictions that might have appeared in an earlier time. Indeed, each one is a born-again Christian who graduated from a church-related college; each then earned a PhD in biology from a major secular research university where evolution is treated as a fact.

Darrel Falk, a Canadian by birth, wavered between his academic and religious explanations before being convinced that evolutionists had it right. "I had known the beauty of Christianity," he says in the article, referring to his graduate-school days. "Now I discovered the beauty of genetics." While a tenured professor at Syracuse University, where his pro-evolution views were welcome, he realized that he wanted closer ties to his Nazarene background, so he sought a position at an evangelical college. That led him to Mt. Vernon Nazarene College, and from there to Point Loma (Nazarene) University in California. While there, he was attacked by the evangelical mover and shaker James Dobson, an alumnus of the college and the founder of Focus on the Family, for what Falk describes in the *Christianity Today* article as "destroying the faith of my students" by describing in his book the way biologists think, which, of course, assumes evolution as their guiding principle.

Falk survived the Dobson challenge and remained at the college, though his views do not exactly fit there — and he no longer teaches biology. He is thus removed from classroom booby traps, but he focuses on the general relationship between science and religion, and for a time served on a project overseen by the prominent geneticist Francis Collins, who ran the National Institutes for Health. Falk calls himself an "evolutionary creationist" and a peacemaker among warring Genesis factions. "We must recognize that we will never reach the point where we will all see Scripture the same way," he is quoted as saying. "When there is division in the church, it will be difficult for the thirsty to find their way to Jesus."

Todd Wood had preserved his "young-earth" creationism through a doctoral program at the University of Virginia that was totally grounded in evolution. As an undergraduate at Liberty University, he'd been safely ensconced in creationism, so the transition to a secular, evolutionist graduate discipline came as a shock. But as things turned out, he didn't regard evolutionary science as the enemy; on the contrary, he admired the voluminous examples of its validity, at least up to a point. He drew the line when it came to acknowledging that humans had descended from apes and other matters that diminished God's direct creation as summarized in Genesis. Though he joined the faculty at faith-based Bryan College, where belief in creationism was not only allowed but required, Wood was nagged by the alleged contradictions he was encountering, and he sought a resolution. He found it by restating the contradiction: he accepted evolution as the material mechanism by which species become more complex, and also accepted the Genesis theology of immediate creation of the original species just a few millennia ago. God's action is accessible by faith; evolution is accessible by the scientific method. Wood took that mindset to a new position as director of creation research at the school. However, he was skeptical that a corps of young and talented students was arising that would continue the creationist project in the future.

By drawing out the unsettling dilemmas of these two professors, *Christianity Today* further broadens the legitimate discussion of a subject that effectively excluded doubts not long before. Other well-known evangelicals have made news by voicing similar doubts. Among the most shocking was the declaration by megachurch wizard Rob Bell that he no longer believed in hell as it was derived from the Bible and understood by many Christians. His book *Love Wins* spells out his arguments against the concept of eternal punishment and in favor of God's love that is so all-encompassing that it borders on universalism, the belief that everyone eventually gets to heaven, not just those certified as born again. It is a gesture toward amnesty that some leading evangelicals scorn as unbiblical. Bell denies being a universalist but says that he values religious truth wherever he finds it. He subsequently resigned from his pastorate of Mars Hill Bible Church — a marquee megachurch that he founded in Grandville, Michigan — in the aftermath of the uproar.

*   *   *

Biblical infallibility still has a following, but my informal review leads me to believe that its appeal is steadily declining and its domain shrinking steadily to the point of insignificance. A common response I get is that the term "inerrancy," in particular, has lost whatever usefulness it might have had as an explanatory tool — both practically and theologically. In dozens of interviews of evangelicals that I conducted, confidence in inerrancy is often halting and reserved, as if it is just harder to go out on that limb, to be *sure* in a world infused with relativity and doubt. It is especially difficult for younger people. Certainty tends to be present but tentative: I have found silent evangelicals who accept bits of recent scholarship — such as the claim that a new ending was attached to Mark's Gospel at a later time — but they are not sure where to draw the line. They no longer feel quite at home with inerrancy, but neither do they have any inclination to surrender to academic approaches that they view as undercutting the Bible's trustworthiness. Nor are they ready to cross over to mainline denominations that they believe have robbed the Bible of its sacredness. They constitute a quiet alternative whose minor allowance for "error" is not welcome in most evangelical circles, even though substantial numbers may basically agree with them in a free and open discussion. The muted split appears to be shifting the ground in the direction of establishing a new standard of inerrancy that will further modify the meaning of "error."

Why, then, do the polls continue to show that more than half of Americans (56 percent in a recent Barna poll) say they believe that the Bible was either directly transmitted or inspired errorless by God? That would seem to indicate that inerrancy still prevails. Perhaps — but in my view that surmise is misleading. It seems to me that many respond to pollsters with a vestige of defensiveness from the days of the Scopes trial, when biblical literalists were ridiculed by perceived atheists. They had seen the extolling of evolution and the attack on literalism as denying that God had anything to do with creation. When pollsters asked whether they accepted science's claims, therefore, it sounded — consciously or unconsciously — like a choice between voting for an option that clearly includes God and one that doesn't. The idea that they can affirm both a role for God and Darwin's theory — as it is being embraced by more church leaders — still seems mutually exclusive. So it seems plausible to me that they voted *for* God rather than *against* evolution.

Nowhere was the fear of defection greater than at Bryan College, the Christian school founded in 1930 in Dayton, Tennessee, just five years after the Scopes trial and named in honor of William Jennings Bryan, the champion of inerrancy at the Scopes trial and an unbending holdout. Ever since it set up shop on a bluff overlooking the town, its central administration and classroom building allegedly built to the dimensions of Noah's Ark, Bryan College has held fast to that lofty stance by requiring faculty members to sign a statement of faith that includes this passage: "The origin of man was by fiat of God in the act of creation as related in the Book of Genesis; that he was created in the image of God; that he sinned and thereby incurred physical and spiritual death." Though that apparently has satisfied literalists for nearly eighty years, the board of trustees grew nervous because some professors were quietly moving toward interpretations of the statement that would allow some agreement with evolutionists. By March 2014, the majority of trustees tried to clamp down on any concession to evolution by tightening the faculty pledge. It now included the following: "We believe that all humanity is descended from Adam and Eve. They are *historical persons* created by God in a special formative act, and not from previously existing life forms" (emphasis added). There is now no room for any kind of qualified Darwinism.

The action has sparked a bitter dispute on the compact, solidly evangelical campus that resounded across the evangelical spectrum and the national news media. Breaking out of its normal quiescence, an alarmed faculty voted "no confidence" in the president by a thirty-to-two margin in a show of defiance. More than three hundred of the school's eight hundred students openly protested against the change, demonstrating in public and signing a petition, an astonishing reaction at a college with a history of conformity to church authority. Trustees on the opposing side resigned. Two tenured professors who were sharply critical of the move soon left, and others were said to be considering the same. At issue were themes that echoed from the prosecution of Scopes: that forcing compliance would cramp academic freedom and stunt healthy inquiry within the church.

That such a blunt countermeasure was happening in Dayton was significant in two respects. First, it became the second stiff test of creationist resolve to put the town in the national spotlight — though, unlike the Scopes trial, which only staged the spectacle, this one was a homegrown confrontation at a college closely integrated into the town. Second, the furor that erupted pointed to profound unease and disagreement among American evangelicals over what biblical literalism was and how Genesis and other Bible texts should be deciphered.

Among the intense observers of this scene was a Bryan graduate who had recently gained a spot in the national spotlight for her book *Evolving in Monkeytown,* which rejected the biblical literalism that she had been raised on right there in Dayton. Rachel Held Evans's book is a full-bore coming-out salvo that upends the pillars of fundamentalism. It is a smart, quick-paced yet good-natured skewering by a young, engaging writer who has not moved away from the surroundings where she has faced disapproving frowns on a daily basis. She was an outstanding student at Bryan, with the added distinction that her father, Dr. Peter A. Held, taught courses in Christian thought and biblical studies there. Her Bible training had included regular treks to summer camps that used methods called "sword drills" to help commit Bible verses to memory. Her affection for her past is palpable, no matter how disillusioned with it she now feels.

In her book, whose title obviously plays on the Scopes trial, Evans never uses the term "inerrancy" as she stakes out positions that directly reject certain tenets. She has come to believe that the inerrancy frame of mind is on its way out. Describing herself as "post-evangelical" in an interview, she no longer sees the Bible as a perfect vehicle for God's message but, in the words of her book, as texts "written down by unholy hands, read by unholy eyes, and processed by unholy origins." She doubts the existence of a biblical worldview and decries literalist efforts to force the Bible into a mold that appears to attain unity, the kind of idolatry Christian Smith and others called "bibliolatry." Especially disturbing, she says, are the misogynist practices derived from biblical passages. Such references are among the "bad" parts of the Bible, which she now recognizes as misrepresenting God and promoting distorted ethics, including its sections on violence.

Many of her fellow citizens find her skepticism jarring, but their reaction has mellowed. She says that she has heard that, at the time her writings went public, some prayer chains petitioned the Lord for her to be "delivered." But on the whole she thinks the protest "wasn't much at all." It was partly because the book rehashes the old, tired Genesis debate of the Scopes era that it didn't excite another round of conflict. It was her next book, on the Bible and gender, that was to rouse sharper debate.

What has struck Evans in Dayton, and elsewhere where she has traveled as a popular author, are the growing numbers of young people who are "struggling with doubts" that they don't feel churches are willing to hear and discuss. That flock of searchers (whom Barna also identifies) is moving far away from the language, practices, and pieties of the Scopes era, beyond the churches — to who knows where? She is part of that generation, still looking from the inside out but aware that the ground beneath her is shifting.

CHAPTER 7

Moses in Cyberspace

To Greg P., a gravel-voiced radio man who has spent thirty-three years pitching the gospel on the rural airwaves, the sight of Bobby Gruenewald stepping onto the stage of the National Religious Broadcasters convention was both auspicious and worrisome. Was this guru of Bible digital downloads more answer or problem? Was he the harbinger of a future that would leave mike jockeys like Greg in the dust, or was he the messenger of hope for a medium that was caught in a technological avalanche? For years Greg has spent his own scarce funds to attend this convention for the camaraderie and the tips for keeping his one-horse station alive. Gruenewald, founder of the world's leading Internet Bible application, YouVersion, comes from another world, one that seems to Greg to be somewhat promising — but also alien. Of that day's speakers, however, Gruenewald was the speaker he was most eager to hear, the most alluring, even though it might leave Greg feeling obsolete.

Gruenewald, for his part, seemed alert to the likelihood that he might be viewed as a brash techie out to impress the social-media dummies, brandishing a high-tech product that would rapidly consign their methods to the scrapheap. He took pains to disabuse them of that attitude right off. His aim, he said in casual, winsome fashion, was the same as theirs: to be a servant of the Lord who followed the lead of the senior pastor on the staff of his futuristic Oklahoma-based church. He was a partner rather than a lone ranger, he assured his listeners. Among his evangelical credentials was an undergraduate degree from Southern Nazarene University outside Oklahoma City.

The audience warmed to his easy-going charm and self-deprecating humor (he drew laughs at the outset by claiming he wasn't "a communicator," offering as proof the fact that his senior minister "had never invited [him] to preach"). Though his stunning success at planting e-Bibles on electronic screens all over the world has gained him a measure of fame in that mission world, he dismissed any suggestion of stardom. Visually, he was the picture of whimsical convention: a mop of blond hair, blue eyes, and a peaches-and-cream complexion give him a youthful look. He wore an open green shirt under a checked sport coat, jeans, and red sneakers. Nothing sensational; nothing vain. Multigenerational American informality. It probably wouldn't surprise them, he claimed, that when he started his venture, he "didn't know much about Bible people" and had a lot to learn from them.

Though his appearance was thus nonthreatening, he embodied a revolutionary possibility that he was in the vanguard of rescuing the Bible from its drift toward obscurity. Cyberspace was doing what radio talk shows, gospel songs, and Scripture interludes could only achieve in a very hit-or-miss fashion: entice millions of people who had been considered highly unlikely readers to open a screen and sample the greatest stories ever told. Scripture, which had been ignored by Bobby's generation like an unrequited lover, was now apparently being embraced by all kinds of customers. Gruenewald's YouVersion Bible, a free download customized in hundreds of languages and versions, has existed only since 2008, but in the span of just five years it had already enrolled over 100 million users, two-thirds of them in the United States. (From there the numbers have continued to zoom upward: more than 158 million, at this writing, toward Gruenewald's next big target of half a billion.) A running tab on its website window posts a new subscriber on an average of about one per second, up to sixty a minute, according to Gruenewald. State-of-the-art feedback shows that during a typical second of a day, 66,000 users are tapped into the online Bible. At that torrid pace, a goal of half a billion downloads seems within easy reach.

With facts like that alone, Gruenewald had the full attention of the assembled broadcasters. He proceeded to tell how YouVersion came about, wrapping the story in assurances that its creation was God-inspired, assurances that were essential if evangelical audiences such as this were to take the subject seriously. Gruenewald said YouVersion came to him in 2006 as a brainstorm while he was standing in the security check-in line at O'Hare airport. It was an answer to a puzzle that had preoccupied him: How could you invent a faster and more appealing means for reviving Bible reading, including his own, which had fallen off?

Bulky print versions of the Bible have prevailed for nearly six hundred years, but despite their continued tactile popularity among traditional religious followers they are steadily losing exclusivity, especially among young people. He was equipped for the task, having honed his computer skills as a former co-owner of a professional wrestling website before joining a church staff as its technology guru. While he was shuffling along the O'Hare security line, the thought of a Bible website popped into his mind and immediately felt like an inspired answer. "This could be the thing God uses to help people get to the Bible," he remembers telling himself. By the time his plane took off, the concept had taken shape, and he'd already tentatively named it.

His church colleagues shared his enthusiasm. LifeChurch.tv, as it is called, is a future-is-now congregation in Edmond, Oklahoma, affiliated with the Evangelical Covenant Church. From there, Sunday worship services are simulcast to gatherings at sixteen widely scattered sites. Its mission, as envisioned by the senior pastor, Craig Groeschel, is to foster a Christian community by appropriating the resources of cyberspace. What emerged from Gruenewald's epiphany was a church-sponsored website steeped in the Bible but limited in scope. It was confined to relatively stationary computers, a decided disadvantage with the on-the-move cyber crowd that now takes the Internet with them. Two weeks before folding, however, the team set its sights on designing a mobile application.

About then, Apple Computer plunked down a golden opportunity by opening its App Store and inviting the first wave of aspiring distributors to compete for a place on its rapidly expanding universe of devices. Gruenewald and his skeleton LifeChurch crew plunged into retooling their product for a coveted spot on iPads and iPhones. The option took off like a rocket. The designers thought that maybe they might attract hundreds, a few thousand at best, during the first sign-up weekend. They got 83,000, an astonishing preview of things to come. From there the race was on — simply to keep up with demand. At Gruenewald's mention of such levels of demand, the broadcasters burst into loud applause.

While YouVersion has taken the lead in downloads and publicity, the Bible App market has sprouted thousands of topflight alternatives with an impressive variety of glossaries, maps, and commentaries. Almost no major Bible advocacy agency is without one, most for free, indicating just how promising evangelists believe they are. Among the more popular: BibleGateway, Bible.IS, Olive Tree Verbum (designed for Catholics), PocketSword, the GloBible, Logos and the NIV Bible. Collectively, they make daily rounds with millions of subscribers across the globe on their mobile devices. The spread and reach have been nothing short of spectacular. Figures on distribution and use are obsolete as soon as they appear. The implications of this eruption are still to be sorted out.

At the NRB convention, Gruenewald insisted it was all about thinking big at a mind-boggling turning point in human history. And he zeroed in on the number-one crisis of Bible ignorance. While Bible-reading has kept heading downward "from the previous generation, from the previous generation, from the previous generation," YouVersion and its competitors claim to be reversing the trend. Gruenewald boldly forecasts that the generations from now on will be "the most biblically literate the world has ever seen." And it seems relatively effortless. Build the app to display the methods of downloading, the choices in editions, reading programs, and accessory programs, and let it be propelled into the digital universe. It is more complicated, of course, but to Greg P. and his fellow radio evangelists, that specter of "success" could make their efforts look paltry.

The razzle-dazzle, high-tech magic and the numbing statistics have clearly not converted everyone to electronic Bibles, of course, but they have established a fault line between old and new ways of promoting and preserving the Bible. The public is obviously reading more on e-screens, but the degree to which this combines with or substitutes for the use of print texts begs further study. The Pew Research Center's yearly surveys of reading habits from 2011 to 2015, for example, show a slow decline in overall book reading during that span — down from 79 to 72 percent — an erosion in print reading from 71 to 63 percent, and a 10 percent increase in e-book readers from an initial baseline of 17 percent. Not surprisingly, e-book readership is greatest among the youngest cohort (34 percent) and lowest among the 65-plus age group (15 percent).

Even as Gruenewald rattles off the mind-boggling figures, understandable doubts hover over the new enterprise. Old-time radio and television operators echo the misgivings of a wider circle of church people. The crowd at the NRB conference was painfully aware of the concrete successes and failures of their own programming. They show up in the generally sagging ratings numbers. As the Internet encroaches further on those strategies, implicitly casting them as outmoded, it is natural for them to defend their traditions and to question how much of the technological glitter is actual gold. They are being advised by Gruenewald and similar enthusiasts that their survival depends on plugging into equipment and social-media techniques, what venues to emphasize (such as Facebook and

Twitter), and what to downplay (such as noninteractive programming and, surprisingly, straight-out preaching). Some of the broadcasters have taken strides in these directions, but others, like Greg P., say that they have neither the money nor the confidence to reinvent themselves.

Religious mom-and-pop radio stations are becoming rare across the radio spectrum. "The door is closing on me," says Greg. He is a former railroad conductor whose independent AM station began as the joint venture of three evangelical churches. "I'll hold out as long as I can," he says, "but the big religious chains, such as Moody, are crowding out people like me. There are still folks out there, especially old shut-ins, who depend on us, so I'll be there as long as I can." Greg spends time during each morning show praying for those who ask him to and explaining as best he can what the King James Bible has to say about everyday problems. But his sense is that he's too slow and too stuck in his ways to keep up.

"Almost time to get out of the way," he said mournfully.

*   *   *

But as dazzling and space-age as the new world appears to be, is it indeed the cure for the Bible's decline? That conundrum goes far beyond the agenda of the National Religious Broadcasters to the entire spectrum of churches that have become alarmed about the crisis and are determined to find solutions. The use of cyberspace for religious purposes raises the same concerns as does the general impact of the shift to digital communications. What possible effects has the switch to new technology had on how readers might absorb and interpret the text?

The late Marshall McLuhan's signature mantra "the medium is the message" has been, by turns, lavishly praised and acerbically derided over the years. Apart from its controversy, though, I think it states a basic truth: that a person's understanding of what is being said, as in the Bible, has been shaped and conditioned by how that information has been passed along — by book, audio device, digital camera, DVD, television, or Internet software. Science has only recently begun to study how Johnny's brain, perception, attention span, reasoning skills, and social behavior have been altered — sometimes startlingly so. Thus it is logical that transmitting the same material over a history and range of media, from smoke signals to iPads, would affect human consciousness in different ways. As a corollary, reading alone, which can reasonably be considered standard for Bible e-readers, doubtless affects both the kinds of material selected (presumably focusing on personal needs) and the interpretation of it, which might differ markedly from that derived from reading it in a group setting. Conservatives, in particular, fret that the habit of sampling Scripture in e-bits fragments the Bible's grand narrative by isolating organic pieces from one another, thus losing context or a fuller view of what belongs where in the whole Bible. Seekers after self-help advice, for example, could narrow the Bible to a collection of personal affirmations that neglect its host of warnings against self-centeredness.

Does it matter, or do these largely hypothetical reservations count for little compared with the prospect of placing the entire Bible on the iPhones, iPads, and similar devices being toted around in pockets, purses, knapsacks, and valises around the world? Isn't the point that people would start reading it? Yes and no, say its promoters. For someone who has never been in deep water before, jumping into a lake could be the first step toward learning to swim; but success depends on such factors as whether the water is warm or cold, filled with lily pads or snags, thick with algae, or driven by a strong current. The conditions will influence the kinds of experiences the new swimmer takes away from practicing the same principles of floating, stroking, kicking, and streamlining. But as diverse as their impressions of what swimming "is," some would argue that at least most of them learn to swim. The "no" part is the caution against taking too lightly the distinctions or lasting effects of their various experiences. Those whose inclinations are closer to biblical literalism will be, as expected, especially concerned that precise meanings and overall Bible story lines can be lost in translation from one medium to another. Failure to keep meanings and story lines intact is tantamount to tampering with the deepest and most soul-searching message a person would ever encounter, thereby inhibiting the opportunity for conversion.

Will reading a chapter from Luke on a mobile phone tend to enhance someone's understanding of the sacred better than reading the same passage in print? Or vice versa? For those who equate success with arriving at a predetermined interpretation, there is little room for diverse outcomes, so that anything that leads the reader astray will be unacceptable. But among the more freethinking, there are no such standards to exclude any means of learning about Scripture. It is much more a personal exploration filtered through the vicissitudes of the Bible's text and the individual's own perceptions. For many of them, there is no "continuous narrative" (more on this in a later chapter), only discrete parts; nor do they claim that one kind of absorbing of the text brings better results than the alternatives because there is no absolute basis on which to judge. The portentous issue of whether the Bible is the inerrant word of God is thereby perhaps easier to bypass entirely with a digital option that lacks a visual connection to ground zero of the debate — that is, the entire print version. Is Scripture, the venerable window to salvation, only viable when in some sense it is permanent and indivisible, or is it a script like most of the Internet's content — that is, a stream of largely unrelated bits?

Though it is still too early to draw firm conclusions, growing research into electronic culture in general indicates that it correlates with rising individualism, isolation, and self-absorption. Johnny, by himself in his room, is preoccupied morning, noon, and night with one screen or another, rarely venturing out and saying little that isn't a direct response to a question. This caricature may be inadequate and unfair, but it is increasingly common. No one disputes that electronic immersion has powerful consequences; but those who feel that it could threaten a "correct" understanding (of the Bible, say) are more distrustful of it than those who argue that everyone naturally reads things differently.

Meanwhile, the Bible app initiative is forging ahead under a mandate that was heard loud and clear at the Orlando NRB conference, which bewailed biblical ignorance. The gathering of evangelical and evangelistic Christians, in a state of low-grade panic, raised and rallied under a new banner that was consecrated in Orlando: ENGAGEMENT. The days were over when handing out record-smashing quantities of elegantly produced Bibles would suffice. The only objective worth talking about now was how to get people hooked on and engrossed in the Bible's substance and subtleties. "Engagement" has become the buzz word for the rising captains of Bible apps, too, because it contributes to their own good and signifies that they are team players in a broader effort to place Bibles foremost in people's minds and hearts (except that, truth to tell, app promoters generally think the future belongs to them, though largely via default).

Like most buzz words, "engagement" promises something that may take a long time to realize — if it ever will. It sounds good as a place to start; yet, unsurprisingly, it still hasn't shown much substance. As the word's history in the realm of matrimony implies, "engagements" do not always result in marriages.

What does engagement mean in the digital realm, where users quickly flip through a lengthening list of apps every day? Does it usually amount to fly-by exposures to slivers of Scripture lost in a deluge of apps? What does measuring aggregate minutes spent with online Scripture add up to? Bible apps are good at collecting that data, but that means almost nothing about reading with depth or comprehension. Launching new reading programs is hopeful, but can they measure effectiveness? Most of the plans are still in the beginning stages, enlisting small numbers of trial-and-error experiments. It is the start of a potential game-changer. Bible activists now admit the gravity of the problem and are eagerly searching for answers. Solutions may be elusive, given the countercrush of society's values and priorities. But they have seized on a slogan that sounds clarion and reasonable, and it could end the distribution mania that has for so long been dominant.

The Bible establishment people — publishers, marketers, promoters, and designers — have often been quick to point out that readers say they favor print versions overwhelmingly (89 percent in one recent survey); but much of that sentiment is a holdover from the past, when the bulky sea of words was not only exclusive but sacred. Except for a few ardent deniers, however, everyone knows that the electronic options are gaining ground fast. Hard numbers of downloads and soft percentages from surveys all point to a rising digital tide — especially among young people — poised to take over the readership. The handwriting on the wall became moveable type centuries ago; now it is passing to digital screens.

Here's how Barna reported those gains in its "State of the Bible 2014" for the American Bible Society. (Remember that these are self-reported figures and represent only those who say they are Bible readers.) In just three years, from 2011 to 2014, the use of smart phones or cell phones for reading the Bible doubled — from 18 percent to 35 percent. Nearly a quarter (24 percent) read Scripture from iPads or Kindles in 2014, twice the number doing so in 2011 (12 percent). The number of Bible downloads like YouVersion continued to soar.

A both/and pattern prevails over the exclusive choice of print or electronic means of reading. Worshipers increasingly bring their digital Bibles to church to track verses that come up during the service (especially in the sermon), or to read instead of the copies of the Bible in the pew racks. For those who spend hours of every day on computer screens, it is a natural extension of habit — quick and easy. At the same time, it makes possible the same kind of distractions, random searches, and compulsive routines that occupy much of their daily attention. And it leaves pastors with the quandary of preaching to a congregation increasingly divided between those who are basically unfamiliar with Bible texts used in sermons and a minority of well-informed members for whom too much reiteration of what they already know can be boring. In the midst of such major shifts, the issue of how reading in digital format influences readers' interpretation of the text's meaning and significance can greatly determine where their faith journey is headed.

Bible professionals often eagerly cite the poll numbers showing that upwards of 90 percent of readers prefer the solid feel and utility of the print version. Both sides — the surveyed readers and the professionals — are voicing their devotion to a cherished life companion, stating a deeply sentimental attachment. But are they clearheaded about this? An enterprising grass-roots group in the United Kingdom thought they were not. The Big Bible Project began as a free-spirited, nonsectarian movement to encourage the formation of small, diverse groups around the county to devote themselves to reading large chunks of Scripture. It worked so well that it not only became an organization that kept its original purpose of bringing back the Bible, but it also fostered survey research. On May 17, 2013, its website reported some results of a survey regarding "why people read on screens." The writer, Tim Hutchings, rejected the claim that print and digital were in competition. When he asked survey subjects, all of whom were dedicated Bible readers, which medium they actually used in everyday life, he says, "most of the people I've spoken with so far happily admit that they just don't use their paper Bibles anymore." Advantages they mentioned were: the e-Bible was easier to carry, to read, to look up related materials, and to compare versions. The disadvantages they cited were the loss of an emotional bond with the source and the fact that it was more difficult to browse and to grasp context. Despite the disadvantages, users still liked the digital Bible better.

Then again, the numbers indicate that Bible-reading of any kind is having less impact on the rest of the reader's life. Though a little more than a third (37 percent) of the readers said they "thought some" about applying the Bible's lessons to their lives, the percentage saying they "thought a lot" dropped eight points, to 57 percent, in just one year.

In terms of sheer volume, the YouVersion worldwide user stats are fantastic in the market of Bible offerings, though Gruenewald repeatedly emphasizes that gains are "small" in comparison with the enormous digital universe, which is still only a fraction of the world's population. At the time he spoke to the broadcasters in 2013, YouVersion was well on its way to topping the 100 million download mark. From the constant cascade of data feedback, the LifeChurch.tv team concluded that users spent 46 billion minutes on the site in 2012 alone, an average of 66,000 per second. Tens of millions passed Bible references on to friends and associates on social media. Every statistic, of course, is eclipsed as soon as it is noted. The team isn't able to determine what portion of the subscribers are already committed to the Bible, as opposed to the highly sought-after newcomers who could be evangelized. More than half a million subscribers have signed up for one or more of YouVersion's scores of structured reading plans. Some simply provide daily passages, others cluster verses and chapters around personal themes, such as work or marriage. From any vantage point, this Bible-occupied cyberspace is a vast wave of elements in constant and dynamic motion.

Gruenewald said that he knew from his experience teaching marketing to college students that the app had to be free. "How could you get people who won't pay ninety-nine cents to download a song they love to pay twenty dollars for a book [a digital Bible] they don't understand?" he told the NRB crowd. The growth spurt bore out his theory, but that left LifeChurch.tv paying the cost of yearly operations, which had climbed above $5 million by 2012 after an initial investment of $20 million for startup operations. Profiteers estimated that YouVersion could fetch up to $200 million on the open market, but Gruenewald rejected their approaches. His yearning was to spread the gospel.

"Although a hundred million sounds like a big number," he told the *Christian Post* as the download counter neared that record, "we know it's nowhere close to what's possible. In fact, we like to say that it *starts* with 100 million. Our faith has expanded to believe that Bible engagement can be transformed not only for this generation, but for generations to come."

That forecast may have been a bit too euphoric, but nothing else has come close to capturing readers faster — or from a broader social, economic, or religious spectrum. YouVersion is the pacesetter and, along with dozens of other top-rated downloads, represents the smash hits of Bible evangelism. They have tweaked much media attention and, for the time being at least, have catapulted the Bible from relative obscurity into the limelight. The 100 millionth download date of July 10, 2013, attracted substantial articles in the *New York Times,* the *Huffington Post,* network television, and a raft of other publications and broadcast outlets. The piece in the *Times* was typical in emphasizing Scripture's historic leap from printed page to the latest technological format, and how Gruenewald and his team had made it work. (It is noteworthy that this account of a major milestone in the annals of religion and religious history appeared in the *Times* business section.)

*   *   *

While flags were flying briskly on the digital front, a sticky wicket appeared to have been overlooked. Downloads were landing like raindrops from an intense storm hitting a parched lawn, but nobody could be sure they were sinking in. Was the electronics option showing the ability to get people hooked on its contents, which print providers had abysmally failed to do? If not, weren't YouVersion and the rest of them merely repeating a halfway measure — distribution without involvement — that print peddlers now reject?

At the Orlando crisis conference, Bible leaders displayed a sackcloth-and-ashes penance for idolizing "distribution" while turning a blind eye to impact. They readily concede by now that Bibles are going unread. They have vowed to rewrite the marketing script to emphasize the new goal of engagement. The digital sensation can't help fascinating them, even if grudgingly, but on the whole they don't know where it belongs in the midst of their newfound urgency to turn a sinking enterprise around. Given the grayness of the climate, it isn't surprising that some see digitized Bibles as a panacea, apparently connecting with segments of the population they have trouble reaching, among them Millennials, the unchurched, the smart set based in technology, the troubled, and the searching. But the excitement and freshness of the electronics surge often masks the most urgent question: Do the new media pull in readers any better than the old one did? If not — if it is a novelty item that app collectors add primarily to say they have one, but barely or never use it — then no great progress has been made. For all its new expertise, it would be just another distribution operation that puts the material out there and leaves it at that.

Bobby Gruenewald has no intention of letting that happen, though, by his own admission, it is the big challenge he has not yet seriously tackled. He is by nature an evangelist, never content with merely "making the sale," but needing to help supply that download as a steppingstone to "winning hearts and minds for Christ" through steady search of the electronic Scripture. The epiphany that burst upon him while he was standing in the O'Hare security line had imbued him with a prophet's passion for responding to a unique moment in God's plan: to utilize the wonders of technology to reach an expanding world population. He has driven himself to answer that call to fulfill a mission that has only now become possible and required. That "delivery" zeal has propelled him like a comet in one direction. Everything else would have to wait. It is the kind of risk that

Bible advocates have to be willing to take at a time when print is on its way out. Perhaps the Gutenberg technology did its job, but now it has lost its edge, giving way to a digital revival. Gruenewald thinks so, and he urges his listeners to jump into the unknown consequences. "God has placed us here at this time like never before in history," he said in Orlando. "He could have chosen to put us here at any time, but chose now." Bible apps are "something God has given us."

The latest gadgetry will become obsolete, too, he said, and will create the need for "the next big thing." Where will it come from? Look within yourselves, he told them, and don't look for answers to outside sources such as Hollywood or Facebook. He pooh-poohed most brainstorming as a futile search. "I can almost guarantee that the next idea, after someone has suggested 'thinking outside the box,' will be a terrible idea," he quipped.

Supply-side issues aside, what are those possessors of tens of millions of apps doing with them? The "receiving" end of digital transactions is finally what matters. It is also the most elusive, despite the torrent of feedback on how many minutes users spend on the site and what sections they are viewing. But how do these data translate into changing a life? Those unknowns and the urgency to follow up on partial information are never far from Gruenewald's mind, and he approaches those quandaries with characteristic candor. The fact is that little has been done to learn what is happening on the other end of cyberspace. "How has this [YouVersion] changed lives?" he asked in private conversation. "Over the several years we have not carried that thought process forward." Bible app producers like him wouldn't be eager to discover that electronics was not changing habits and lives better than print had done, of course, but Gruenewald's attention is fixed on seizing a colossal opportunity to turn the water of technology into the wine of biblical devotion. As to the degree to which the water is doing that, he said, "We've not circled back to that." He trusts the course it is taking.

"If what we're part of doing now could transform a generation," he said, "then it would be seen to have a purpose. The factors make sense to me. Reports show that people are less interested in church or the Bible. The Bible app is an indication of a countertrend. What would it mean if this became the most Bible-engaged generation in history? Breaking the patterns of individualism and relativism?"

Research into whether digital versions are accomplishing that is virtually nonexistent. By necessity, Gruenewald has given his time and energies simply to keeping a fledgling system going with a small staff and popular demand far exceeding expectations. That kind of frantic activity keeps Gruenewald running in place, but it also appeals to his technological aptitude. Discovering the extent to which the result is making disciples does not come easily to him — nor perhaps to the bulk of techies in the field. "I'm not great at being heady," he said. "I like to engage in this on a more practical level, so I don't know that I've spent enough time on [the app's influence on users]. If we play this out fully, we'll have to look closely at the theory that, if we distribute a book, they'll read it."

Since few are reading the stack of printed versions of the Bible that are already out there, the chances that weak readers will dive into an app seem like a long shot. The gamble is that the electronics medium alone will enhance the Bible's status in contemporary culture, giving it a stamp of approval in company with music videos and medical advice. If digital apps are actually being habitually consumed by readers, unlike books that are obtained and discarded, then getting those apps installed will be the most compelling task. The momentum will presumably finish the job almost by itself.

Nobody thinks it will be that easy. You can lead horses to water, but you can't presume how many will drink it. On the other hand, it may be possible to inculcate habits that will favor it. For a start, YouVersion, NIV, and other major Bible apps promote reading plans (four hundred in 2013) to help ease the entry of newcomers into the mammoth scope and complexity of Scripture by breaking it down into digestible portions. You can take it in bits and pieces each day — at a pace that will allow you to get your bearings and find direction. Some of these plans are geared to particular themes, such as motherhood or finding a life partner or anxiety, directing the reader to verses and sections meant to be relevant. Others supervise reading the entire Bible or specialize in areas of theology and ethics. Neophytes can begin mapping its vastness, grasping its syntax, and discerning patterns of history and prophecy. Veterans will deepen their knowledge. The initial reports from the field are encouraging, though the numbers are small. By 2013, for example, the more than 500,000 people YouVersion had attracted to its plans represented only one half of 1 percent of all subscribers. Millions more might be using their own plans, but there was as yet no way to identify them in the surging river of user data.

Those who do sign up for plans aren't entirely left on their own. They are prompted by email messages if they haven't read their designated serving of the Bible so as to condition them to daily practice. To combat boredom and density, YouVersion sometimes rearranges the text in an effort to foreground material that has most attracted readers and to backload the duller stuff. (*Huffington Post* gave an article on that practice the title "The App of God: Getting 100 Million Downloads Is More Psychology Than Miracle" [August 19, 2013]). The gentle nudging is not meant to intrude but to go beyond superficial customer satisfaction to patterns of behavior that actually change lives. That certainly has happened, but the extent to which and profundity with which it has done so across the YouVersion universe is still a haunting mystery. How do digital marvels mold readers into better examples of the biblical or the Christian life — if they do?

As the most sought-after Bible app, YouVersion has achieved a level of name recognition that makes it nearly synonymous with the product itself, something like the way "Kodak" was at one time equated with cameras in general. It is a player in an energized new drive to rekindle an embrace of the Bible. Focus on its rapid expansion has enhanced its standing by exemplifying the premium America places on "growth." That reputation can be parlayed into benefits for other newcomers in Bible resurgence.

So it was that YouVersion became associated with a new game show, called *America's Bible Challenge* and created by the Game Show Network. It is a sweet, square, folksy Bible contest between two unfailingly cheerful teams and hosted by Jeff Foxworthy (comedian, popularizer of the phrase "you might be a redneck," and host of television's *Are You Smarter than a Fifth Grader?*). The toughness of the questions, however, left many avowed Christians scratching their heads. Television critics mostly either gave it a pass or thought it too cornball; but it immediately shot to the top of the cable charts as the highest-rated original show in the history of cable TV (1.7 million viewers the first week, close to that the remainder of the first season). By the second season, the show added YouVersion as a resource that contestants could use to search for answers. Thrilled by the size of response (much of it the result of an effective campaign by evangelical churches to rally their members to watch it), the network made the show a central feature in its lineup: the perennial favorite game-show format had become the vehicle for biblical content — quite a considerable feat.

The other collaboration involved YouVersion's highly touted docudrama *The Bible* during the 2013 Lenten season on the History Channel. The ambitious ten-hour series, produced by the husband-wife team of Mark Burnett (creator of *The Survivor*) and actress Roma Downey, helicoptered over the huge biblical terrain, touching down in chosen spots and sometimes rearranging and falsifying events. It was a smash hit (despite taking a drubbing from most reviewers), drawing 13 million viewers to its first segment, averaging 11 million over several weeks, owing again to its large prompted audience of evangelicals. Gruenewald saw the opportunity to advance both his aims and those of the series by placing notices for YouVersion prominently on the series.

*　　*　　*

Collaborations among the vanguard of Bible fixers indicate both widespread alarm concerning the Bible's shrinking public profile and a drive to counteract the losses. They use the latest devices and communications techniques. Maybe they're regaining ground, maybe not.

By the middle of 2014, a quirkier issue had bubbled up: If George Washington had used an iPad with a Bible app instead of a leather-bound version of Scripture, would he have been invalidly sworn in, thereby tainting all of presidential history? In other words, does a Bible made of electrons qualify as the real thing that public officials put their hand on while taking the oath? Stringent guardians of tradition were skeptical. If the text of God's Word was bundled with all sorts of other materials, sacred and/or profane, that might compromise scriptural purity, they argued. We'd best be cautious, even resistant.

By then, however, there were at least three publicized cases where downloaded Scripture had served that purpose. In May 2014, Suzi LeVine chose to use her iPad installation when she was sworn in as US Ambassador to Switzerland and Lichtenstein (two countries that we might imagine to be neutral about such things). That stirred up a little curiosity and some fussiness. A Long Island official took his oath by swearing on something similar when nobody had remembered to bring a print Bible. The same thing happened when a group of firefighters were inducted into their department in Atlantic City, New Jersey.

Common sense and the law rendered it a moot point, as most people suspected it would be all along. The switch made no legal difference whatsoever, since the Constitution says nothing about having to use a Bible or any other book. Presidents have chosen to use one or more Bibles to signify their respect for the majority religion, and the habit has spread to the point where now it may seem required, but the legal church-state separation line is clear. You could use practically anything or nothing as a prop. Look for the pace of digital users to rise, and the possibility of using something other than the Bible to increase.

CHAPTER 8

Who Says What the Bible Says?

The Society of Biblical Literature (SBL) is to the Bible what the Centers for Disease Control are to infectious diseases: both are the places to go for the latest scientific bulletins about alien cultures. Other groups of scholars examine the Bible from different starting points, such as inerrancy or applying its messages to everyday use by the faithful. But no organization devotes itself so pointedly to wide-open study of Scripture on such rigorous historical and linguistic grounds, what has been the field known as "higher criticism" since the time of its appearance early in the nineteenth century in Germany. The SBL became the most visible American clearinghouse for that brand of academic scrutiny, which removed the Bible from its pedestal as the direct word from God and put it into a laboratory, where scholars explore it primarily as a work cobbled together by mortals with God-consciousness, flaws and all, much as they would dissect any ancient document.

Using modern analytical tools, the higher critics found layers of writings, rewritings, blending, copying, contradictions, and mistranslations in manuscripts that Christianity had with rare exceptions believed to be the single voice of a transcendent God. The previously unassailable sacred book was suddenly questionable. You could entertain the idea that when writing styles didn't match within a text, the reason could be that portions of several sources had been combined. Words thought to mean one thing might mean something else when linguistic experts got involved. Images assumed to be unique to Scripture were found to have existed in neighboring contemporaneous cultures. Archaeological evidence became more crucial. Would uncovered remains verify that Joshua fought the battle of Jericho? Did the laws of nature permit or deny miracles, or were they meant symbolically? The authenticity of everything was up for grabs, even the question of Jesus's existence. The Enlightenment's zeal for rational explanations and doubts about otherworldliness had come home to roost among a smattering of Biblicists who embraced it as progress; the larger share of Christians scorned it as an attack on the Bible's sacredness. The defenders' instincts were right: in the hands of the modernists, the Bible did lose much of its specialness and authority. Growing research exposed its human thumbprints, identifying it increasingly as a document fashioned by mortals, dwelling on interaction with the divine, shaped in its myriad parts by contemporary forces of events and cultures. To rank-and-file Christians, then and now, such tampering with the Bible's special place is a threat to their faith and therefore anathema.

Then came Charles Darwin with a theory of almost everything, which said, in effect, that Genesis had it wrong about creation, at least as a factually trustworthy account. Darwin's *Origin of the Species* rattled many Christians' confidence in the underpinnings of Holy Writ. Bitter debate and sharp controversy flared from the very beginning of this intrusion of science into religion; its practitioners, after all, were challenging the written guarantor of the public's faith. This small band of innovators was sometimes beleaguered and shouted down. But the movement proved unstoppable, given the growing hegemony of science itself, and in 1880 the fledgling predecessor of the SBL held its first meeting in New York City. Eight founders attended. They included noted Biblicists of the time, most of whom taught in Protestant seminaries that had at least traces of liberalism. Harvard, Yale, and Chicago had their own divinity schools, while others existed within the precincts of Columbia, Princeton, and Penn. The wrenching church splits caused by the Civil War confined most critical biblical research to Northern states, where greater openness to secular humanist influences fostered more challenges to tradition.

That handful of founders might have felt both astounded and vindicated had they been able to watch the swarm of humanity that streamed through Chicago's McCormick Place in late November 2012 for the combined gathering of SBL and the American Academy of Religion. The ranks of SBL members had swollen to over 8,300 — two-thirds of them faculty and students — from the US and increasingly from other countries (ninety-four in 2012). They had come to rub elbows with fellow specialists in Bible texts, archaeology, classical literature, and Ancient Near East studies, and to hear each other's latest findings — all the while searching for jobs and/or advancing their careers.

The widening panoply of the Bible's place within America's intellectual centers was on display, prompted by an array of motives: secular, professional, entrepreneurial, evangelistic, pre- and postmodernist, humanitarian, esoteric, egalitarian, and more. As the Reformation had more or less wished, the Bible had been snatched from the grip of church authorities and was on the loose. It was an intriguing picture of chaos.

There was nothing close to a stereotypical biblical scholar to match those male professors in dark suits from the old days. Among them now were: bearded, agnostic Bible department chairmen; newly tenured women bringing fresh insights; mid-career men with gym-trimmed torsos carrying their papooses in back pouches and toting volumes on Gnosticism; Jewish experts on the New Testament; magnetic mentors of young faculty and graduate students, some in jeans and blue blazers, others in skirts and blouses hinting at world religions. The markings: stars of David, visages of Buddha, words and symbols of Muslim Arabic, along with pectoral crosses and a smattering of clerical collars (an option almost exclusively exercised by ordained males rather than their female counterparts) — all of it underscoring the degree to which Christianity has lost its nearly sole proprietorship of Scripture. What role could the Bible play in pluralism of this kind, with its wide assortment of interpreters and appropriators, such as Dan Brown (*The Da Vinci Code*) and Michele Roberts (*The Secret Gospel of Mary Magdalene*), whose fictitious tales, loosely based on Bible references, appealed to readers who, knowing little to nothing about the Bible itself, were invited to accept these stories as "gospel"?

The conventional tent of Biblicists has rapidly expanded, too. Higher criticism was for many years occupied with using the ballooning knowledge of the history and culture of biblical times to better comprehend the sources and settings from which Scripture arose. It is analogous to the difference between studying Samoans as a self-contained island people and seeing them as part of a complex South Seas civilization whose separate islanders share traditions. Likewise, philologists were making great strides in deciphering ancient languages; the effect was that words and passages in standard Bible translations could be understood more precisely. Literary research uncovered mixtures of styles and places where whole texts had either been lifted from one source and dropped into another or appeared elsewhere in a different form. The two versions of the Ten Commandments, for example, could be explained as having arisen from two different traditions that were, however, commonly grounded in a long stretch of oral transmission that preceded both of them. Errors in translation could be corrected as linguistic competence grew. The results were often unsettling, especially when they called into question cherished beliefs. Archaeology was the other major difference-maker. Ancient ruins could determine the accuracy and chronology of the Bible's accounts. What remains of King David's reign? Did Joshua knock down the walls of Jericho? Did early Christians incorporate Jewish symbols in worship? Extensive archaeological digs verified accounts and broadened understanding of them; but sometimes they challenged those beliefs.

Those original research preferences served the mostly Protestant preoccupation with getting the Bible's message right. As the centerpiece of their faith — and guided by the *sola Scriptura* banner of the Reformation — attaining the correct wording and meaning was supremely important — but seldom achieved. The rigors of higher criticism stretched that process beyond anything previously imaginable, dissecting Scripture empirically in ways that were never before so revealing of hidden or mistaken aspects of its contents. It became subject to new kinds of "truths," and traditionalists generally refused to accept them.

As it approached the turn of the twenty-first century, the Society of Biblical Literature felt the repercussions of academic specialization and emerging areas of study. Many younger scholars chose to view the Bible from vantage points that grew out of their personal experience and sense of contemporary urgency: among them women's studies; environmentalism; LBGT issues; African American culture; globalization; Islam, Buddhism, and other religions; Middle East studies; the Bible as literature; race-and-class tensions; and poverty. As more looked at the Bible through the prisms of those interests, the SBL expanded and further diversified and specialized. Not everyone cheered. Some saw in these new directions the makings of "identity studies" — an offshoot of "identity politics" — which operated from bases that were too narrow and prone to personal bias, and thus academically questionable. Continued splicing into ever more discrete subject areas accelerated fragmentation within the SBL, skeptics argued, further weakening its ability to cohere around common aims, values, and discussions.

But academic disciplines relentlessly subdivide everywhere, and the curriculum-trending dog was wagging its SBL tail, since most members were faculty members at colleges and universities where the creation of hybrid fields of study had been proceeding apace. They were expected to treat both the Bible and their special area of study with objectivity and the critical tools being adopted in other disciplines. But objectivity would prove to be a difficult standard to uphold. What might there be in the biblical text that had overtly or covertly affected the status of women, African Americans, migrant workers, gays and lesbians? How had its contents been used and misused? Would scholars truly honor the Bible's texts, or would they succumb to the temptation to selectively excise portions or twist their meanings to support their own viewpoints? These and other questions hovered in the background.

The infusion of new energies enriched the SBL's makeup and diluted its concentration on the old staples of higher criticism. The relative like-mindedness of earlier decades faded, and the various study areas, like those in the universities where members taught, grew more remote from one another. Other than the value they collectively placed on the Bible, there was less that they held in common as they pursued an expanding universe of subjects in different scholarly voices. They engaged with Scripture largely individually in one fascinating way or another: they were moved by personal piety, love of literature, religious history or ancient languages, and other passions — not because Bible-related careers offered academic stardom or financial rewards.

Chicago's gargantuan McCormick Place housed the SBL convention in November 2012, and it symbolized both the connection and the disconnection among participants. The purposeful knots of religionists streamed back and forth along broad, austere corridors like passengers on an autobahn — clutching their laptops, iPads, briefcases, valises, and small children while walking to sessions and meetings sometimes located as much as a half hour's walk apart within the far-flung center, the nation's biggest convention site. They wore smiles, stepped briskly, and exuberantly greeted old friends. The 10,000 registrants were dwarfed by their surroundings, stretched thinly across acres of interior space. They huddled for an hour or two in mostly small clusters to hear accomplished colleagues offer thoughts and discoveries about subjects that most of them lived and breathed on a daily basis. Bringing them something new could be a daunting challenge. The rows of meeting rooms, exits off the main corridors, were painted in conversation-friendly medium green with the uplifting touch of a yellow rectangle on the front wall and a focus piece in the form of an altar-like table overhung with blue cloth. While one room might entertain a fresh take on the prophet Ezekiel's visions, an adjoining one could be hosting a panel on Native American syncretism or a dazzling new discovery about Ugaritic ritualism. Academics being academics, practically no claim made in countless papers read at the convention went unchallenged. Rounds of debate over such claims, there and later, could indicate that the presenter had struck pay dirt.

Fragmented though it may have been, with various squadrons of experts heading in separate directions, the overall climate was cordial and respectful, even robust. Whatever the centrifugal effect of their specialties, they were often bonded by common university, seminary, and graduate school department connections and grateful for each other's contributions, even though they might not understand much about them. Hundreds of student attendees found their way through the labyrinth and welcomed the adventure. Nowhere in this scene of eager scurrying about were there obvious signs of a rebellion that threatened the SBL's core identity.

*   *   *

Though the SBL has always promoted scholarship, its efforts to meet the ever-stricter tests imposed by academic research expose a chronic tension. Compared to researchers in other fields, scholars of the Bible and religion are more apt to be suspected of letting their faith-based beliefs distort or limit their studies (for example, can a devout believer in the physical resurrection of Jesus fairly judge the evidence for and against?) rather than letting facts speak for themselves. All scholars face that restraint to some degree. Disputes over separating fact from opinion show up all the time. But in disciplines other than religion, those who are personally devoted to a variety of other beliefs — libertarianism, atheism, astrology, or other life-meaning alternatives — are seldom assumed to inject their beliefs into their studies. Religionists are widely suspected of avoiding research that might conflict with the teachings of their faith or of selecting only findings that support those teachings. Reason and critical analysis will thus take a back seat to unquestioned convictions. Under that regimen, prior belief in the physical resurrection of Jesus will eliminate all other possibilities from the start. On those grounds, biblical scholarship — and the scholars who practice it — has struggled to earn respect in modern universities. Fairly or not, increasing respect depends considerably on turning that reputation around, convincing university colleagues that their work is as sound and nonsectarian as that produced by the best scholars.

It is an uphill slog. Religion professors commonly report that their departments rate low on prestige within their institutions. They may succeed on an individual basis, but in general they suffer from the perception that their subject lacks academic authenticity. Accordingly, they tend to receive fewer institutional rewards and advancement. All the more reason that SBL members who are most invested in raising the stature of Bible studies are alarmed by what they see as signs that others among them allow their convictions to influence their studies.

The argument concerning whether faith is compatible with reason has, of course, raged in the church since the dawn of the Age of Reason, the Enlightenment. Some said that they could live in peace together; others swore that reason (primarily associated with provable cause/effect relationships and law-abiding explanations of reality) is fundamentally at odds with faith's reliance on otherworldly sources. Many believers contend that reason and faith are not opposed, rather that they are two distinct means of grasping the whole of reality: that there are distinct ways of knowing that are equally true — by rational investigation and suprarational transmission of spiritual revelation. And so on. Though that perspective has a long history and still holds true among most evangelicals, it is virtually anathema in conventional research circles. In the SBL, such work is called "confessional," connoting an unholy mingling of preaching and learning, and its presence is an embarrassment to the strict research side of the discipline.

A similar divide exists concerning history as a test of religious truth. If no proof can be found for the Bible's version of the Israelites' invasion of the Holy Land, does that mean that the events never took place? If there is nothing to back up the story of Mary and Joseph's flight to Egypt with the baby Jesus, does that falsify a major portion of the birth narratives? Even some of the strongest defenders of biblical infallibility defer to the archaeologists' findings — or lack of them — but stick with their principle that the Bible is historically accurate. The more strictly scientific among the Biblicists argue that the facts are undeniable and that the Bible is thick with mythology.

The long-simmering tensions between the two camps, fueled chiefly by professional aspirations rather than personal frictions (in fact, many regard each other highly on personal grounds while having no use for each other's research), burst into the open in a 2006 broadside in the *Chronicle of Higher Education* entitled "What's Wrong with the Society of Biblical Literature?" The author is Jacques Berlinerblau, a Georgetown University professor with dual doctorates in sociology and Ancient Near East languages. In a nimble, spicy style, he skewers what he takes to be a growing menace of evangelistic elements in a society supposedly devoted to probing the Bible without fear or favor.

Berlinerblau wades straight into the troubled waters. Bible scholarship is crumbling at secular universities, he declares, even though logically it should be on the upswing because public enthusiasm for Scripture is rising. Likewise, the field is no longer producing public intellectuals, such as Hannah Arendt and Bernard Lewis, who once raised the level of religious and biblical studies. The SBL should have the clout of other public-interest centers, such as the Brookings Institution, but does not. Why? Berlinerblau lays blame squarely on the SBL for failing to uphold tough academic standards and instead allowing too much that is uncritical, even promotional, to compromise objectivity. The Society thus flunks the key test as a legitimate academic society: instead of concentrating on let-the-chips-fall-where-they-may research, he argues, it has become largely a Bible-friendly forum that protects *beliefs* about Scripture rather than doing its proper job of honest scrutiny, scholarship that is neither friendly nor unfriendly to the Bible or religion. "The SBL should be to the Bible what FIFA is to soccer," he contends.

Berlinerblau urges the SBL to stick to biblical criticism by shunning a contrary tendency to advocate or promote the Bible, much as the American Astronomical Society separates itself from the unscientific practice of astrology by confining itself to proof-based discoveries. For Berlinerblau, it is a back-to-basics strategy that will raise the SBL's stature. The Society has to make greater allowance for heretics ("some of the very best thinking in the history of biblical scholarship has come forth precisely from heretics"), dissidents, and atheists. Up to now, he says, most research under the Society's aegis clusters under just two specialties: archaeology and Near Eastern languages. It is time, he says, to expand that study especially to the touchier territory of how Scripture is to be interpreted (the field of hermeneutics), which, as everyone in the SBL knows, is where frictions arise and thus, in Berlinerblau's opinion, where the SBL has neglected to encourage harmony.

By trumpeting his grievances in the *Chronicle,* a widely circulated touchstone of higher education, Berlinerblau gained a far wider hearing than if he had gone the in-house route; hence he thrust the troubles of a little-known organization onto the national stage. The shock caused by this smudging of a benign reputation may not have risen to the level of "What's Wrong with Mom?" but it did stir things up. On its face, the move played to the advantage of the adherents of strict academic standards within the Society by inviting the professional sympathies of thousands of like-minded professors and other educators who are accustomed to reading the publication.

Meanwhile, at least a fifth of Bible scholars who were members of SBL at the time (19 percent, according to the executive director of the SBL) were employed by religiously related institutions, mainly Christian colleges, universities, and seminaries, which favor scholarship that fosters faith and growth as disciples over knowledge for knowledge's sake. Many of those institutions require faculty members to pledge in writing that they will safeguard certain convictions: the belief that Jesus was born to a virgin; the physical resurrection of Jesus; the reality of miracles; and the belief that the Bible is wholly true. Promising to uphold those convictions could keep a scholar from exploring those subjects or others for fear of running afoul of institutional authority. That has not inhibited everyone by any means, but the standards are widely thought to have had a restraining effect. On a more positive note, many who serve religiously based institutions see nothing wrong with using the central tenets of their faith as the yardstick with which to measure challenges, not the other way around. The conformity is nothing more than submission of one's life and work to God's bidding; their efforts as scholars thus rightly contribute to the spreading of the gospel. They are doing *theology* ("talking of God"), not independent research apart from that commitment. It is an act of faith and needs to meet the beliefs that undergird that faith: to them, research has a higher calling that achieves meaning when it contributes not to the fund of factual learning but to the building up of the church. To them, that is "fair-minded research," and they blanch at the notion that enlisting academic skills to further spiritual ends is considered detrimental to the SBL.

The implication that "believers" who practice promotional "theology" are improperly squatting on the turf of "critical scholarship" agitates the higher-criticism establishment, but the alleged squatters shrewdly keep showing up and unobtrusively pursuing their mission. Unless the higher critics were to take some kind of initiative, they assume, for good reason, that they have established a niche that will keep growing, given their expanding influence in biblical studies.

It remains unclear how much Berlinerblau's scolding was a response to the jolting decision the American Academy of Religion (AAR) had made three years earlier to stop holding its annual conventions jointly with the SBL (it took effect in 2008); but that rejection had worsened the overall atmosphere. The AAR was much larger, broader in scope, and more academically prestigious. Within the SBL, the AAR's linkage of its annual meetings had borne traces of condescension toward the SBL, suggestions that the Bible enterprise was a tolerated sidekick rather than an esteemed partner

because of the doubts about the SBL's scholarly authenticity that Berlinerblau detailed. The sudden break (unilateral and with no prior consulting)
stunned the SBL and symbolized for many of its members the latent desire
of the AAR to sever ties with "the Bible people." The SBL's sorest insecu-
rities surfaced regarding its perception as the inferior partner, sometimes
patronized and demeaned by the very organization it felt closest to. Among
the SBL's leadership, the decision heaped further disrespect on biblical
studies and the Bible itself.

The SBL's executive director at that time, Kent Richards, decried
the split and the disregard behind it as "a great sorrow. Why? What does
this benefit anybody?" Exposing the nerve, he added, "Sometimes people think, well, they're Bible scholars, they must be Bible thumpers." Prof.
Karen L. King of Harvard said the break had stirred much "resentment"
and indicated "how little we know about each other. It's astounding really.
People don't understand what other people do." Biblicists heard "Oh,
you're an SBL type" as a slight. There was "a lot at stake in separation,"
Prof. King said, owing to the expansion of the Society's participants to include such fields as the history of Jewish thought, sociology, and religion
and violence. "The Bible doesn't stand on its own," she said.

The AAR tried to soothe frayed feelings and said its decision was
mostly for financial reasons; but the wound had been inflicted, placing
the Bible even further from the main intellectual currents of the religious
mainstream scholarship that the AAR purported, at least, to represent.

*   *   *

Two years after the "divorce" went into effect, the second major shoe
dropped when a distinguished Hebrew Bible scholar at University of
California–Berkeley abruptly quit the SBL and said why in an anguished
column entitled "Farewell to SBL: Faith the Reason in Biblical Studies"
in the July/August 2010 issue of the *Biblical Archaeological Review*. Prof.
Ronald Hendel's target was similar to Berlinerblau's: too much unscientif-
ically grounded research was finding its way into the Society's programs
and materials; too many conversion-minded and faith-based groups were
being invited to society functions (Pentecostal organizations were singled
out by both Hendel and Berlinerblau), further lowering SBL standards.

The particular burr in Hendel's saddle was that the Society had
erased from its mission statement the phrase "critical investigation of
the classical Bible," which he and many others regarded as a sign of gen-

uine scholarly commitment, and replaced it with a vow to "foster biblical scholarship," which he considered a weasley loophole permitting sloppy or preachy submissions.

Critical inquiry, which Hendel equated with "reason," had been "deliberately deleted as a criterion for the SBL," he wrote stingingly. "The views of creationists, snake-handlers, and faith healers now count among the kinds of biblical scholarship that the Society seeks to foster." Therefore, he did not want to "belong to a professional society where people want to convert me and where they hint in their book reviews that I'm going to hell."

Fans and foes of that declaration quickly filled cyberspace and print space with sharp debate, from "good riddance" from those who accused him of anti-Christian bias, to "good going" from admirers who applauded his candor and considered his critique of the SBL overdue. In many respects it had rebroadcast Berlinerblau's points — which had been much heard but not much acted on. This second round of scourging by a highly regarded scholar took the remnants from Berlinerblau's opening alarm and rolled them into something that was to gain greater momentum.

It rolled right over conservative sensibilities. Among the outcries was a blast from the Associates for Biblical Research (ABR), an Akron, Pennsylvania, group dedicated to using archaeological discoveries to buttress their faith in the inerrancy of the Bible and its historical accuracy. Hendel's article "betrays nothing less than an anti-Christian bias" and "continued irrational acceptance" of "anti-supernatural assumptions," wrote Henry B. Smith, the ABR's development director, in August 2010 on the group's official website. Among Smith's points was that Hendel was wrong to extol the faculty of reason as the prime locater of truth, because reason itself is deeply flawed by sin. All Hendel had really done, in Smith's view, was to "expose his humanistic, anti-God philosophy."

Not surprisingly, champions of conventional scientific research cheered. Prof. Kenneth Atkinson, a biblical scholar at the University of Northern Iowa, told an SBL audience just months after the dispute flared that nothing less than "the future, but the very nature of our field" is at stake. "Should evangelical scholars and those with deep faith commitments be allowed to participate in SBL?" he asked. Could the Society "remain an academic society without a litmus test?" No on both counts. Valid scholarship could not abide those who, with "fixed religious presuppositions or fear of a critical examination of the biblical text, cannot fully engage in biblical scholarship." Bible study has to be undaunted; nothing is beyond criticism or reexamination.

As Hendel was unfurling his rebuff in the periodical, John Kutsko was adjusting his office chair as the new executive director of the SBL. It turned out to be a fortuitous choice. In Kutsko the SBL had a seasoned Biblicist with an undergraduate degree from evangelical Gordon College and a PhD from Harvard. He had made his bones as a scientifically based scholar with deep appreciation for similar scholars and their concerns, but he also brought an understanding of evangelicals. Having arrived as Hendel's splash roiled the waters, Kutsko put aside the adjustment cushion to which he was entitled and, alert to the seriousness of the issue, acted swiftly and adroitly to address it.

In a message to the entire membership, Kutsko thanked Hendel for sparking the discussion by offering "honest comments" and "sincere concerns that are widely shared in varying degrees." He conceded that Hendel had put his finger on a hot-button issue, to wit, that "personal faith commitments trumping critical inquiry" had been "a historic challenge in our field." Everyone has to lend a hand in upholding the rules: "We are all stakeholders in the shared ownership of our organization."

On the question of whether the SBL had permitted squatters on its turf, Kutsko's answer was enigmatic, except perhaps to insiders, who were attuned to the code words Kutsko may have used. He implied that there had been lapses, but he claimed they did not represent "so much intentional slippage of scholarly rigor as an uncertainty and perhaps even a sense of discomfort at the 'fairness' of critiques toward colleagues and diverse affiliations and methodologies." Was he trying to say that the flow of new members from other countries and different fields of study made it harder to judge whether they were critically kosher? Or was he simply fudging the sticky issue so as to leave it to further debate?

Vowing to shore up criteria for acceptable scholarship, Kutsko sought to assure members that everyone speaking or planning programs at SBL events would be obliged to "abide by the standards of critical scholarship, inquiry, and discussion." He urged them to hash over these matters, including whether to reenter the words "critical inquiry" at their next meeting (they were not restored).

In phone interviews Kutsko stood firm in his defense of higher criticism (it showed how text translation had changed over time); he bemoaned the decline in teaching jobs for Biblicists; and he insisted that the SBL do a better job selling the value of Bible study to universities and colleges where it is having a hard time holding on (70 percent of the teachers of Bible in colleges are nontenured adjuncts). To illustrate how crucial it was for students to get a firm grasp of the Bible's actual contents, he compared its impact on the course of human behavior to that of Shakespeare. "Shakespeare," he said, "doesn't kill people."

Despite the "apocalyptic" depiction of SBL woes in the media, he said, "members don't bear that out." Like the Bible itself, he said, the membership is a complex blend doing good work in the nooks and crannies of society without notable rancor.

*   *   *

All but forgotten in the SBL's recent bout of dyspepsia was the indigestion caused by the Jesus Seminar from 1985 to 1995. The Seminar began with a half dozen liberal scholars convened by the late Robert W. Funk (with financial support from the Westar Institute); dozens more soon joined. It was a Trojan horse of sorts, designed as an academically sound project with a religio-political subtext. Funk boldly took on perhaps the most emotionally loaded contents of the New Testament, if not the whole Bible, the hundreds of cherished sayings of Jesus, and proposed to judge whether they were authentic, doubtful, or counterfeit. Funk, an accomplished scholar who had taught at Vanderbilt and had once been executive director of the SBL, foresaw clamor bursting from the confrontation between sobering facts with which modern Biblicists demystified and discredited the Bible and a general public largely ignorant of such claims against a biblical text they believed to be sacred. That unmasking, the Seminar's activists hoped, would combat the Christian Right's conviction that the Bible was entirely credible and could be used selectively and literally to stamp its policies with divine approval. The Seminar insisted that it was far more complicated than that, that Scripture had been doctored, in effect, and that teaching biblical literalism was a perversion of truth.

Funk's instincts as a promoter served him well. The Seminar created a buzz by gathering conspicuously every six months or so to review a batch of sayings, armed with arguments and papers that enticed growing media coverage. After hearing each other out, they cast colored beads in quasi–game-show fashion to vote whether or not they were persuaded that Jesus had actually spoken the particular sayings in question. Red signified confidence that he had; pink meant that the words sounded like they were Jesus's words, but for some reason they were not; gray conveyed the belief that the quotation had been imported from elsewhere and placed in Jesus's mouth; and black signified that the words had nothing to do with Jesus.

The final scorecard stunned even hardcore historical-critical practitioners. Of the 1,030 passages examined in the four Gospels, just twenty-six made the cut as real sayings of Jesus. More than four out of five (82 percent) received less than the top seal of approval. From the viewpoint of unsuspecting believers, who trusted that the Bible was made of whole cloth, that could be quite a shock; defenders of a whole, uncorrupted Bible rushed to knock down the Seminar's propositions.

According to the bead counts, Jesus's famous scene with the woman at the well didn't originally contain Jesus's reply to her question about when the Messiah would come by saying, "I who speak to you am He" (John 4:25-26); he never spoke of heaven and hell in the following way: "Then they will go away to eternal punishment, but the righteous to eternal life"; he never uttered this reverent vow to save mankind: "This is my blood of the covenant which is poured out for many for the forgiveness of sins"; and the words "the Virgin will be with child and will give birth to a son" were not recorded as referring particularly to him. One single saying in the Gospel of Mark was voted to be authentic. John's Gospel was judged to have absolutely none. The Beatitudes — in fact, the Sermon on the Mount as a whole — were deemed similar to what Jesus would have said, but voters decided he had not done so in those words.

Lane McGaughy, a courtly professor of New Testament who aided the Jesus Seminar from its beginnings and once served as the SBL's executive director, experienced all the storms that raged around the venture before and after it concluded in 1995. He remained steadfast in his praise of what it had done. At lunch one day, the amiable, learned Bible veteran hailed the Seminar for "changing the conversation" by cracking the wall of denial that the Bible was anything less than it appeared to be. Despite much pooh-poohing by detractors of the Seminar's makeup (not enough heavyweights and nonliberals), its tactics (frivolous and superficial), and its fractious conclusions (radical, nowhere near reflecting consensus among Biblicists), McGaughy voiced confidence that "its findings are widely accepted" and explained that the Seminar's results simplified a much more fluid definition of what was "real" and what wasn't in New Testament times, compared to the more exacting standards that are applied today. His allowance that the ancient mentality permeating Jesus's sayings didn't lend itself to strict modern analytical categories seemed to be at least a tacit admission that the Seminar's method sidestepped a core axiom of spiritual life: that faith evokes its own facts, such as incarnations and resurrections.

"In those times," McGaughy said, referring to the Jesus era, "no difference was made between what Jesus said and what his followers said he said. Modern historians and scholars don't allow sources that cannot be verified." Seminar scholars are among those who believe that another document exists — which they call "Q" — that certain Gospel writers had as a resource to weave into their own versions. Such a document is vouched for circumstantially, but it has never, in fact, been found. Evangelicals generally do not believe that it exists, but it is crucial to McGaughy's point: "Luke [the presumed Gospel writer] uses Mark's Gospel [assumed to have been written first and thus available to Luke]. Mark, at about age seventy, had decided he'd write a version of Jesus that he felt comfortable with. Luke took it and the Q source and said, 'I'm going to look into it myself.' He took it from there."

The Seminar's original desire to topple the Christian Right's effectiveness in selling inerrancy as standard Christian teaching had intensified as the public's declining knowledge of the Bible made it less possible to tell whether that claim was true or false. In addition, inerrantists had refused to concede anything to historical-critical research conclusions. The Jesus Seminar hoped to put a dent in that impression by publishing and broadcasting its counterclaims as widely as possible.

Whether the Seminar realized it or not, the bead strategy perhaps did more than anything to advance that cause. Its public image was whimsical (probably unintentionally so) and fanciful, inviting the imagination to create a virtual logo that stuck in the mind, a form of branding that enlarged the Seminar's place on the public's radar screen. Funk and his associates were primed to jump on that advantage to gain a foothold on media turf that was dominated by evangelicals. It worked — attracting admirers and foes. Conservative Christians were predictably outraged, attacking the project as sacrilege and anti-Christian. The Seminar had given them one target in particular that brought scorn: its rejection of anything supernatural. If a verse or a setting were couched in something miraculous, it was summarily dismissed as something that could not have happened. Fans of the Seminar said it was time to tell the truth about the Bible's human designs.

There was plenty of yelping at what the iconoclastic Seminar had laid bare, and not only from livid conservatives. The project was renegade and irreverent enough to rouse edgy cheers and jeers. It was like the proverbial skunk at the lawn party or the uncle spouting distasteful family history at the Thanksgiving reunion. Even the Jesus Seminar's launching pad, the SBL, kept it at arm's length — because, McGaughy contended, "it was too radical." If the initiative had been embraced, he conjectures, it could have "given historical criticism its own American identity" and would have reversed a generic American hostility toward higher criticism that had lasted nearly two centuries.

Luke Timothy Johnson, a leading Catholic scholar of the New Testament, is among those whose popularity and reputation would have lent valuable support — or even benign neutrality — to the Seminar. Instead, he became its bitter foe. In an article for the liberal Protestant journal *The Christian Century,* "The Jesus Seminar's Misguided Quest for the Historical Jesus," he denounces the project for relying too much on sheer facts from the past to dictate conclusions when many other factors, such as the living faith of the church, deserve more attention. And there is for liberals this insidious comparison: the Seminar's "obsessive concern with historicity and its extreme liberalism merely represents the opposite of fundamentalism." He heaps further scorn on it as a crass "entrepreneurial venture guided by Robert Funk."

Yet conservative reactions reflect the burden of defending the fortress of biblical literalism that the Seminar has flattened. Not surprisingly, defenders ranged from moderates, who attempted to answer the Seminar on its own terms, to enraged fundamentalists, who condemned the project for undermining the Bible and desecrating Jesus, defaming Christianity, and leading astray Christians and non-Christians alike. There were enough heaps of ridicule and outrage to block the sun from view. But the flurry of responses did include some substantive, scholarly, and irenic contributions that offered further discussion.

Among them was a collection of essays by the Bible faculty at the widely respected evangelical Biola University in California, entitled *Jesus Under Fire.* The contributors questioned the Jesus Seminar's methods and strove to trip up its members. But that book and others like it showed just how pungent the Seminar's brew had been. Apart from the debate about its credibility and worth, the Seminar had jolted a wide spectrum of Biblicists one way or the other and seemed virtually certain to accelerate the spread of skepticism and biblical illiteracy. How could it not? Because the findings had the potency of science behind them and had landed the first blows, its impact was more than likely to outpace the responses.

Several members with long SBL histories saw a link between that surge of piquant liberalism, with the furor it triggered, and its more recent troubles. The Jesus Seminar's boldness, even as it became more peripheral to the SBL, set in motion a pendulum swing in a conservative direction that became more hospitable to the kind of "believer friendly" participation that Berlinerblau and Hendel both decried.

Debate over Jesus's words came down to the yawning gap that separated those who measure their studies through the lens of faith commitments from those who measure their studies by the criteria of modern scholarly rigor — apart from their faith or lack thereof. As compelling as the attacks of the faith-firsters were on the Seminar, my limited survey shows that they achieved no solid success defeating the Seminar on its own terms. Nor would they be expected to, because they begin from a wholly different place: a pledge to uphold the tenets of a prior faith and to accept a supernatural, miracle-filled world — neither of which the Seminar in general allowed to frame its inquiries. The ongoing struggle between the transcendent and the secular, faith as a self-validating factor in deciding truth as opposed to sole dependence on material (empirical) evidence, and vastly opposing views on whether historical-critical research is compatible with "belief" — all these continue to divide Biblicists. It does not look like the lion is about to lie down with the lamb anytime soon.

Love it or detest it, the Jesus Seminar's colors and content carved a stream of thought into the subconscious of both sides in such a way that it persisted for some time. Historical-critical researchers rode its momentum even if they objected to aspects of it; faith-based scholars saw the wolf at the door no matter how strenuously or effectively they fought it.

*   *   *

Perhaps the following recent discussion at Yale Divinity School might have taken place even without the Jesus Seminar's audacity and quirks, but the Seminar's legacy made it less remarkable. At a late afternoon forum, Prof. Joel Baden, a resident faculty member who teaches Hebrew Bible, expanded on the theme of his cutting-edge book *The Historical David: The Real Life of an Invented Hero,* which takes a new look at an old biblical giant. For Jews, David occupies the highest rung in their ancient past, generally credited with coalescing the nation of Israel and founding its religious practices in Jerusalem. He is likewise celebrated by Christians as a larger-than-life figure, due in large part to the tales the Bible tells about him, from his upset victory over Goliath to his romantic escapades with Bathsheba.

For nearly an hour, under questioning from one of his Yale colleagues, Prof. John Collins, Baden sought to strip legend from reality as he'd found it, reducing the Bible's portrayal of a majestic king to a real, mortal man whose profile was vastly inflated and sanitized by writers bent on creating a leader of mythic proportions. Baden personified the intensity and exactitude of the modern, objective scholar, his attention squarely on which elements of the story, if any, could be rationally verified (or rejected) historically — that is, via literary analysis. It was not being evaluated as a source of faith.

Baden is a trim, youthful-looking man with beard and glasses. He connects bits of knowledge with alacrity and in an engaging manner, allowing that it is probable that a real-life model for the fully realized biblical David existed and that he actually became king, though Baden agrees that there is no proof of that from outside the Bible. For that matter, some of the most cherished legends about David, such as the one ascribing to him authorship of dozens of the Psalms, couldn't be traced to Scripture either.

Over time, various writers reworked the story of David to fashion him into the figure who would be deserving of the reverence, adulation, and inspiration that his reputation had acquired. That increasingly fictitious, sanitized *story,* Baden says, has taken the bare bones of the *history* that underlay the account and conflated it. Whereas the original tales of David, in the two books of Samuel written at a time that was close to the events, were detailed and alluded to David's gross misdeeds, the recasting of David's life by the writer of Chronicles centuries later left out parts that portrayed David as less than perfect by covering up his less flattering history.

A question by Collins, who injected himself into the conversation as a clever skeptic, provided the session's most arresting moment. Does it personally matter to Baden, he asked, whether any of this material is true or false? It sounds like an exchange that might have occurred in a department faculty meeting between an older, mentoring senior professor admiringly testing a junior colleague.

"No," Baden replied slowly, smiling wanly. His answer is deliciously ambiguous. It is certainly a nod of allegiance to the conventions of critical scholarship. If objectivity is the goal, then it makes no difference whether the outcome of the study shows the text to be historically true or false. But as I observed him at that meeting, his reply yielded another plausible meaning, perhaps one that was impressing itself on him unwittingly. It is a quality of extrarational, suspended judgment, a gauzy hint that beyond his research hovers something ethereal that is of great significance. Baden said nothing to indicate he imputes anything transcendent to David's story, and so far as I am aware I wasn't looking for it. But perhaps for that moment, the scholarly need for "unbelief" had coexisted with a scholar's "belief," where David's life somehow touched something ineffable.

CHAPTER 9

Canon Fodder

Charles Stanley has survived the minefield of television evangelism with a style that goes against type. His gentlemanly manner and soothing baritone delivery, marks of his Virginia upbringing, contrast with the prevalent image of media preachers as boisterous and wired. Since 1972, as the newly installed pastor of First Baptist Church in Atlanta, Rev. Stanley has pitched his biblical sermons to that broad band of seekers, shut-ins, and skeptics who rarely if ever darken a church door, with a notable ability to keep them watching. He is there every week behind a spare pulpit, with his lean frame and full head of hair, his leather-bound Bible at the ready, exhorting in commonsense language those in the crowded pews at his feet and the millions on the airwaves to come to Christ.

Now in his eighties, he has outlasted a horde of media ministers who have died or have lost their bright-lights perches to financial and ratings failures or, more famously, to sexual temptation or other violations of the Ten Commandments. A few years ago, Stanley did suffer an internal church skirmish when his marriage fell apart; but that seems almost quaint by comparison to other TV evangelists who have gone down in flames. After the dust settled, the church urged him to stay — on the condition that he not remarry. His pulpit appeal defies easy definition, but it stands out as a calm, reasonable approach that invites viewers looking for an alternative to preachers who shout and set off sirens of judgment. In Stanley they have a man with the bearing of a judge, a benign visage that reminds people of Don Knotts and Mr. Rogers, and a voice whose cadences sound more like deep thoughts than sales pitches.

His sermons draw from daily news events, social trends, popular books, and, most of all, Scripture. Above everything else, Charles Stanley sees the world through the lens of total confidence in every word of the Bible. The Bible is "God's book," he says during a television sermon in which he vows to validate the "existence of God" against the claims of deists, materialists, and atheists. "God's book," he says, "is absolutely true."

Heads must have nodded across the waves of listeners as I heard him utter that judgment one Sunday morning from behind his plain wooden pulpit. It is a salt-of-the-earth conviction that ripples across a wide swath of humanity, including many who don't believe it but want to. Stanley's expansive audience is mostly on the conservative/evangelical end of the Protestant spectrum, but his sermons have elements that entice borderline mainline Protestants and Catholics, as well as "nones" (those with no church affiliation), to listen. It is roughly similar to the crossover effect that Billy Graham achieved.

Stanley's personal talents and charms could go only so far in persuading fence sitters to jump to his side and accept his core message. Somewhere along the line there is one condition: they have to be willing to accept Stanley's definition of the Bible as infallible and stamped with God's specific purpose and design. Though he imparts that message without rancor or fundamentalist hardness, it asks for a commitment that repudiates a staple of scientific/secularist thinking that comes naturally to many of the undecided.

Stanley stands in the nexus between old-fashioned piety that believes in miracles no matter what science says and the secular disconnect from transcendence that I have discussed earlier. To the one side of him is sophisticated academic learning that rejects otherworldliness, and on the other side the sea of ordinary Christians who live most of their lives in thrall to secular principles but are not ready to give up entirely on otherworldliness. For his part, Stanley isn't about to broker the differences between the two; he is solidly on his side of the divide. But he is one of the few highly visible preachers whose congregation in its broadest sense is inclusive enough to afford that opportunity had he chosen to exercise it.

*   *   *

As it is, Charles Stanley's theological and biblical assumptions — and those of evangelicals who share them — are eons distant from those exercised in the rarefied climate of biblical scholarship and teaching at the leading universities and research centers. Scholars at the high end of research are delving into areas of criticism and combining fields of knowledge in such a way that they are, on a practical basis, in an orbit of their own, neither better nor worse than the less erudite ranks of common believers — but remote from them.

That gulf between professor and pew has occupied a good deal of my attention in this book, and it will receive more attention below. But first, what is stirring among the professors that might be news, even shocking news, to the lay masses?

One is the continuing scuffle over *canon,* though for most laypeople the word itself gives no clue to the drama behind this seemingly obscure subject. It refers in a general way to a collection of books recognized by authorities as the best of their kind in portraying the nature of a certain subject or historical period. A well-known canon of Western literature, for example, consists of the works regarded as the most authentic expressions of Western culture, highlighted by such luminaries as William Shakespeare, John Milton, Mark Twain, and James Joyce. In other words, if you are seeking to understand that civilization, go to those books. In recent decades, a backlash against the alleged bias against marginalized people and the elitism of race, class, and gender of that canon have knocked it off its pedestal, exemplifying the human factors that can make and break such lists.

Even the Bible has been assembled in parts, added to and taken from, and approved with different ingredients by various Christian traditions. I'm not qualified to judge the rights and wrongs of the arguments that swirl around that subject; instead, my purpose is to outline the contours of the debate and suggest that, like a faraway El Niño, it affects the whole climate system.

Either there has or hasn't been a conscious effort by pioneering Christians to designate a set of writings by those close to Jesus and the earliest apostles as a genuine, God-given guide to what Christians are called to believe and how they should practice that faith in their everyday lives. If it happened that way, initially over the span of two hundred years or so, certain books were added to or stricken from the list until, by AD 400, a more or less stable canon received the church's stamp of approval. There was plenty to choose from. The Gospels of Matthew and John, the Acts of the Apostles, and the Apocalypse of John made the cut, for example, whereas the Gospels of the Ebionites and of Thomas, the Acts of Paul, and the Apocalypse of Peter did not. Scholars are still combing through those early centuries with the tools of historical criticism to find more clues to an ever-bigger picture. It has been an impressive achievement. Subjects previously downplayed or excluded — from the treatment of women and slaves to how Roman occupation affected Christian character — are now on the agenda. Greater inquiry into what qualified a text for being accepted or rejected (in theological, political, and social terms), more careful analysis of which fragments or whole texts made their way to certain churches, and a closer look at the influence of surrounding cultures' religions and morality (particularly Jewish) expanded the scope and injected new energy and debate into those studies.

The uncovering of the Dead Sea Scrolls and the Nag Hammadi Gnostic Gospels helped propel the momentum. There were crossovers from the Qumran scrolls and the Hebrew Bible. Many striking features of such newfound Gnostic texts as the Gospels of Thomas and of Mary, perhaps most strikingly related to the role of women, sharpened speculation that those and other books might have been rejected without just cause. More broadly, the deepening of research and emergence of new texts quite naturally brings into question the very concept of an established canon. Why these and not those? Historical, archaeological, and literary-critical advances have taken the canon probe in new directions.

Biblicists were also under the sway of the megawave known as "postmodernism," or "deconstruction," which prevailed within Western intellectual currents. It can receive only brief mention here, but in a nutshell its overall point is that the West has wrongly trusted reason as a path to truth and that historical truth (among others) is impossible because screens of subjective perception and collective self-interest distort interpretation at every stage, inexorably shifting its meaning as it wends its way through personal and cultural filters. The centerpieces of the objectivist-rationalist Enlightenment were thus under siege. The Bible isn't immune to this critique, of course, so those Biblicists most persuaded by the new movement applied its doubts about certainty and historical validity to the stories and lessons of Scripture. Relatively speaking, there were no "answers," just more questions, illusions behind illusions.

Postmodernist skepticism deepened the split between modernists and traditionalists, of course, but still the canon question has remained. Has a divinely bundled textbook been provided to instruct the church in what Christianity is supposed to be, or not?

My scan of the fat volume of attempts by experts to answer that question is nowhere near complete or conclusive, but it is unfailingly fascinating. A parade of superior minds using the best analytical tools have been uncovering the intricate web of activities that finally bound tiny pods of Christians into a semblance of a connected church during the first four centuries after

Christ. That formation was made possible by — and, in turn, contributed to the creation of — twenty-seven books that were adopted as the New Testament. The steps toward that end unfolded unevenly over a distant stretch of Mediterranean countries and regions in which the new faith was being tried out by largely independent groups of followers. All roads might lead to Rome, so to speak, but their diverse paths and occasional conjunctions left travelers with a diverse mix of perceptions and conceptions of what was normal. The underlying question was how the New Testament was put together, why those texts were granted authority — and what kind of authority — and whether it was regarded as an appointed "canon" (or rule) aglow with divine authorship or a collection of wise, spiritually rich testimonies that was certified as the source of guidelines for leading a Christian life.

Early Christianity detectives had much to show for their efforts, but, like Stephen Hawking and other theoretical physicists in their pursuit of the universe's ultimate secrets, they lacked a "theory of everything." They appeared to be getting closer but needed further breakthroughs, such as the discovery of hitherto unknown documents or other revealing remains. But there would be no reversion by highly trained scholars to the "everything" answer provided by biblical literalism — except among the dwindling group of holdouts.

The science-friendly Biblicists were sounding more confident than ever that they were on the right side of history, to the extent that they could be sardonic about those who clung to the supernatural myths. R. A. Baker, a biblical scholar, dismissed miraculous explanations for the canon's existence in an "Early Christian History" blog: "The NT was not dropped from heaven. The NT was not delivered by an angel." Nor was it dug up in a farmer's field as Joseph Smith described discovering the Book of Mormon. Nor were all twenty-seven New Testament books found undamaged in clay jars, as were the Dead Sea Scrolls. "The New Testament canon developed, or evolved, over the course of 250-300 years of Christian history," Baker says. Success in uncovering that process reinforces the "historical validity" of its origins.

Another prevalent assumption is that simply doing historical criticism puts a dent in presumptions of canonical purity. Forming the canon is redefined as a decidedly human process of trial, error, bias, churchly horse-trading, and gradual packaging, unlike previous conceptions, which held that the canon was fixed by godly arrangement and would last forever. By general consensus, the template of what became the basic standard was approved in AD 367 by the renowned theologian Athanasius of Egypt in his Festal Letter. That didn't mean uniformity: books were added and subtracted by various branches of the church, but the structure was essentially in place. However, many recent scholars contend that, like other canons, the biblical canon cannot retain that stability because it is subject to the changing historical forces that will, by turns, strengthen and weaken it. Over the past 150 years, the upsurge in the desire to get down and dirty with the facts in and around biblical accounts has been born of the larger impulse to revisit the past with modern precision. For Christians, the particular incentive is a hunger to find the historical Jesus.

Flip Schutte, a professor of Bible at the University of Pretoria (South Africa), put his shoulder to the wheel of that human history in his review in the leading South African theological journal *HTS* of *The Canon Debate,* a landmark collection of essays by thirty leading canon scholars. "Canons aren't eternal," Schutte flatly declares. Drawing on convictions shared by a sizable portion of scholars, he describes a six-stage process whereby canons are born, become established, lose credibility, and finally disintegrate. He believes that the biblical canon has lost clout and is in the throes of "disintegration" because "we don't read the Bible anymore as if it is a divine oracle that speaks firsthand of God. It has lost its unconditional status as 'Word of God.'" He adds, however, that a holiness of the canon will persist in some way as long as "there are believers who can relate to the Christian myths" (supernatural claims) and who can "through these myths experience God."

Most significantly, Schutte is among those progressive Biblicists who speak of a "canon behind the canon" as the spiritual reality to which Scripture in a secondary role points and to which it offers footnotes. Hence it doesn't matter whether the Bible has been under construction over centuries by people who have added their own interpretations. It could be a rough draft of the Holy Spirit's movement through history as the taproot of life and faith. The "canon behind the canon" is the presence of Jesus Christ. Schutte's review of the 662-page, definitive *Canon Debate* mostly plows familiar ground, but he singles out a fellow progressive, Robert Funk, founder of the Jesus Seminar, as a grand exception, one who says that Christianity "was a movement of spirit — not a book."

*   *   *

To say yes to the authentic canon is to declare that, despite the scoffing of postmodernists, all parts of the Bible are connected, warts and all, by a common theme and a unified message. For Christians, the Hebrew Bible is not to be discarded in favor of the New Testament but is to be searched for signs and prophecies that point precisely to fulfillment in events recorded in the New Testament: the coming of Jesus, his death and resurrection, and the budding of the first churches. History is important, but the revelation reflected in the Gospels outweighs inconsistencies and contradictions in the other biblical accounts. The "yeses" are thus not restricted to those who insist that the Bible has no errors. That, I think, has become a key factor in responses to the crisis concerning the plummeting of Bible knowledge and reading. Given the choice between promoting a canon that insists on inerrancy and an approach that puts inerrancy aside, at least for the time being, many evangelicals have been willing to downplay inerrancy for what they see as a greater good (all inerrantists may be canonists, but not all canonists are inerrantists). Word-for-word accuracy of God's transcription doesn't count for much if there is no trust that the whole book is heaven's own blueprint, the whole being greater than its parts. And it is tougher to sell that belief when fewer people are reading less and less of it.

For many "yeses," therefore, whatever their attachment to inerrancy, it is more urgent to first win acceptance of the Bible as a package, the way a solar power agent needs to market the "idea" of the source before attending to the details. Accordingly, the Bible might first be seen as a jigsaw puzzle by a Single Designer, who melded its irregular pieces into a single design that depicts nothing less than the salvation of the world. Or it might be seen as a roller-coaster ride — from the reversal of fortunes in the Garden of Eden to the fires of final judgment and redemption. Or as a book of short stories bearing the consciousness of one author rather than a collection of stories by a variety of writers with diverse mentalities.

By orientation, the "yeses" gravitate to the Evangelical Theological Society (ETS), a conservative rival of the Society of Biblical Literature that customarily meets just before the SBL's annual assembly, and in the same city, so that its members can attend both meetings. Canon advocates are in good company at the ETS, not only because they generally share the presuppositions on the biblical canon, but also because they find support for their blending of personal faith into their scholarship in the service of the church's mission. In this corner, Bible research belongs within the community of believers from which Scripture has arisen in the first place. To the extent that its members see it that way, they exemplify the kind of "believer" Biblicists whose work both Ron Hendel and Jacques Berlinerblau protested as violating the objective standards of the SBL.

To say no to the authentic canon is to deny that the Bible has any underlying theme or organizing principle on the grounds that historical examination shows the Bible to be a bundle of largely heterodox materials that often duplicate or clash with each other, that are historically fabricated or incorrect, and that contain generous amounts of fiction (albeit fiction that is itself a testimony to truth). As they see it, the Bible resembles more what the American founders first envisioned in the Articles of Confederation: autonomous entities with some common interests, knit together rather than joined at the hip (as the later United States was envisioned by the Constitution). Secular-minded researchers argue that the New Testament is shot through with personal agendas by its authors and that, along with its supernatural worldview, it doesn't begin to qualify as a Great Books collection published by the Holy Spirit — or if it is, that doesn't speak well of the Holy Spirit's organizing talents.

Postmodernist skepticism about certainty notwithstanding, the rationally minded "nos" have, by almost all accounts, gained a much larger following in recent decades than the "yeses" have, especially among the ranks of Bible scholars within secular institutions. Canon defenders are plainly caught in a major gravitational shift that further removes faith-alone claims from the realm of possibility — even among Biblicists. Canon still has its impressive supporters, but it has lost ground in the big picture, along with inerrancy. A third branch of that mindset, the field of biblical theology, is also fading; it has long sought to trace how primary Christian beliefs can be drawn from the Bible's own inner history.

Yet, while historical critics have the upper hand among scholars, the theologically grounded minority shows much vitality. Some, such as Stanley Hauerwas, a mover and shaker in Christian ethics, are comfortable living with a paradox. He accepts the results of the historians as significant but not superior to the "revealed" wisdom and truth that gave birth to the church and have sustained it since. That mystery is the soul of Christianity, he says, brought about by the life, death, and resurrection of Christ, to which the biblical writings testify and by which they bond its followers. Whatever the problems with the text, they cannot supplant or nullify the essence of that mystery, according to the canonists. To some of them, the Bible's communal origins and nature imply that Scripture is properly studied only within the church among those who grasp that mystery.

In his book on that subject, *Unleashing the Scripture,* Hauerwas insists, in his typically provocative manner, that individuals cannot adequately grasp the Bible by themselves but need the company of committed Christians, who share its spiritual premises and implementation. Hauerwas says, only somewhat hyperbolically, that the "only thing we can do is take the Bible away from everyone. The idea that you can read the Bible on your own is a deeply corrupting presumption." That goes for scholars as well, Hauerwas says. Scripture is a byproduct of the faith of the first believers, not the source of it; it is the messenger, not itself the message. At the same time, since the Bible is the enhancer of faith, not its genesis, it is not to be worshiped, though it often has been. That is an error of idolatry called "biblicism," a scourge that Christian Smith warns about in his recent book *The Bible Made Impossible: Why Biblicism Is Not a Truly Evangelical Reading of Scripture.*

The split between the two sides is deep and wide, but less and less hostile or competitive. Rather than clash, they appear to be moving in opposite directions according to the methods they use and the answers they seek. Disputes between empiricists and inerrantists have burned much hotter as winner-take-all combat on a wider scale. That struggle is slowing and temporizing as inerrancy has lost its appeal, but it hasn't arrived at the live-and-let-live stage that the canon debate seems to have achieved. It looks as though they will go their separate ways with their own goals: one hunting down the physical facts to disprove the existence of a canon, the other professing a mystery that overrides those facts and knits together a divinely appointed narrative.

(I have consciously avoided the elephant in the room, which the reader has undoubtedly noticed: it's about facts. Believers in inerrancy defend biblical events, people, and places as historical fact. Their faith depends on that conviction: that the virgin birth and the resurrection, among other things, really happened. The historical-critical practitioners — to varying degrees, and partly or wholly — deny that those claims can be proven objectively. And therein the confusion and the conundrum. Literalists cannot say that exact accuracy is irrelevant because they say it is. What they call "facts" are, by commonsense standards, more like products of wishful thinking. On the other hand, historians cannot always be 100 percent sure that important elements of data are not missing.)

Whether secularized twenty-first-century listeners can fathom such a supernatural founding poses a huge challenge. Without the Bible as an elevated authority that fortifies faith claims, evangelism gets harder, and the power of the Bible wanes. Under pressure from biblical myth-busters and the spread of agnosticism ushered in by the secular age described by Charles Taylor, the Bible is being reduced closer to "ordinary" status, cataloged increasingly as a work of great literature and Ancient Near Eastern history rather than as a sacred testimony to the Christian path to salvation.

Meanwhile, in secular higher education, Bible courses are being phased out in favor of the insertion of a sample of readings from the Bible into literature courses, where it is one among many reading assignments. Departments of religion that once showed at least tacit sympathy for religion as "true" are being transformed into departments of religious studies, which require objective approaches that effectively rule out the discussion of personal convictions or any talk of religion as a life choice. Students in religion classes usually have no idea whether or not their professors have anything beyond an academic interest in religion. The silence is believed to be a safeguard against proselytizing. In the process, it stigmatizes the search for religion as "truth" as a lesser occupation and inhibits considering it as such.

*　　*　　*

Wherever they personally stand on the divine inspiration of Scripture or the legitimacy of canon, Biblicists with advanced degrees who are affiliated with teaching, research, or religious institutions travel in a stratosphere far removed from the places where choirs sing, babies are baptized, and church councils struggle to stay alive, or at least stanch the losses. Bibles are planted in the pew racks of many of those spaces, for use in worship or reading during personal quiet time. Often they are like sentinels guarding a tradition of individual encounter that has mostly given way to communal behaviorism such as watching verses dance on overhead screens and singing biblical paraphrases in high-pitched gospel singsong at the direction of a stylized Christian rock band. Or they appear in more sedate Protestant settings, where pew Bibles are more like loyal pets keeping vigil as the appointed lessons of the day are imparted from the altar in more stentorian fashion. Trends suggest that neither kind of churchgoer knows a whole lot about the context or finer meaning of the passages that are explicated.

As in many fields, research has yielded startling discoveries that ordinary Christians know little or nothing about, unless they are among the handful who read esoteric academic journals. In many specialty areas — medicine, American history, and climatology as examples — discoveries have nearly always found their way to the public as new products, innovative methods, or stunning revisions of how we see things (the moon wasn't made of cheese, it turned out; Columbus didn't discover America;

and carbon dioxide caused climate change). Bible scholarship's harvest, by comparison, though it can be equally jarring, seldom finds its way into congregations, either because it risks trampling on such cherished beliefs as the immaculate conception or because there is so little demand for contrary claims. Believers are, by and large, satisfied with understanding the Bible as it is presented by the particular church they attend: literally recorded from God, flawed by its purely human sources, a volume of myths, a source of spiritual truth through metaphor, and so on. And they are not looking to complicate things by asking questions about historical accuracy or the correct definition of common but archaic references in the text.

That tendency to superimpose faith on history rather than history on faith is one barrier to accepting the revolution going on among the scholars. The resistance to reports that shattered folk Christianity's take on the Bible is prevalent, so far as I can tell, among a wide range of Christians for whom Scripture is seen as an immutable island of safety in a sea of frightful modern change. I find that true even among people who have scant knowledge of the Bible's actual content but keep it fondly in mental reserve as an all-purpose insurance backup, and who devoutly uphold passages that aren't in it ("God helps those who help themselves" being a favorite). It is often repeated that the Bible has disappeared from public life; in fact, it seems to me that it has receded from individual and private life to nearly the same degree. During the celebration of the King James Version's four hundredth birthday in 2011, a British Bible revivalist, a person who has directed the Evangelical Alliance UK, lamented that, "despite owning more Bibles per household than we will ever use," Western nations "are slowly starving to death because we have lost our appetite for Scripture." The "gotcha" polls on biblical knowledge regularly supply ammunition for his claim. Yet distant, absentee nostalgia for the Good Book in pristine form — that is, without upsetting discoveries — seems hardly to have abated.

I believe the hitch is that the Christian church cannot ignore the truth about the Bible, wherever it came from, without weakening the credibility of the New Testament's alleged eyewitness accounts. Without that mooring, the church seems certain to establish its authority elsewhere and drift in another direction. As I have mentioned above, it is difficult to deny that such a shift is taking place as elements of American Christianity bypass the Bible both personally and institutionally. The rising alternative, it appears, is to focus directly on Jesus as the source of personal faith, though Jesus has always been considered incomprehensible without the Bible's testimony. In place of Scripture, seekers are drawn to glimpses and anecdotes about Jesus told in an assortment of visual media, some produced by the churches, others woven into popular music, film, and fiction. Among the quick profiles is a stylized Jesus in the self-help mode who dispenses personal comfort. He is ever-loving, -approving, -encouraging, and -compassionate, utterly removed from the figure who spoke in the Sermon on the Mount the "hard sayings" about sacrifice and against self-centeredness.

As most serious Bible scholars spiral further from fanciful or mythic depictions and burrow further into the historical substrata, the very survival of the inherited church seems to require acceptance of these scholarly challenges to adapt Christianity in whatever ways deemed necessary to appeal with integrity to the secular, empirical world of the future. But it has not worked out that way for reasons on both sides. The ever-more-esoteric directions taken by scholars under the sway of academic mandates to specialize have taken them to places increasingly distant from the pews. Many in the pew don't even want to hear about it.

Nor is it entirely self-evident that they need to listen, though the contemporary age's concept of progress assumes that they should. From another vantage point, however, historical-critical additives are not crucial to sustaining the vitality of faith. Dr. Andrew Village, professor of "practical and empirical theology" at York Saint John University in England, has studied the interaction between high-end research and ordinary congregations and has found patterns that are both intriguing and unsettling. Among the findings he reported to the Society of Biblical Literature convention in Chicago in 2012, for example, was a matching of church members — and the composition of congregations as a whole — with Jungian personality types as identified by the widely used Myers-Briggs screening. Churches with a distinctly conservative profile were most likely to exhibit "thinking," or logical, preferences for certainty, whereas liberals leaned toward a "feeling" character, which sought compromise. The outcome basically confirms some stereotypes, which link conservatives with unwavering conviction and liberals with relativity; but it also underscores at least the inherent compatibility between conservatism and the usual object of its scorn, scholarly rationalism, which produces historical-critical results.

In his ground-breaking book *The Bible and Lay People*, Village examines how regular church people interpret Scripture (exercising what scholars formally call "hermeneutics"), turning many preconceptions into arresting paradoxes. How should experts instruct congregations in the trailblazing discoveries? Does it do more harm than good to disabuse congregants of basic assumptions? First, Village berates "the academy," despite "all its sophisticated developments in biblical scholarship in the last 50 years," for being "largely ignorant of what other people do with the Bible," adding that scholars have only recently become "aware that there are any 'ordinary' readers at all." The search for accuracy and composition has fallen "into the hands of academic theologians," who have removed its study even further from Christian commoners.

Perhaps his most significant conclusion is that, when traditionally minded congregants are "educated" about challenging discoveries, they do become less literalistic; but the impact rarely dislodges their faith in basic biblical literalism or supernatural interventions. (Village uses "literalist" as a catchall term, not one restricted to believers in strict inerrancy.) Village's most striking conclusion is that literalists often find the "truth" of biblical texts by virtue of their faith-filled intuition more readily than liberals do with their stores of information. The tough test for liberals is to find new meaning in a Bible that has been rampantly redefined and dissected.

Village is hardly alone in accusing academia of hijacking cutting-edge Bible study. Leading scholar/believers, such as Luke Timothy Johnson, protest that the Bible has been wrenched from its rightful home in the body of the church and subjected to an alien discipline governed by scientific and postmodernist thinking. Johnson refers to it more broadly as the "academic captivity of the churches." Hauerwas, like Johnson, doesn't object to historical criticism itself, but thinks that its adherence to academic (secular) standards makes it generally useless for churches. At the hands of the historical-critical approach, the Bible, in effect, would lie in ruins — reduced to a heap of fragments.

Kathleen O'Connor zeroes in on the premise of contemporary research: it applies the motto inspired by the scientific method, the idea that study begins with skepticism and works its way to greater certainty by trial and error, rather than starting with faith that certain outcomes will be achieved. Study in the setting of the church involves theology, she said in an interview, and "theology needs more than the hermeneutics [interpretive criteria] of suspicion." It also needs the "hermeneutics of hunger that engages the content of Christian tradition." Bible scholarship, she observed, is missing "sophisticated study of the theological dimensions of Bible texts." The prolonged absence of such study has made Bible research "incapable of speaking to our present," she said. Bible exegesis (uncovering as close to an exact meaning of words and passages as possible) is "no more than historiography and history of literature. For me the challenge is what the text *meant* and what it *means now*. We should expand our methods beyond the historical-critical approach, put the Bible back together as a literary and theological document."

Complaints like these are coming from insiders, friends, and colleagues of religious-studies faculties devoted to strict academic rules. While relatively few in number, they signal a strain of restlessness that may someday challenge the dominance of rigorous objectivism and skepticism in favor of greater acceptance of faith factors within religious experience. Meanwhile, scores of prominent evangelicals and other conservative Christians still regularly brand historical criticism as a scourge. In their view, liberal/empirical scholars are sabotaging the Bible and undermining faith. To some, it is nothing less than a satanic shaking of sacred pillars. Or, in a milder version, it is close-mindedness that rejects mysticism without adequate reason.

But trust in science's methods is not going away, and the chasm between professor and pew shows every indication of widening further. The trends are deeply ingrained. Decades ago, top Biblicists were already declaring that ordinary congregants weren't equipped to decipher the Bible's enigmatic language. Expert research requires years of study and practice that nonspecialists lack almost entirely. Van Harvey, then head of Stanford University's religious studies department, said flatly in a 1985 interview that "the lay person has simply been disqualified from having *any right to a judgment* regarding the truth or falsity of certain historical claims" (emphasis added). By historical standards, "there is scarcely a popularly held belief about Jesus that is not regarded with considerable skepticism," he declared.

In terms of sophistication, then, Bible scholars have soared ahead of churchgoers in roughly the same way physicians' levels and depths of learning have long since raced beyond common people's understanding of medicine. The difference is that the physician has to deliver the results of that learning to real patients, however obliquely or partially. What's more, patients tend to accept the diagnoses, welcome the reports, and integrate the therapies into their treatment. Bible scholars, by contrast, work alone and offer the fruits of their expertise mostly to each other — or in some cases, in simplified fashion, to a broader audience.

* * *

Leaving aside the unwavering biblical literalists, most American Christians are probably open in varying degrees to the revisions and challenges offered by academic scholars. I say that because the research principles of science are so pervasive and credible that they are almost universally accepted, no matter what a person's religious convictions are. Celebrated advances such as the Salk vaccine and the Hubble telescope implicitly endorsed the scientific steps that produced them as a source of truth. But if such openness exists, it is almost entirely dormant and inoperative, alien and independent — as though the refined scholar were saying to the congregant, "The Bible isn't what you think it is." And the congregant replies to the refined scholar: "The Bible isn't what *you* think it is either." Neither acknowledges much need for the other.

My helicopter view of the scene has led me to the opposite conclusion, which is that each needs the other, and that prolonging the silent stalemate will seriously hurt both. Some kind of fence-mending is, in my view, indispensable for getting the Bible back in circulation. Otherwise, church and Bible seem likely to continue spinning away from each other.

I don't mean that everyone on both sides will seek a creative resolution. On the religious side, unshakable literalists will no doubt exclude themselves, as will liberals who have written off the Bible as their religious compass. Among researchers, there are those who want little or nothing to do with religious institutions that threaten their commitment to academic standards. But to that broad middle ground of Christians, including evangelicals who have eased away from strict inerrancy and liberals who wonder what role the Bible still plays, a meeting of minds seems urgent. Few doubt that the higher criticism of the modern university has dealt a severe blow to the Bible's authority by justifiably shattering the traditional picture of where it came from, when it was written, and how its contents can be described. Also, few doubt any longer that current images of the Bible fail to attract readers: either conservative absolutism that brooks no dissent or liberal "no confidence" in the rubble of disillusion. Can a blending of new scholarship and old faith authentically revitalize its authority?

I'm not suggesting that the Bible's text be rewritten or color-coded (from red for "most certainly happened" to gray for "most certainly didn't") or that its language always matches its meaning in the original setting, but that the Bible itself be rebranded, so to speak. As of this writing, that brand is fuzzy, contradictory, and generally foreign to the receptors inside contemporary human heads. The idea would be that the major players among that large band of more-or-less mainstream Christians would put their minds together to come up with a clear "pitch," as it were, that would replace current confusion about the Bible's identity in a way that would allow for historical and linguistic honesty while remaining receptive to metaphor as equivalent truth-telling and claims of mystery. So far as I can tell, the Bible never brands itself in any specific way; it never describes itself either as a collection of factual accounts or as a patchwork of myth, legend, and history. It never says what it is or declares itself to be the truth; rather, it functions as a conduit for truths.

The compelling motive, as I see it, is that the Bible's brand may be conceived and marketed so as to appeal to the secular mind of the age while keeping room for the mysteries of faith. Its overall selling points: it is historically and linguistically accurate, distinguishing verifiable fact from spiritually rich fiction to meet the expectations of the secular mind while remaining hospitable to the testimony of things beyond the scope of measurable reality. The famed paleontologist Stephen Jay Gould made a vigorous attempt in that general direction in his book *Rocks of Ages,* in which he argues that science and religion complement each other: science explains the physical world; religion addresses meaning and morality. He calls his theory "Non-Overlapping Magisteria," granting both areas of inquiry equal footing and mutual independence.

Without a joint repackaging effort, it is difficult to see how the Bible can be credible to a contemporary worldview marked by empiricism and a temporal orientation that expects historical validity. That doesn't necessarily preclude openness to aspects of scriptural witness, such as the resurrection, that do not easily fit that means of inquiry. Is it mere wishful thinking that the great objective-subjective divide can be bridged? Perhaps, but without an attempt to define the Bible legitimately to adapt "truth" to the Zeitgeist, will the Bible continue to disappear into the past? If people find no reason to pick it up, beyond normal human recalcitrance, will it any longer be an engine moving the church into the future? Things can be redefined by science without losing their character: consider Pluto, downgraded from planet to dwarf planet in 2006. Subsequently, interest in it appears to have even increased.

Scholars have risked their fates by moving their tents farther from the sanctuaries. Ever since the seventeenth century, Bible study has become an academic specialty, originally in German universities. Among its purposes, as Michael C. Legaspi brilliantly notes in *The Death of Scripture and the Rise of Biblical Studies,* was to stop warring factions from bending the Bible to their own purposes by restoring the text's correct wording and facts. What began in part as a peacemaking effort closely tied to the church became over the centuries a cottage industry in thrall to the universities in the grip of the Enlightenment's this-worldly reasoning. At one time scholars principally served the church, which, in turn, underwrote their work; but that connection has attenuated. The thought occurs that Bible scholarship has for centuries been able to justify its existence on the basis of its constituency, the church, in the wider world. This established its usefulness to the common good. But it has grown more autonomous, with weaker links to religious institutions (except in cases of the universities Bible scholars work for), thus presumably more vulnerable. Will universities continue to support research that demonstrates academic excellence but lacks practical application? As I have discussed above, Bible scholars often complain that their discipline ranks low in academic prestige. Perhaps an initiative to tailor their research results to the churches' need to update the Bible's image — on the way to a style of collaboration that wouldn't violate scholarly standards — would enable revival on both sides and allow Bible scholarship to strengthen its rationale.

Cooperation could by this analysis give both congregants and scholars cause for optimism by alleviating the threats both face. The road will be fraught with obstacles, but it would be worse still, it seems, to stand still, to see Bibles go unread for lack of clarity and credibility, and to see scholars recede further into isolation from the churches that provided their original reason for being. That does not require scholars to embrace otherworldly concepts they find unacceptable or congregants to forswear their faith. It would be a venture in trust that something better can be found to reestablish the Bible's ability to reach the public and that superb scholarship can gain appreciation.

Will O'Brien is living proof that bringing the Bible to the tough corners of the world could result in a hybrid view of Scripture that resists easy classification. His two jobs, one as director of a forty-nine-unit homeless shelter in downtown Philadelphia, the other as coordinator of an atypical school of theology, have stretched him in opposite directions. On the one hand, he is indebted to historical criticism for setting the record straight; on the other, he has become less willing to insist on historical accuracy of passages that hold special meaning to him. His guiding principle is that the focus should be on what the biblical author intended to say. As to whether the setting is accurate, O'Brien says that he is "not comfortable saying 'this didn't happen.'"

O'Brien is an engaging, energetic man in his fifties, with youthful good looks and silvery hair. His passion for social justice is infectious; it first led him to civil rights and peace causes nearly three decades ago. He is a barely reconstructed product of that era of heightened religious activism, a direction to which he was drawn during his undergraduate years at Notre Dame. After working as an editor for *The Other Side,* an ecumenical magazine with a countercultural edge, O'Brien went on to press a tough struggle to secure a high-rise building for homeless and mentally impaired people known as Project Home. Along with that came a new appreciation for the "healing" stories conveyed by the Gospels. He became more inclined to take them at face value, regardless of the scholarly fine points. Meanwhile, his leadership of the Alternative Seminary, as the theological school is called, brings the challenge of finding the biblical understanding of human rights concerns such as racism, sexism, homophobia, and militarism and to view them through the biblical lens of justice. What sets the school apart, O'Brien believes, is that it drills deeper into the interpretation of biblical texts than college and seminary courses usually do, in part by encouraging students to relate their thoughts and experiences to the passages under study. Its leftist political leanings derive from Latin American liberation theology. The curriculum remains flexible to allow responses to emerging issues. A sampling of recent course offerings includes "The Economy of God: Biblical Economics and Our World"; "Reading the Bible into the Lives of Sexual Minorities"; and "The Way of Jesus for Our World Today."

The seminary's affinity for well-placed irreverence was summed up in a quotation on its website from the grandly acerbic Søren Kierkegaard:

> The matter is quite simple. The Bible is very easy to understand. But we Christians are a bunch of scheming swindlers. We pretend to be unable to understand it because we know very well that the minute we understand we are obliged to act accordingly. . . . My God, you will say, if I do that my whole life will be ruined. Herein lies the real place of Christian scholarship. [It] is the Church's prodigious invention to defend itself against the Bible, to ensure that we can continue to be good Christians without the Bible coming too close.

On a Saturday morning in December 2012, O'Brien was leading a one-day seminar called "Peace on Earth and the Politics of Christmas" in a brightly lit reception room of the shelter, once a casket factory. His survey of the familiar stories was aimed at debunking myths about the Christmas stories and pointing to the disguised exaltation of otherwise defenseless poor and lowly servants like Mary and Joseph at the expense of the oppressive Romans. Salvation is at hand in the narrative of the common and ordinary, a harbinger of hope for liberations to come.

With a brisk deftness, O'Brien brushed aside literal readings of the birth accounts in Luke and Matthew, noting, of course, that Mark and John say nothing about it and that the two existing versions are radically different. (In Luke, for example, the angel tells Mary that she will deliver the Holy One; in Matthew, the announcement is made to Joseph. Likewise, shepherds come calling in Luke, while "wise men" stop by in Matthew.) Tools of historical-critical research are properly used "in service to the church," he allowed, but that school of thought tends to become "an arrogant, rational worldview" that imposes a tyranny of its own.

He straddled the line between two preconceptions, two ways of seeing that commingled among the people in his class. "Biblical scholarship tries to figure out what's historical," he said, referring again to the birth stories. But that search should not overlook the reports of mysterious happenings, such as angels guiding shepherds. "There are witnesses and testimonies of faithful people," he observed. The test is whether those testimonies change lives. "Does their testimony reflect on experiences I have that make me live in a certain way?" The research tools help understand prior experience but cannot substitute for it. "I have an experience of Jesus. At the seminary we open the text and use scholarly tools to look at it."

For some in the audience, young Christian urban interns grounded in inerrancy, these were unsettling claims, and O'Brien, accordingly, stepped cautiously but firmly. Later, some of these recent college graduates were in shock; others weren't ready to dismiss O'Brien's analysis out of hand.

After the session, O'Brien said that he customarily guides the group through the puzzles in the stories by switching from evoking unblemished tradition to invoking the glare of modern scholarship. "No matter how stimulating the scholarship," he reflected, "if I'm in a housing project with an old African American woman reading from her King James Version to nurture her faith and survive, I'm going to honor that."

CHAPTER 10

The Eye of the Bible Beholder

"Where you stand depends on where you sit," the aphorism attributed to Rufus E. Miles Jr., is nowhere more applicable than in the practice of Bible reading. Every instance entails filtering ancient writings through the jumble of thoughts and feelings laden with daily trials, joys, obsessions, and ambitions. The constant flow and interaction of conscious awareness plays against the backdrop of deeply held perceptions and convictions about how life works.

Humanity, therefore, has projected a steady stream of unique personal perceptions onto a text that is obscure and confusing in itself. Perplexity meets perplexity and spawns ever-new conceptual hybrids. To read the Bible is to interpret it through individual screens. It sparks conversation between strangers, each of whom, as a rule, is encased in language and symbolism understood only dimly by the other. To some, this endless blossoming of plausible meanings is a blessing of riches; to others, it spins out of control into chaos, running far afield of the fixed answers they have relied on to anchor their faith. It stands to reason, therefore, that a nurse practitioner in an urban hospital encounters the Bible's mysteries with a cluster of sensibilities quite distinct from those of a highway construction worker, soybean farmer, or tax lawyer.

Following the aphorism's logic, your idea of what the Bible means depends to a certain degree on whether you sit, on any particular Sunday morning, in an austere multipurpose room in Otisville Federal Prison or in the elegant, colonial-style sanctuary of First Presbyterian Church in Bethlehem, Pennsylvania. Individually, people's "stands" on how they hear the Bible's messages that day may find considerable commonality, but the chapter-opening aphorism implies that they may diverge to an even greater degree across group lines and within their own groups — partly because they "sit" in such different places in worship and in life.

For inmates in the upstate New York prison, the Protestant chapel service first requires unstacking hard plastic chairs and arranging them casually into two sections for fellow worshipers in a floodlit, unadorned multipurpose hall. Soon gospel sounds arise from a duo of drums and saxophone, reverberating off the austere walls as upwards of seventy-five men in tan uniforms arrive and mingle, greeting each other and exchanging smiles, fist-bumps, handclasps, and words of spiritual uplift before finding seats. On a side wall at the entryway stands a row of metal cabinets for each of the faith groups that share the facility: among them, Muslims, Protestants, Jews, Catholics, and Rastafarians. On a nearby table are two boxes, a pink one asking for "prayer requests," and a yellow one inviting reports of "prayers answered." At the forefront, attached to polished wood panels, are two framed collages of colored glass — purple, blue, and yellow — facing each other to form the sides of an extended triangular semblance of sacred space. Otherwise, a plain pulpit at the head of the assembly comes closest to any kind of actual religious symbolism.

More than one hundred miles away, Presbyterians begin filing into their gleaming white sanctuary well before the start of worship, many escorted to red-cushioned pews by ushers sporting lapel carnations. Waves of chords from composers like Buxtehude, Bach, and Messiaen, played on the superb Moeller pipe organ, wash over them, and sunlight glows through vintage stained-glass windows. For attendees at the traditional 10:15 service (a rock music alternative has preceded it downstairs), going to church is still the occasion for a semiformal style of dress, now rapidly giving way to casual wear almost everywhere. At one time, of course, "dressing up" was standard among Protestants to show respect for "ascending" to the Lord's house from the ordinariness of life. Men wore suits or sport coats, slacks, dress shirts, and ties; women wore skirts and blouses or dresses (with allowance for smart suits).

The sprawling church complex on forty-two acres of land is a throwback to an era when religion thrived in America and Protestants often held the reins of civic and religious life. Members who were top brass at Bethlehem Steel have largely underwritten the imposing colonial-style structure, which was dedicated in 1957, and help cushion its finances (total assets stood at more than $8 million at the end of 2012). A half-dozen clergy, along with about fifty full- and part-time staff members, minister to more than 2,600 members, most of them solidly middle class and above, for whom dozens of educational, spiritual, and cultural programs are geared to age clusters and interests. The church's chancel choir is an attraction in itself, widely renowned for its breadth and quality under the direction of Greg Funfgeld, conductor of the internationally celebrated Bethlehem Bach Choir.

In the midst of general church decline in the mainline Protestant denominations, First Presbyterian remains strong and confident that it can preserve and even renew its vitality. Its voice is as upbeat as its character is upscale. Its leaders are unshakably positive about the church's future and have dedicated most of the church's resources to internal growth. But beneath the climate of good cheer lurks a potential danger: a split over gays in the ministry that could profoundly shake the congregation. The friction, notably understated, stems from how they interpret the Bible — or neglect to.

*   *   *

At Otisville, a low-lying complex hidden in the hills, it was Father's Day, an acutely painful time for the many inmates who have never known their fathers or were haunted by memories of fathers who harmed them. Some are also remorseful about having repeated the neglect by leaving and/or mistreating their own children. The very word "father" evokes the God of the Bible, whose image, particularly as judge, can be more alienating than comforting. But some testify that cultivating faith in that God has allowed them to overcome their guilt and to discover for the first time what it means to be a father or a son.

The prison chaplain at Otisville, Jeremy Myers, has made time in the Sunday morning service for those who want to unburden themselves or tell illuminating stories about themselves. A half dozen men have responded, each one testifying to the Bible's influence in turning his life around. Learning what God as "Father" really means, Leon says, has led to cooperative experiences where younger men allow older men to "father them as sons" and, in turn, "younger men teach them [older men] to be fathers." Hidalgo, choking back tears, says that he was forty-five years old before meeting his father for the first time. Two years later his father died, but not before they had made their peace. "I forgave him," Hidalgo says. "God gave me strength to forgive, and so did my father. There were reasons my father was not there for me and I haven't been there for my kids."

Mitch's past holds a father he says he still fears, no matter how hard he tries to banish the memories. God has since become his "real father, a heavenly father in whom I can put my trust, and that has made all the difference," he says, his voice trailing off in a prayerful whisper. Behind Mitch, stepping up to the microphone, is Richie, who sums up the self-sacrificing nature of parenthood by quoting Jesus: "What man among you," Jesus asks, "if his son asks for bread, would give him a stone?" (Matthew 7:9). Like many of Jesus's utterances, the answer is in the question. Mitch continues as if giving the homily: "Your father in heaven loves you more than you could ever know."

Richie can dip into a storehouse of verses and portions of chapters across the span of the Old and New Testaments, and he does so without the least hint of boastfulness, the words of Scripture rolling off his tongue smoothly, conversationally, and without dramatic inflection. In a climate of deepening Bible ignorance, he is unusual, but in Otisville many others belong in his league. Clusters of men take their Bibles into the yard to study together, asking and answering questions about the texts under review. They are mostly biblical literalists, though the word or concept as such does not come up among them; to their credit, they are among the fraction of Americans who tend to know literally the words of the text being interpreted. Frayed Bible covers and countless underlinings are clues to their hours of poring over its pages. Well-meaning Christians who like to quote the Bible must do so with care around this group, because they can pick up gaps or errors in an instant. The chaplain vouches for this, having been gently admonished on more than one occasion; and he contrasts their proficiency to the dismal ignorance of the Bible by guards and administrators. While some of that Bible expertise among inmates can be attributed to an inadequate supply of prison reading materials, the motives clearly go much deeper than that.

That's because the Bible has something that most of these men crave: the promise of rescue. Rescue from sicknesses of mind, body, and spirit; rescue from habits and addictions; rescue from the revolving door — in short, rescue from the "selves" that have caused them misery. Similar demons vex every human being, of course, but for many inmates prison has stripped away the blinders and distractions of the outside world that have kept them from confronting the challenge. For those who grab hold, Bible study is the opposite of a fanciful palliative or soft assurance. It is a path toward personal truth, exchanging illusions and quick remedies for soul-searching and self-scrutiny, and trading cynicism and resentment for peace and compassion — toward oneself and others. A tall order, to be sure, and never finished, but life-giving and rescuing, according to their own accounts.

George, a wiry, studious man with thick-framed glasses and a broad grin, has gone that way. During his current sentence for robbery (he has served previous stretches on similar charges) he says he "caught fire" from the Bible. He'd had no religious background, but soon "others were coming to me with their Bible questions," and that caused him to search Scripture more diligently. He was being called on to be a teacher, and that culminated in a vow he made to himself one day: "No new believer will go un-nurtured."

Sunday services exemplify the inmate-centered character of the chapel programs. Chaplain Myers is the duly ordained official in charge, and he does the preaching; but almost everything else about worship is purposely left to participants. Though Myers was in charge of virtually everything at the Christian and Missionary Alliance church he once pastored, he has become largely an onlooker and facilitator at Otisville. He entered the Otisville chaplaincy in his mid-thirties with a full head of revivalist steam, looking to establish a "Bible college in prison." But he ran into an already fixed routine whose worship preferences mostly diverge from his. The men offer prayers and testimony, and they sing, shout, and speak in tongues by themselves — joyously. Myers has accepted more of an adjunct role, admitting that the style of worship the men practice — boisterous Pentecostalism — clashes with the more sedate and orderly services in his own tradition. He sometimes leaves the scene during the peaks of singing and clapping. Agreeing to disagree seems perfectly acceptable on both sides.

In some respects, Myers embodies the renegade traits so prevalent in this and every prison, though his were derived in circumstances vastly different from most of theirs. Having grown up the second oldest of ten siblings in the household of a Montana pastor, he had been schooled in the inerrancy of the Bible and groomed to someday replace his father in his home church. But after attending Moody Bible Institute in Chicago, he had gone to Dallas Theological Seminary, a bastion of conservatism. Ironically, it was there that a course in Genesis convinced him that its origins were more complex than simple dictation from God, as he'd been led to believe. In the meantime, he had become disillusioned by how the seminary's fundamentalism treated women and gays. He dropped out of Dallas, but went into the ministry with those quandaries unresolved, eventually leaving the pastorate and the good graces of his father, from whom he had become estranged. Like so many of the men in his prison congregation, Myers would not be speaking to his own father on this day set aside for fathers. Like them, whom he describes as wounded by rejection, he has both given and received rejection of his own, and this is an unspoken link between them.

Myers writes perceptively and compellingly about his struggles with Scripture and the church on an engaging website-blog entitled "Till He Comes." It is a side of him quite apart from his prison duties; his prison ministry he keeps distant from the thousand or so daily visitors to the site. His blog offerings come across as salty, rigorous efforts to test the waters of biblical higher criticism while holding fast to the infallible Bible of his up-bringing. What makes his books and articles fascinating and informative is his exceptional intelligence and his superb writing skills. His commentaries on Bible texts are full of insight and reasonable advocacy. He is a person who has strained to stay balanced on a theological tightrope: he seems to be resisting a strong urge to join Peter Enns and Rob Bell, who have rejected biblical literalism outright. Myers no longer fastens onto any single inter-pretation as sufficient. He has come to view the skirmishing among the competing schools of thought (literalist to metaphorical) as a monumental waste of time because it diverts attention from the more serious issue of so many people knowing nothing of the Bible, let alone the squabbles among its interpreters. Much of his creative energy seems devoted to defending a strain of ambivalence he doesn't care to indulge. But undoubtedly it is difficult to reject a commitment that has been a way of life.

It is possible to envision Myers as a "progressive" evangelical in a setting where theological exploration combines with teaching and commu-nity outreach. For example, he speaks fondly of the Simple Way ministry in Philadelphia, part of a wider movement of groups dedicated to urban ministry and living prayerfully together in poor neighborhoods. But he isn't there yet, by his own admission, because he is concerned about the broader interests of his wife and three young daughters.

Though he left the church ministry, he hurried back to retrieve his credentials in order to qualify as a federal prison chaplain. He more than satisfied the Bureau of Prisons' desired experience and skills: among them, openness, approachability, knowledge, attentiveness, acceptance of reli-gious differences, and physical fitness (including a short haircut). Three years after becoming a prison chaplain, however, on that Father's Day in 2012, his light-brown hair falls to his shoulders and is tied back in a ponytail. He also wears a mustache and goatee. Myers explains that he discovered there was nothing in prison rules against growing long hair, so he'd done it in an effort to avoid being seen "as just another cop who was there to make sure they stayed in line."

But it hasn't turned out that way, he believes, and he feels that he is even more the outsider looking in, the one who stands in the midst of their exuberance and praise — without sharing their joy. Preaching, once the mainstay of his ministry, has become an onerous task for him. For one thing, everything he says has to be translated into Spanish for the 10-15 percent of the Latino worshipers. That requires halting every five or six words for interpreting, and that makes it impossible to gain the momentum needed for effective preaching. His sermons are recycled versions of ones he first delivered years ago, and he is quite frank in admitting that he isn't sure he still believes some of what he said back then. Or that preaching itself has much value, though the men tend to listen closely to his views on the Bible lessons.

Sometimes they check out his interpretation with a Bible fundamentalist who had begun making regular Tuesday-night visits to the men long before Myers arrived. One time, an offhanded comment about suicide landed him in trouble. Talking about the biblical story of Samson taking his own life, Myers ventured to say that, on the basis of his reading of Scripture, "God loves us so much that he doesn't keep us out of heaven for committing suicide." Listeners were shocked. In the prison climate, suicide is widely considered a taboo subject because it can be a temptation to the hopeless among them. Angry inmates took Myers's comment to their Tuesday counselor, who promptly denounced suicide as sinful. "He's been here longer than me," Myers says. "Who's going to win that battle?"

On that Father's Day, the chaplain preaches on the Bible's sobering insistence on rooting out one's personal faults before pointing fingers at others. Pleas for self-improvement are prison boilerplate, to say the least, but no less applicable because of that. Two Scripture readings bolster his point: the well-known parable Jesus told to warn against judging others in the sixth chapter of Luke; and Saint Paul's stinging reminder in the second chapter of his Epistle to the Romans against speaking one way and acting another ("While you preach against stealing, do you steal?").

Both passages speak of refusing to clean up one's own act as blindness and bringing judgment on oneself. The vivid image from the parable is the contrast between ignoring the "speck" in one's own eye while shouting about the "log" in the other person's. "Think first about yourselves in one part of your life — personal holiness," Chaplain Myers says. "Root sin out of your own life before trying to root sin out of other people." Jesus's wry comment about the "blind leading the blind" would probably have made his hearers "chuckle," he continued, adopting a folksy tone, but the serious point is that we all inevitably have blind spots about our failings, just as our driver's ed teacher taught us we'd have operating a car. "We see other people sin and we condemn them," he says, pausing to allow the Spanish translator to catch up. "But Jesus says 'be careful.'" And beware of hypocrisy, he adds, using as examples "a pastor who is preaching against homosexuality and turns out to be renting boys" and "a pastor who preaches against greed and is taking from the offering plate."

"Don't try to be God to someone else," he sums up. "Apply the Scriptures to yourself first."

Another round of singing, testifying, and praying brings the service to a close, and a cluster of the men stay behind to talk about their experiences with Scripture. Many say they've heard the sermon as a special form of the prodding they often hear within the walls to better their inner and outer selves. The difference is that in this small subgroup of the thousand-inmate population, the Bible is credited with helping some men achieve that end by aiding their transformation. A man named Carl speaks as one of them. He "stopped running" from himself and had "totally surrendered to the one who speaks through the Scripture," he says. "I read it every day because I need to be filled with the Spirit every day to survive, to keep my mind fixed and full of [God's] spirit." Bryce, a hefty man with a bushy white beard, has careened from one kind of "bad behavior to another" for decades before "being awakened by an evangelist in prison," a person who steered him to a lifeline, the Bible. "It's so much more than stories," he says heavily. "It's the whole lesson in life, so much grace. I had fallen away from church, discouraged by bad examples I saw in it. Now I'm back."

Perhaps, a cynic might say, such testimonies are given with one eye fixed on convincing a parole board that those seeking release are worthy of it by virtue of a transformation of their souls. Those aims are both plausible and sensible, measured by their quality of sincerity. Rescue from personal misery is commensurate with rescue from a jail cell.

*   *   *

By comparison, First Presbyterian is relatively devoid of personal drama and raw emotion, though its Sunday morning alternative "praise service" now features a gospel rock band, spirited singing of contemporary music, and personal appeals for embracing Christ. The traditional service is a comforting reassurance for many that all is well in a sanctuary of familiar decorum and order of worship. Among the estimated twelve hundred worshipers who come to First Presbyterian on an average Sunday, a third or so choose the more expressive service of praise.

Presbyterianism stands solidly on the Bible as the backbone of its creeds and the wellspring of its celebrated tradition of preaching. For the time being, First Presbyterian belongs to the larger of the two biggest American branches: the more liberal Presbyterian Church (USA), which originally emerged as the Northern entity in the church's split over slavery before the Civil War, and the Presbyterian Church in America, which is rooted in the Southern side of that break. The PCUSA is much larger (1.7 million compared to the PCA's 367,000 at the end of 2013); but the PCUSA has suffered sharp losses in the wider backlash against Protestant progressivism and is down 400,000 members since 2013.

In principle, both denominations believe that the Bible is the source of true growth and vitality; but neither body can any longer expect many members to read it or know much about it. At the same time, the PCUSA branch has been in turmoil over the decision by its supreme governing body to permit the ordination of practicing homosexuals. Dozens of its churches have left the church body in protest, and First Presbyterian of Bethlehem is close to doing the same. The church has already put one foot in the rebel camp by joining the Fellowship of Presbyterians, a dissenter lobby group that is putting pressure on the denomination to reverse policy — but has not yet formed a separate denomination. A decision by the membership on whether to cut ties with its long-time alliance has been in the works.

"First Prez," as it's commonly called in "just folks" jargon, has a solidly conservative reputation, though naturally not every parishioner in it fits that profile. Among the implications of that image is that major decisions are justified on biblical grounds. In 2012 the stumbling block was homosexuality; in 2011 the General Assembly ratified ordination for gays and lesbians who were in same-sex relationships after a sufficient number of local presbyteries approved it, dropping the definition of marriage as exclusively male-female couples, but stopping short of explicitly recognizing same-sex marriage. They took that step the following year, when clergy were allowed to marry same-sex partners, over the loud objections of opponents, who included a sizable portion of First Presbyterian's members. Alarm over that decision sparked the congregation's intention to split from the PCUSA.

The choice is momentous, and not least because it involves the equivalent of turning a large freighter around in an open sea. It means reassigning and juggling sizable chunks of money from one church organization to another; negotiating terms of departure from the local jurisdiction (presbytery), a move that could be fractious and personally wounding; and a shift in the congregation's identity. Its growing reputation as a church that shuns both homosexual clergy and same-sex marriage might attract more like-minded Christians, but it risks taking on a negative image (a rejecting rather than accepting church) that would otherwise stifle the church's growth. From what I have witnessed elsewhere, a climate of exclusion and negativity, strictly on a pragmatic basis, isn't conducive to church vitality and can indicate an enclave in retreat. However, that is not what secessionists generally think. They argue that the church is returning to an "authentic" fidelity to the truth of the Bible and that such trust will provide rewards of its own. Though the general public is trending swiftly toward acceptance of same-sex equality, the Presbyterian secessionists contend that they are not on the wrong side of history, but that pop culture is on the wrong side of God's will.

Presumably, in keeping with the terms of the debate, the issue will indeed be settled on biblical grounds, and the one who is chiefly in charge of laying the foundation is the head pastor, Rev. Alf Halvorson, a thoughtful and genial native Minnesotan in his fifties with a stocky build, receding blond hair, and a welcoming smile. He is decidedly among the disgruntled Presbyterians and, like many others, paints the issue in much broader terms than opposition to gay ordination. It has to do with the "authority of Scripture" in general and "whether Jesus is the way to salvation," Pastor Alf wrote to the congregation about the dispute.

To the heart of the matter: "I am for a national sexual ethic for all officers [clergy included] for many reasons," Pastor Alf wrote. "Some say the issue of sexuality is so murky in Scripture that we can't know God's will here; but with such an important issue, I do not believe God has left us without clear guidance from Scripture. The Bible does address our sexuality. I don't believe we can endorse the ordination change [acceptance of openly homosexual clergy] in light of a plain Reformed reading of the Scripture. I affirm the previous standard as a challenge for all of us, whether heterosexual or homosexual."

It was a firm conclusion reached by inference rather than rigorous analysis of Scripture passages that applied to the debate. "Some" say the Bible's references to homosexuality aren't definitive but "murky." The pastor swept those claims aside by declaration ("I do not believe God has left us without clear guidance from Scripture") without explaining his reasoning based on the actual references. The key phrase is "plain Re-formed reading of the Scripture." As I have alluded to earlier in this book, it is a respected Protestant tradition that affirms the ability of Christians without great learning or wisdom to understand the Bible's message. The truth is available equally to the sophisticated and to the simple. Meticulous research meanwhile has peeled back the many layers of complexity that separate the ancient mentality and framework of thinking from our own, raising doubts about the ability of modern minds to grasp the meaning of Scripture from a distant past. What did the alleged references to homo-sexuality mean two millennia ago when no such distinct sexual category was recognized? Were some expressions of same-sex eroticism acceptable while others, such as cult-like behavior or prostitution, proscribed? Were the biblical passages that are used today to condemn all active homosexu-ality originally intended to declare all or only some of that sexual behavior sinful? Those issues make a correct "simple reading" tougher, according to Halvorson's opponents.

No matter what the national church does, First Presbyterian has stuck by the old prohibitions in selecting its own leaders. Officers will still be required to live up to the "covenant of marriage between a man and a woman or chastity in singleness." The reason is that clergy are "held to a higher standard"; but Halvorson allows homosexuals to teach in the Sunday school. In fact, a lesbian couple had recently asked the church to baptize their child, and the church agreed to do so while informing them that as members they wouldn't be eligible to be chosen leaders. "We are a big tent," Pastor Alf has written. "Everyone is welcome, but some just can't be officers."

Arguments that may have been adopted from Scripture to buttress the pastor's position are not spelled out. Among the myriad denomina-tions, no one surpasses Presbyterians in applying reason to Scripture in defining its theology. In this case, the reasoning appeared to be bypassed or set aside. It is as if a summary judgment is all that's necessary. Gen-erally speaking, the church's clergy and staff have no illusions that most members understand the broader outlines of Scripture, let alone nuances; on the whole, the laity is willing to accept the verdict of "experts," mostly clergy, regarding the Bible's position on controversial matters rather than exploring matters themselves. So Pastor Halvorson's summary judgment has no doubt convinced many members on its face.

Biblical illiteracy is thought to be as common at First Presbyterian as at any mainstream church, and Rev. Cody Sandahl is striving to alleviate it. Sandahl, a University of Texas graduate, avid basketball player, and former computer professional, was added to the staff in 2009, fresh from Austin Theological Seminary, where his father was a fellow student, having worked previously as a Pepsi bottler. The younger Sandahl is smart, relaxed, good-humored, and has good "people skills," with expressive facial features that congregants connect with. He is the kind of student that seminaries feel fortunate to get these days. On the hot-button question of same-sex marriage, he makes an obligatory though passionless case in support of Halvorson's position; later he says that he could "live with it either way."

The unpretentious young minister has been struck by how little "Bible awareness" there is in Pennsylvania compared to what he has been used to in Texas. Texans are more likely to believe that reading the Bible is "normal," whereas Pennsylvanians are skittish about being caught doing so, lest they be labeled "Bible thumpers" or be seen as having "lower intelligence."

Against the overall backdrop of Bible-shunning, First Presbyterian appears to share that ennui by slackening its efforts to promote Bible-reading until recently — and that at the instigation of Cody Sandahl. His plan is to reverse that trend by coaxing a large portion of the congregation to read and discuss the Bible in small groups. The strategy anticipates resistance from those who plead that Scripture is too dense, perplexing, or stuffed with boring filler like dietary laws and archaic figures of speech. Sandahl's answer is one that has found favor in many other churches faced with similar reluctance: to substitute a book that, in effect, cuts and splices the actual Bible text (from the New International Version) to form it into a running narrative — like a novel. To streamline it in that way, the designers leave out parts they think interrupt the narrative's flow and trim other sections to quicken the pace of the journey from the creation in Genesis to the grand finale in Revelation. It is thus an exercise in reading the Bible without actually being exposed to the full dimensions of the Bible. Rather than tramping through thick patches of ordinances in Numbers or twisted plot lines in 1 Kings, the reader can be whisked along on a limited-access interstate highway from the start of the stage-managed trip to the end.

That chosen book is *The Story: The Bible as One Continuous Story of God and His People* (published in 2007 by Zondervan, an evangelically oriented publishing house and major Bible promoter); the book was launched in an attempt to entice readers who are not disposed to read the entire thing. The hope is that *The Story* will succeed as a compromise, where a preceding ambitious abridgment, *The Reader's Digest Bible,* fizzled during the 1970s, a time when slackening Bible reading received much less attention.

Besides being a satisfactory primer for the scripturally limited (and the American hankering for shortcuts), *The Story* also serves as a way to view the Bible as a chronological account knit together by divine plan — the *canon* claim that events are consciously linked to convey God's actions over time in bringing about salvation and final judgment. The components extracted from the NIV largely eliminate texts that dispute that story line, distract from a seamless design, or cause moral controversy. Discordant or unharmonious themes have also been stricken. Among the materials eliminated: the entire "wisdom literature" books of Job, Ecclesiastes, and Song of Songs, each of which jostles moral complacency in its own way; sections of Genesis, such as the demise of Sodom and Gomorrah and Noah's drunken nakedness; the bloody conquests of occupants of lands that stood between the Hebrews and the Promised Land; most of the Psalms and Proverbs. The full versions of the four Gospels are compressed into summaries, a truncating that includes bypassing almost all of Jesus's social justice injunctions in the centerpiece Sermon on the Mount in Matthew and Luke. As for Saint Paul, his Epistles are also either melted down or, in the case of his two Epistles to Timothy and his Epistle to the Philippians, dumped. That might have excited the famed apostle's irascible side.

But it is best reckoned as a tradeoff: exchanging a complete Bible that will likely gain little traction for an edited, faster-reading adventure that might attract a popular following. The response has supported that choice. Within three weeks of the publisher's announcement of the challenge, nearly eight hundred copies of *The Story* were sold or otherwise distributed across the age spectrum to the dozens of small groups that would discuss its thirty-one chapters.

An early-morning gathering of men is one of those groups. A half dozen or more meet for prayer and discussion for ninety minutes, starting at 6:00 a.m., in an upstairs parlor of First Presbyterian. Most are retired managers and professionals, and though they've known each other a long time, their leader says that they balk at talking about themselves. Holding his open hands far from one another, he says, "We're about this far apart. They don't like getting that personal. We try to reduce the gap. But guys don't like to talk about their personal lives."

Ironically, this morning's topic is intensely personal, a virtual seminar in the mysteries of human relationships. It is the immortal portrait of Ruth told in the ninth chapter of *The Story*. The portrait is essentially a web of Ruth's attachments of mind and heart. She is the Moabite woman who has converted to Judaism, the religion of her first husband, who has died; she then stands sacrificially by her widowed mother-in-law, who later guides her to her second husband, Boaz, a landholding Israelite. Ruth is beloved as an exemplar of loyalty, well worthy of the Jewish life she has chosen and to which she as an "outsider" is warmly welcomed. The slim account is a coveted pearl in the Hebrew Bible, loved for its emotional and spiritual power. Its attraction far surpasses the issues of whether it is based on an actual historical figure (it isn't, according to many scholars) or the need to identify who wrote it and when.

No one in the sunrise group has previously read about Ruth and her closest in-law, Naomi — or claimed to know anything about it. They have gladly taken the project on, though, and since chapter 9, "Faith of a Foreign Woman," is scheduled for the day, they take the subject in stride. Overall, their leader says, *The Story* is "a good book to start with rather than get bogged down in the Bible. It tries to tell the basic narrative."

He invites "personal concerns" at the outset, and a series of prayer requests pour forth, most for those in failing health: a mother with a threatening blood clot, a neighbor with a severe heart attack, a young man with throat cancer. Ruth is something of a puzzle to most of these men. On the whole, they see Ruth as someone who deserves to be judged well because she plays by the society's rules, ultimately getting rewarded by her marriage to a good provider, Boaz. But there is also some feeling that Ruth's otherwise admirable character might have been clouded a bit by what appears to be her scheme to attract the well-heeled Boaz into her arms (with a little help from Naomi). Maybe not so perfectly noble after all. They imagine that a woman's group looking at the same narrative might focus instead on the place of women in that society.

The past is past, however, and the circumstances of the story strike these men as so distant from their own that they find little to compare with themselves — even if they wanted to get personal in ways their leader wouldn't expect them to. That line is about to be dramatically crossed. A question from the study guide asks how their responses to personal tests compare to Ruth's courage in standing up for her convictions. They can relate to that; memories spring to the fore.

The leader/moderator sets the tone. Speaking about himself in front of others is a "question of courage," he says. "I don't think of myself as a fearful man. But I don't think of myself as a courageous man either."

One soft-spoken man with a ruddy complexion tells of a tense moment one night in a small evangelical church where, as its education director, he invited a spokesman for Planned Parenthood to speak. By his own admission, he had not adequately considered the consequences of asking a proponent of a woman's right to choose abortion, one of the topics sure to come up, to talk to a largely anti-abortion congregation. Noting the deepening grimaces on the faces of church members as the spokesperson advocated women's own decisions on matters of abortion and other hot-button subjects, the education director became increasingly uneasy about offering his usual prayer to close the program. He made a halting attempt, then backed off. "I was supposed to pray at the end and couldn't," he recalls apologetically. "I just couldn't. Maybe I could have handled it different."

Another anecdote follows immediately from a nattily dressed elderly man with a yellow bow tie and penetrating eyes. He was driving down a city street on a dark night when an oncoming car without headlights approached on the other side. He'd thought of flashing his lights to alert the other driver, the customary signal, but hadn't done so. "I felt bad for days," he said, though his daughter offered consolation by reciting a rumor she'd heard about a gang that initiated new members into the gang in part by making them drive without lights and to vandalize the first car that flashed its lights. Weeks later now, it was still unclear to the man with the yellow bow tie what he was supposed to do or whether his decision somehow reflected a lack of courage in the face of perhaps a dark premonition. "If the Holy Spirit tells you to do something, do it," he ventured. "But if he doesn't, you've got to pay attention."

A stout man with a mustache and a gruff voice chimed in. Recently, just before Christmas, he had been in the checkout line of a Dollar Store, behind a woman with three small children and a few holiday items to pay for. She offered a government assistance card as a method of payment, but the cashier said there was no money left on the card. The woman nervously searched her purse for cash but came up way short. "It occurred to me to give her the money she needed," he said forlornly. "I felt prompted to do so by the Holy Spirit. But I didn't." He saw her again outside the store. "She actually apologized for holding up the line," he said. "I again held back from giving her the money and I still feel guilty." He couldn't say what kind of courage he was lacking, but he was sure that's what it was.

Had these men who'd been described as keeping their personal lives to themselves heard or felt something in Ruth's story to loosen their tongues? Had "sitting" with her story affected where they "stood" in telling their own? The evidence was circumstantial, to be sure, but persuasive. It reminded me of a parallel change of heart described by an African professor who'd taught a seminar on the story of Ruth at the University of KwaZulu-Natal. Of the seven students, three were men. They read, analyzed, and prayed over the text. The most striking outcome, Prof. Helen Efthimiadis-Keith said, was that some men found their own stereotypes about women in Ruth's story and were "embarrassed how men treated women" in contemporary surroundings. "One said, 'God wanted me to see what it was like being Ruth,'" the professor said. "They wanted to invite others to that kind of Bible. A transformation took place."

At the peak of *The Story's* promotion, about a thousand of First Presbyterian's congregants had copies, nearly half of the total and close to the average twelve hundred weekly attendees. Sandahl was pleased, though his measure of the depth and scope of that engagement was based mostly on anecdotes. In connection with this effort to "evangelize" the whole membership with awareness of the Bible, he had set up a contest to award the best-written personal accounts of their experience with the book. Only a handful of entries showed up, and most of them made no reference to the Bible. Three months after launching the campaign to promote the Bible with a Bible Lite, Sandahl estimated that a fifth of those who began the process, about two hundred parishioners, were still reading it.

CHAPTER 11

The Fragility of Teaching and Learning Scripture

The youngsters squirm out of the pews and scramble to the chancel of the cozy Lutheran church. While the purple-robed choir director, Clara Phillips, deftly herds them, they flutter waves to parents, giggle among themselves, hop around at will, and generally fidget. Ms. Phillips then fixes their attention long enough for them to respond to the first plunks of the piano, singing forth in one-part disharmony:

> Jesus loves me! this I know,
> For the Bible tells me so.
> Little ones to him belong;
> They are weak but he is strong.
>   [Refrain:]
>   Yes, Jesus loves me;
>   The Bible tells me so.

These carefree vocalists triumphantly added to a string of renditions of the song that has been the unofficial Sunday school anthem for more than 150 years, since Anna Bartlett Warren wrote the words (1860) and William Batchelder Bradbury set them to music (1862), as the blood from the Civil War flowed torrentially. Since then it has been both a capsule summary of what Christianity is about and a visceral assurance that it's trustworthy.

Jesus is no less the focus of Christian faith since that song was first sung, of course, but its bedrock assertion that "the Bible tells me so" — fully and sufficiently — is no longer taken for granted. Consider this: fewer people are looking to the Bible for anything these days, yet the figure of Jesus looms as large, perhaps even larger, than it ever has in the public mind. Thus it can be reasonably inferred that the images of Jesus floating around in the psychic landscape have been based at least in part on sources other than the Bible. The explanation that I have found most plausible for this phenomenon is that another Jesus has entered America's collective consciousness. The form that he has taken follows the long history of shaping Jesus to suit the human needs and longings of a particular age and time. Generally speaking, the contemporary age has been acutely beset by emptiness and self-doubt. The Jesus envisioned as the remedy for this is the Jesus of the Warm Embrace. He loves us unconditionally and unceasingly, forgives even before we confess, and encourages us to be everything we can be. He is the totally accepting friend we thought we'd never have.

Projecting such attributes onto Jesus is nothing new, to say the least, but cyberspace has enlarged its scope and appeal. Jesus of the Warm Embrace is not the product of one — or even a few — designers. It is the commingling of hopes and desires from myriad contributors — from therapists to filmmakers and poets. The Internet and social media are suffused with this Jesus, who, as one interviewee says, "has loved everyone since about 1975." An urgent, silent plea has gone up for a healer who will fix the broken places of the nation's heart, mind, and soul. Not surprisingly, the desired Jesus fills imaginations and visions: he abounds in uplift and approval. He speaks none of the harsh judgments and warnings such as those that the Bible reports he uttered during his lifetime — about the rich, the greedy, the selfish, and the oppressive. Only gays and pro-choice advocates are sometimes left out of his Warm Embrace, at least according to some of his followers. Otherwise, never a discouraging or critical word. Naturally, not all Jesus imagery fits neatly into this upbeat mold. There is the occasional Mel Gibson, whose blockbuster hit *The Passion of the Christ* binged on agony and anti-Semitism, plus occasionally the old-time butt-kicking preachers who still dangle the feet of unbelievers over the pits of hell. But overall the Master is infinitely kinder and gentler than when he was viewed by the whole story in the Bible. The savior of this age, fashioned by human projections, floats freely in cyberspace, showing up in counseling sessions, television specials, Christian fiction, therapy tapes, movies, college classrooms, quasi-scholarly books, and positive-thinking sermons — everywhere conforming to the preference for assurance and the aversion to thorough self-inventory. The results can be charming flights of fancy. My favorite is the Jesus of the television show *South Park,* a wholesome, kindly, and self-effacing young man who befriends the kids and conducts his own talk show, *Jesus and Friends,* as a warm-hearted public service.

By default, then, Christianity is retaining a Christ-centeredness that is, however, depending less on the Bible itself and more on a popularized version of Jesus as the World's Greatest Guy. Innumerable Internet sites present Jesus caricatures styled by their creators to promote their own ideas that are seldom subjected to any significant critique from the Bible itself. There has never been consensus on how the Bible defines Jesus; interpretations have differed widely from the very beginnings of the Christian church, but the Bible has always been the principal reference point. Now, as the huge bestseller *The Da Vinci Code* makes clear, whole scenarios purporting to rewrite the founding premises of Christianity can be invented practically from whole cloth. Without even any passing knowledge of the Bible, readers are more likely to believe the "facts" of that fictional thriller than the facts contained in the original documents. The Bible has its own fictions, to be sure, but it is the most profound original document.

Suffice it to say, there is a good chance that the Jesus who is celebrated in the popular mind, media platforms, and upbeat church ministries bears little resemblance to the Jesus of the Gospels. Getting the profile from those original sources has always been an imposing educational task. The Gospels and Paul's Epistles form only a fragmentary biography of Jesus, one that in its entirety contains contradictions and enigmas. The Roman Catholic Church settled the matter by restricting custody of the Bible and its interpretation to the clergy, who would then pass along official judgments about it on a more or less need-to-know basis. Biblical language and lore infused the culture, often wrapped in folklore and superstition, but the laity's primary focus was on the sacraments as wellsprings of grace.

The Reformers' *sola Scriptura* cause and their distrust of hierarchy placed a much heavier burden on Protestants to instill the Bible's materials as the foundation of faith. It is not the object of faith, as has been pointed out, but the primary witness to the events in the Old and New Testaments that gives substance to that faith. The mandate fell largely to preachers such as Jonathan Edwards, who elaborated magnificently on its passages; to regular reading of Scripture by ordinary parishioners; and to organized Bible study, which took many forms. By the nineteenth century, the form that stood out the most was the distinctly American feature called Sunday school. On weekday nights (typically Wednesdays) and Sundays, groups arranged by age met to absorb prepared basics, much as Catholics memorized lessons in the catechism. Teaching was quintessentially one-way — from the allegedly better-informed to the lesser-informed.

That format has continued to the present day, grounded in the presumption that the teacher has hold of an interpretation that governs the direction of the study. Assuming, for this discussion, that anyone telling others what the Bible means is doing so from a point of view that differs from a large number of possible perspectives, the one-way format is inevitably an exercise in bringing others over to the teacher's authoritative view or, one might say, indoctrination. In practice, that breaks down when members of the class make effective challenges, but in general the dynamic follows the pattern of active leadership and passive students.

In the century and a half since Darwin's *Origin of the Species* upended Genesis and higher criticism exposed the Bible to an MRI kind of investigation, it has become increasingly important to locate the teacher's posture on these matters and the method by which he or she conducts the class. Learning about the Bible takes place within a framework of ideas about where the Bible comes from (God alone, human alone, some kind of amalgam) and the way it is interpreted (fixed meaning and revelation, multiple meanings and open-endedness), knit together by a single and divine canonical narrative or forming a miscellany of reflections on encounters with divinity. As I have noted earlier, greater sophistication in scholarship has both enlivened discussion of how much weight Scripture should be given, in whole or in part, and exposed more links to other religious traditions.

Along the way in writing this book, I discovered effective teaching and learning under a mind-boggling mixture of settings and purposes. Every technique and type of human exchange — from rote learning to free-for-all — has spurred lively, provocative experiences between speakers and listeners. Each is undertaken within an encroaching secularity where even the most Bible-saturated religious schools go back to basics. Erosion is everywhere, making the task of the preacher and teacher even more consequential. Any of that multiplicity of styles could serendipitously initiate someone into the scintillating world of the Bible or bring it to life for the first time.

* * *

At Shiloh Church, eighty miles from New York City, a quartet of early arrivals for their weekly plunge into Scripture raved about the fish cakes, yams, and cornbread they had consumed at a diner on the way, a new place opened by a fellow church member who had come back from a serious illness. They had tried it for the first time, and on the basis of their enthusiasm a bright future could be predicted for their friend's venture.

The two men and two women sat by themselves in the bright, polished-wood-paneled sanctuary, but as the 7:30 starting time neared dozens of others filled the pews around them and kept trickling in. Nearly everyone brought a Bible, and the study leader, Pastor Juanita Davis, the widow of the church founder and the mother of the current pastor, readied her notes and exchanged greetings from a podium at the front. Gospel music from a guitar, electronic organ, and drum set, along with three singers, lifted the tempo and alertness of many of the Wednesday night regulars, who were tired from a full day of work. Above the pulpit of the hexagonally structured church, whose main floor sloped from back to front, was a banner that read: "Get Your House In Order: Faith, Family, Finances, Future, Fitness."

Bible studies come both front-loaded and freewheeling. Academically inclined churches often present portions of Scripture and expect the group to dig out its subtleties. Shiloh belongs to a different category: it defines the theme to be discussed right away, and it summons upwards of twenty passages to reinforce the point. The theme this Wednesday night was "Praise as Warfare": it was about calling on God to overcome adversity.

Theirs is Bible study within the contours of a full worship service. To wholly enter into it, you must take direction and have confidence that the leader's understanding of the readings is correct. So far as it's possible to tell, this gathering has no trouble meeting those prerequisites. This Bible study represents a respite from the rigors of their daily lives, and they take direction with expectations that a balm will that day, too, be found in the region of Gilead.

Under the guidance of Pastor Davis, those assembled for Bible study roam through pieces of Revelation, Ephesians, Romans, a half dozen Psalms, Isaiah, and Matthew's Gospel for reasons why it is good to praise God. First and foremost, the pastor assures them, praising God dispels common troubles, such as losing a job or breaking up with a loved one. A trusting heart knows that, but it needs constant reminding. It is all about focusing in the right direction, accepting and receiving God's help rather than relying on yourself. "When you sound your praises, let them go — the blessings come." She continues: "God is not a waiter who comes to take your order. You were created to praise God. God gets excited when you praise him."

No matter what the dismay or abuse from an ill wind, the very act of offering praise to God "builds you up and makes you feel good." Her comments are studded with Scripture quotes and touches of whimsy to undergird every point; readers are scrambling in their Bibles to keep up with her references. From Psalm 40: "You have called me out of darkness into the marvelous light" means: "You can praise Him through everything" instead of "talking back to the boss, being angry with your wife, or snapping at rebellious kids." She recalls the older generations who sang praises "even though they didn't know where their next meal was coming from and had no money in their pockets."

From 2 Chronicles comes the report of the small Hebrew army overcoming a far superior force when they successfully prayed to God to confuse the enemy. The bottom line is to let God take care of the daily struggles: "God says this is not your battle. God will fight the battle for you."

"What's the battle in your life?" she asks. "Job, family, children, finances? The victory has already been won."

She suggests that they need to sing the hymn "I Know I've Been Changed." Musicians and people respond with gusto and shouts of gratitude. Pastor Davis ends with the famous example of Joshua's victory at Jericho, when the people trusted God's promise that parading joyfully around the city with his army would be enough to knock down the city's walls. "You don't have to fight, just march. If Joshua's men hadn't done that, and said what they were really thinking, those walls would never have come down."

"Rise from your seats," Pastor Davis implores them, "picture the walls in your lives and, praying to and praising God, declare to your pewmates, 'The walls are down!'" The Bible studiers do so, going from one to another for the many minutes it takes to reach a natural finish. The theme is praise, but the subject is the struggles that mire the mind, heart, and soul in everyday troubles.

*   *   *

Far away, in Georgia, Anna Carter Florence prefers studying the Bible with more chaos than sure-footedness. To her, its texts are ripe with meanings rather than nuggets of single, predetermined interpretations, and as a professor of preaching at Columbia Theological Seminary she has an important role in advancing that point of view.

Preaching, as it has usually been practiced, is derived from pieces of Scripture, so it makes a great deal of difference how the preacher views those ingredients. Prof. Florence ardently believes that the best way is simply to avoid adopting what others have already concluded in favor of immersing oneself in the text without presuppositions. Live inside of it until "something sticks in you," and that "is where the sermon begins," she emphasizes in a prestigious series of lectures she gave at Yale.

The invitation to Florence to deliver the lectures was recognition of the attention she has received for generating a fresh look at the long history of relating Scripture to preaching, particularly within liberal Protestant circles. She has brought youth, creativity, and enthusiasm to a field that was in need of rejuvenation and pragmatic solutions to problems that are not very susceptible to old strategies.

Her search has adopted the postmodernist assumption that human beings are incapable of ultimate truth, but that approximations of it can be distilled through one's "experience." That is no easy alternative: it requires a deep dive and often an exhausting exploration. No matter how keen the preacher's interpretation, she says, it should not be, de facto, the final word. It should be the launching pad for the congregation's search for its own version of the truth from those same Scripture portions. Too many church members feel obliged to accept the authority of the preacher without doing their own investigation. Scripture should speak personally through everyone who studies it by hearing sermons and/or participating in other Bible study sessions.

Prof. Florence's plea to seminarians is to overturn that habit of ascribing Bible-learning solely to the clergy, leaving the church with "a well-stocked refrigerator only the preacher can use" by dint of training and reputation. Congregants thereby forfeit the scriptural nourishment they can gain on their own. "Entitlement-driven members don't know how to fend for themselves," she lamented in an interview. "They want someone to wait on them. And they lack the will to change." On the other hand, some shy away from Bible study because they feel ignorant. "One man in South Carolina said, 'I can't go — I don't know any of the answers,'" she recalled. "And that was a progressive church!"

Her effort to turn that around by equipping her students to try an entirely new means was triggered by a class she'd attended during her days as a Yale undergraduate. A course in repertory theater introduced her to the rewards of climbing into a series of roles and sharing insights with other players. The story became fuller and richer as she heard other views and exchanged roles to see the same things from different angles. A few years later she saw the potential for using that method in the church to enliven the Bible.

Prof. Florence had been raised Presbyterian, accustomed to the minister's keeping the Bible in a religious "refrigerator" of sorts for selective usage; but with this new tool she explored how the repertory style might enliven the process of learning the Bible. For such a change to take place, it was necessary for the clergy-to-be at Columbia Seminary to free themselves from the straitjacketing that the "refrigerator" model would otherwise impose on them. In keeping with custom, they'd be expected to be the resident Bible "experts" — with primary access to the refrigerator. But it was time to rescue the Bible from the refrigerator, "to stop talking about the Bible's text and learn to live with it."

Prof. Florence's reorientation relies largely on liberating students from looking for the one "right" interpretation of a Scripture story, which is, in turn, a result of being "totally dependent on the [interpretation of] the preacher." (Confidence in the pastor is good in itself, but in this case the price could be the perpetuation of biblical illiteracy.) Florence nudges them to take a passage and run with it, without preconditions, such as a need to fit their results into a sermon. Just go with where your imagination takes you, she urges them, though it might not be conventional. Treat Scripture as art, not as an assignment hemmed in by inhibitions. "Text is a wild thing," she ventures. "It takes you where the wild things are." These folks are not doing what is ordinarily called "Bible study," which is a one-way kind of conversation; yet they are getting beyond the surface. She advises them: "Make mischief with the text; be less burdened by the outcome — be open to something new." Discussing their personal adventures together can allow them to "discover the Scripture that's in the Scripture, for us to rehearse until something true emerges." It is a mystery: "Get into a text and stay in it" (which is reminiscent of the monastic prayer practices like the Ignatian "Spiritual Exercises"), "and remember, the text looks at you more than you read the text. Stay in the scene until you have something to say."

That "something to say" is the pearl of great price, something to work with from within the heart and soul, not a witty or erudite academic conclusion. It is the only legitimate source for preaching to people who are developing similar sensibilities. That way, she insists, it gets real. The key to unlocking Scripture and climbing inside is to look at the verbs. The verbs take the reader directly to the setting and can collapse the time between then and now. Using the anguishing story of the woman accused of adultery (John 8), Florence underscores the evocative verbs: they "bring" the woman whom they have "caught" in the act; they "make" her stand as if it were a trial; Jesus "bends down and writes" figures in the dirt and asks her accusers who among them has not "sinned." One by one, they "go away."

Florence teaches a class where all the parts of a biblical text are acted out and roles are interchanged. In the previous spring semester, the class had dramatized the contents of Mark's Gospel, the Book of Esther (which included enacting Purim in a synagogue), and Paul's two Epistles to Timothy — exhaustive repertory-theater style.

For those inclined to crawl inside Scripture in search of revelations, Florence's approach promises to be exciting and provocative. Whether many will be attracted to it or will be willing to devote the time and rigorous honesty it demands is doubtful, in light of the laity's drift away from the Bible. But perhaps its very character as a "radical" option will magnify its appeal.

Where such approaches are used, student-actors attempt to decipher Scripture, to make of it what they can from the inside. More commonly, students experience it the other way around: Scripture takes the measure of them. The interpretation of Scripture is commonly agreed on; the hard part is measuring how it applies to the inner tangles of one's own life. As Prof. Florence notes, the Bible may uncover more about you than you uncover in the Bible.

*   *   *

Good Samaritan Church (the name has been changed for privacy reasons) has followed the latter path. Spiritual and moral injunctions are derived from the Bible as standards by which members examine their own behavior as Christians. Though this process is often scoffed at by elements of the wider culture, who see it as self-destructive, that description does not fit my experience of the Bible-study groups where I have sampled it.

Seated in a circle in a dimly lit, low-ceilinged auditorium on a Sunday morning are a group of men, dressed mostly in black, brown, and gray suits; they hail from such varied backgrounds as insurance, car repair, office management, warehouse service, and farming. Most are veteran church members who know each other well from years of Bible study. They are at ease with being called fundamentalists, though it isn't a term they use militantly or with prideful identity. It is just where they suppose they've been tabbed in the sorting-out process. They are far less interested in nailing down biblical principles than in using scriptural mandates, as they see them, to conform better to living as God wants them to in the midst of their struggles. The mandates are not of the kind that urge individual success on a financial or professional basis; rather, they are lessons in spiritual discipline.

One Sunday in October 2012, for example, their pastor has assigned them the topic "long-suffering," both the kind God shows and the kind God calls on mortals to emulate. The Hebrew Bible lays out the problem. God can perform the miracle of leading his people out of Egypt, can deliver manna to feed them in the desert, can chisel Ten Commandments on two tablets for Moses on Mount Sinai (though once, alarmed at the golden calf created by the people below, he threatens to "destroy them and blot out their name" [Deuteronomy 9:14]), and can demolish the Canaanites. But for all the powers of punishment God claims, he concedes that he cannot force anyone to do his bidding. The people keep breaking the commandments and refusing to go along with the Almighty's program. So, like any organizer of lesser stature, God is constantly frazzled as he waits for some cooperation. He gets mad, then relents, and some progress may take place. Between successes, however, God stands by helplessly, fussing and fuming, but ultimately always reverting to loving them again. The suffering is real and long, and the results are unpredictable. Learning to get through it without enacting hatred and revenge, as God shows, is thus the soul of faithfulness and compassion. It becomes a virtue.

That is the example for how humans are to endure the dry patches, the wrenching uncertainties, the bitter disappointments, and the agonizing waits. At Good Samaritan Church, as with so many other evangelical churches, the unshakable premise is that God's ways, however inscrutable, are always right simply because he chose them. He sees his people rebel and procrastinate and complain, and it causes him to suffer — for a long time, if need be. His followers are expected to act similarly, turning aside from their natural compulsions to go berserk in order to hold open the possibilities for peace and resolution.

The Good Samaritan group is given minimal direction by a designated leader, Stan, a soft-spoken man with silver-framed glasses. Stan introduces the topic with the observation that "long-suffering" is mentioned in twenty-seven places in the Bible, singling out Numbers and Jeremiah in particular. No special text serves as the anchor for discussion, but all eight participants are invited to read one or two that mean something to them. It is an open forum.

Ted jumps into an aspect of the topic that appears familiar to everyone there. It is the suffering felt in a prolonged effort to rescue the unbeliever through the acceptance of Christ as his or her personal savior. It is understood as a labor of love that combines God's suffering with theirs. Winning souls is at the heart of the church's motivation to bring salvation to the world and, not coincidentally, to increase the membership rolls of the church, which has hovered around 250 for several years.

Ted's hopes have been for the conversion of a man named Leo. Over many months Leo had been in the throes of a fatal illness, and Ted had reached out to him with Bible reading, personal sharing, prayer, and "even a little preaching" — to reach Leo's soft spot — but as he felt that the moment was nigh, it slipped away. "I was trying to talk to him about salvation one day," Ted said. "And he looked up at me and said, 'Let's just let it go while we're still friends.'" It was their last talk before Leo died, and Ted's remorse, as others in the group point out, sounds very much like being long-suffering.

Sean speaks less charitably about his prospect, a man named John, who is thought to be unsaved because he is "too selfish." In a tone of pique, Sean says he worries about John's fate because "John wants to do everything his way." Another group member says that he's been looking for "signs of redemption" in another hard case, a man dying of emphysema.

"Long-suffering" doesn't always bring expected rewards, says George, a dignified elderly man whose stature is complemented by a calm presence, craggy features, and a silver cross crowned with thorns pinned to the lapel of his three-piece black suit. But it is a "gift that God has given us" to go on. And nobody should forget, he cautions, that no matter how saved anyone feels, they all fall short of doing his will. "God is also looking down from the cross at us, waiting for us to come to him."

Another man suggests that, though God shows that quality in abundance, "the Bible never says God is patient." George looks away, perhaps thinking about it but not inclined to contradict it.

The trials closer to home bring out another dimension. Finding purpose in suffering is a major challenge, says Maurice. "Particularly when I was young, I had a hard time getting used to the fact that what I'd hoped for just wasn't going to happen. And now, if my wife were to die, it wouldn't matter how patient I've been." The man next to him nodded, slowly saying, "If my wife died, I'd be miserable — horrible. Sometimes things don't fall into a box we feel is acceptable." It was the closest to doubt of any expression.

Long-suffering has been Tim's lot as he has followed the growth of his children with trepidation and continues to be anxious about them, since they seldom go to church now that they are on their own.

No one was more caught in the grip of acute suffering than Stefan, a man in his mid-thirties with wavy blond hair and an open blue-and-white striped shirt. For months, he says, he lived with the shock that his wife had committed adultery with a member of the church. He wanted her "to repent," but she had not. As the others listened attentively, Stefan unloaded a litany of accusation and blame against her, churning his suffering into anger. It was the raw stuff of hurt that seemed to have none of the redeeming value others had attached to their trials.

After a pause, Geoffrey spoke up to offer balance and a place to rest the case for the time being.

"We've got to be careful about the heart," he said. "We are so quick to judge that we forget there is evil in our hearts. Yet God welcomes us over and over, helps us find unity in the church, because people are going to wrong us and we're going to wrong other people."

Brad had remained quiet during the hour-and-a-half session, but later he said that it had alerted him for the first time to the burdens he carried from knocking on doors in nearby neighborhoods. At the minister's urging, he had joined a weekly effort by the church to attract the unchurched to Bible study at Good Samaritan as a prelude, perhaps, to winning them for Christ. He had last gone out with the team of two dozen members four nights before, after a long day working as an accounting manager in a utility company. He'd been doing this for a number of years and had seen people's resistance to strangers at their door zoom since 9/11, which he said he understood. Of the twelve homes he'd tried that night, five answered. Did they go to church? And a standard evangelical bottom-line question: Do you know where you'll go when you die? If not, God has a plan you might be interested in. If the answer was yes, that often ended the conversation. Brad, who is anything but a pushy person, says that he can never quite recover from the many doors slammed in his face or the hostile replies to his invitations. Some people who seemed to be in obvious need stayed in his mind, though they didn't welcome him. He longed to bring the assurance of God's love to all those who seemed lost, lonely, and sick. Some he visited many times, he said, not expecting specific results, which rarely happened anyway — but because it felt right. Quite possibly he was receiving as much or more than he was giving.

These days, he didn't generally expect even those who let him in the door to be familiar with the Bible. What concerned him, however, was that many members of Good Samaritan knew less and less about it. Attendance at Bible study was about half of what it was a few years before. The usual causes were invoked: busy schedules, digital and video distractions, losing the habit of daily devotions, and reliance on the preacher's Bible-studded sermons to get what they needed. "A lot of people have turned away from the Bible and toward sin," he said grimly. "They're so busy with other things that they don't have the time. I don't know how long God's hand of mercy will be on us, but a lot of people don't have a good grasp of Scripture. We can get a lot of head knowledge, but unless we spend the personal time with prayer and Scripture, we won't be on the same page."

*   *   *

Another type of warning about Bible study came from the dais of a church in Naples, Florida: "Never teach a child something they'll have to un-learn." The words were those of Marcus Borg, spoken from a podium at the United Church of Christ. Borg, a guru of Christian progressivism, had been brought in for a three-day teach-in on the virtues of steering clear of biblical and theological literalism. Borg's provocative critiques and incisive analyses made him a leading light in his field. He wrote twenty influential and popular books, among them his defining theological work *Jesus: A New Vision,* which emphasized Jesus's humanity, and his last book, a memoir entitled *Convictions: How I Learned What Matters Most.* For decades he held forth as a distinguished professor at Oregon State University, lectured around the world, and was a principal founder of the Jesus Seminar.

The Naples church was a liberal oasis in a posh city with deeply conservative strains of politics and religion. Most churches saw the Bible as fact, so Borg's starting presumption that Scripture is essentially metaphorical ("I am the vine, you are the branches") rather than objective truth (that we are, in fact, branches of a grape plant) gave his seminar a distinctly alternative appeal for those looking for something different. This was the tourist season, when Florida churches sponsored headliner programs to attract visitors looking for something other than bingo or square dancing. This program scored well, with near-capacity audiences on hand for Borg's talks. Many said they'd welcomed the chance to be with like-minded Christians and to hear Borg in particular.

Borg laid down his marker. His interpretation of the Bible was "historical and metaphorical," he said, which generally ruled out taking it at face value. Its stories "are not so much about whether [the events] happened" but "setting ancient text in ancient context," searching for what the language meant at the time it was written. That involved "more than the literal meaning of language"; a figure of speech characterized something else, as when "dark horse" referred to a competitor whose chances of winning a race are generally overlooked. Metaphors — and allegories, their longer, more complex equivalents — appear throughout the Bible as memorable sketches of things hidden just behind them; artful, catchy, pungent images of concrete realities. Psalm 23's picture of the Lord as "my shepherd," for instance, doesn't describe Jesus's actual occupation but evokes a poignant image to evoke God's care and compassion.

In the roughly three thousand years since biblical texts were first written, constant shifts in language and cultural forms make it challenging to understand why metaphors were used. Some obviously became more obscure than others — to the point of becoming incomprehensible. At bottom lies the prolonged debate about whether many of these verbal devices are metaphors at all. To Borg and other progressives, for example, the miracles of the New Testament, including Jesus's restoration of physical and psychic ills and his own resurrection, were not factual reports but allegorical allusions to Jesus's power to heal inner, broken spirits and revive life in the midst of death.

What he called "common Christianity" was largely an American Protestant distortion that further escalated after World War II. It was the "heaven and hell" variety built on a warped view of the Bible's teachings driven by two biblical corruptions in particular: first, that salvation was about getting into heaven; second, that qualifying as a good Christian was primarily a matter of "believing" in certain statements (Do you believe Christ died for your sins? Do you believe Christ will come again?), sometimes called creeds, without a corresponding need to turn personal behavior upside down, if necessary, to follow Jesus. As Borg told his Naples audience, this kind of checklist Christianity (in the vein of a TV quiz show) provides a mental test to gain the afterlife that implicitly insists on compliance with the Ten Commandments in personal behavior but demands few changes in inner states of consciousness. Confessing sins and believing that Jesus has "paid for your sins" is the key. Therefore, Borg sees it essentially as a cognitive, strategic process, like applying for a fishing license: that is, cut and dried, agreeing with a set of literal propositions that can be truthful without altering motives and behavior. "You can believe all the right things," he quipped, "and still be a jerk."

The wrong turn, in Borg's estimation, had stemmed from a colossal misunderstanding of "salvation" in Scripture. Read accurately, he said, it wasn't about an *afterlife* or heavenly reward but about *this life* and bettering it. The focus has been tragically misplaced. Biblically speaking, being saved means undergoing thorough renewal via Christ's spirit. "Transformation," the true purpose, becomes possible by entering a living, trusting relationship with Christ. Whereas "what you believe doesn't have any necessary effect on character or behavior," Borg drilled home, "what you give your heart to and pledge your loyalty to (Christ, that is) intrinsically changes you; it transforms the self and the world."

Transformation, as he used the concept, is about moving from "sickness to wholeness," from "self-preoccupation to compassionate engagement," from a "world of injustice to a world of justice, nonviolence, and peace." Being "born again" is the "perfect metaphor" for the Christian life, for the "radical transformation of the spirit" created by "relationship with God that's not just psychological." It is political as well as personal. The Bible is "pervasively political" in promoting a this-worldly drive for justice and an end to suffering. In the Hebrew Bible, the central metaphor is the "Exodus," the liberation from bondage, Borg says. In the New Testament, Jesus confers salvation by healing the agonies of those he meets along the way, and he pays relatively little attention to sin.

Marcus Borg's death in January 2015 marked the loss of a major advocate of historical-critical Bible scholarship whose ability to befriend those on the conservative and evangelical side with whom he disagreed had bolstered a search for common ground. At Naples, he delivered four lectures and struck up dialogue in long question-and-answer follow-ups. He was a lion among the older wave of new interpreters, a scholar of right-brain sensibilities who said that he didn't reject the idea of an afterlife but that it wasn't either his or the Bible's main concern.

Evidence of Borg's ability to speak to a spectrum of views was the presence at the Naples seminar of critics such as Bob. Taking time from his work as an electrician, he had driven fifty miles to hear someone whose perspective on the Bible differed from his own in nearly every respect. Since his teens, Bob said, he'd regarded the Scriptures as nothing less than "inspired" by God and utterly credible as history. He allowed for some expressions as "symbolic," but he had no room for Borg's claims that the stories of Jonah and the whale, the crossing of the Red Sea, and Jesus's raising of Lazarus from the dead weren't actual events but metaphors for deeper contemplation. He had read about Borg, and he felt that he owed it to himself to listen to someone who would challenge him.

At the end of the two-day seminar, Bob said that he hadn't altered his views or accepted Borg's, but he had stopped fighting one battle: his compulsion to "prove" the divine authority of the Bible. Something in what Borg said led him to conclude that something more urgent and practical was at stake. People Bob knew at his Christian and Missionary Alliance church weren't "asking about the nature and authority of the Bible as a philosophical or theological question," he'd realized. "They don't care so much whether it's true, but *whether it works*." Sooner or later, he thought, it would be necessary to pin down the "truth of the Bible," but he'd hit upon something more urgent: to establish a "biblical worldview" that was faithful to Scripture and produced sound results.

* * *

Gary Swanson was in no small measure a pragmatist himself, as his topic for the evening's Bible class made clear: "Making Good Decisions" — and, by implication, ducking bad ones. The person he chose to represent the bad guy was Judas, whose betrayal of Jesus in the Gospels made him a compelling — perhaps indisputable — villain. The "good guy" figure was far less obvious, in fact something of a surprise: Thomas, as in "Doubting Thomas," whose reputation for wavering might have been thought to eliminate him. Notwithstanding, the stage was set.

Swanson sat in a director's chair in a nearly empty production room within Studio City in Hollywood, the set for the filming of CBS shows such as *CSI*. He looked out at a group comprised of technicians, actors, and facilitators from the surrounding movie and television studios. Most were in their late twenties to early forties and had finished work for the day. Swanson had founded the study group on a regular Thursday-night basis several years earlier. On this night, nearly forty people sat in three concentric circles of chairs ready for Swanson to put them through their paces.

This is another of the highly directed studies where little is left to chance. The difference is the element of performance art that Swanson brings to it. He perches on the stereotypical director's seat with a mischievous look in his eyes, ready to assert his presumed, readily granted position of authority. He presides like an orchestra conductor — a gray-bearded, burly six-footer at that. He directs the study with aplomb, moving adroitly from one biblical verse to another, steering discussion smoothly and injecting incisive comments blended with wit and good-natured remarks.

Swanson, a voluble, gregarious, sometimes bombastic man, has undergone Baptist conversion. He describes himself as "driven" and leaves no doubt that his talents as a salesman would have made him capable of peddling refrigerators to those proverbial Eskimos. At the time of his conversion, and beyond, he had become an inveterate reader of the Bible, including a chapter of Proverbs and five Psalms a day, and a dedicated daily listener to four or five radio preachers. Somewhere along the line he'd hankered to be an actor and as a young man went to California to try his luck.

He migrated to Hollywood from Ohio, after success in financial services, for the explicit purpose of planting a beachhead of righteousness in a film industry he decries as drowning in sin and evil. His initiative is called Tinseltown Ministries, and it consists of another study group on Wednesday nights in addition to this one. Swanson sees his mission as "spiritual warfare" against perversions of every kind to rescue young people caught in the throes of Hollywood's snares, degradations, and crushing defeats.

Like any good conductor, Swanson coordinates rhythms and sudden changes in his directions. His opening gambit sets the tone. Referring to Adam and Eve, he asks, "How many rules did they have in the Garden? One stinking rule. What did they do?" In loud unison the group shouts, "They broke it." And they laugh.

It is a familiar routine that underscores human folly as a chief talking point, serving as Exhibit A in the gallery of bad decisions. Adam and Eve paid a price for their wrong choice, of course, being made to grow their own food, to face death, to lose direct contact with God, to watch out for devouring predators, and so forth. But at least they weren't threatened with eternal damnation. Nobody was that lucky after Christ came, he said, because anyone, like Judas, who betrayed or refused him would "go to hell." By giving himself to Satan's wiles, Judas betrayed Jesus and thereby sealed his doom. Could he be saved? If Judas were totally owned by Satan, Swanson said, there was "no way to get to Jesus." On the other hand, anyone who is "truly saved can't be truly possessed." Who knew the whole story in Judas's case? Maybe "all Judas had to do was to ask Jesus, 'Will you save me?' "

One detail remained. If the Gospel account of Judas's act of suicide was true, was taking your own life enough by itself to block admission to heaven? No, Swanson said, there was no biblical base to that. "The unpardonable sin is denying Jesus until you die." No respite from that.

Thomas, then, was the improbable bearer of good news. Over the centuries he's been unfairly slighted, Swanson said. The temptation is to think that Thomas failed where the rest of us would have passed with flying colors. Seeing the risen Lord, Thomas couldn't believe it without touching his wounds. Swanson was full of praise, first for Thomas's honesty in admitting he needed help believing, accepting the evidence he found, and exclaiming, "My Lord and my God." Unlike Judas, Thomas repented. His heart was good, as was his decision.

Throughout the study group, Swanson steers without coercion. He elicits support for his talking points, though he invites no others (Judas, for example, has been subjected to a multitude of interpretations). Swanson is often exuberant when someone gets the point.

He brings them home to where they started the discussion. Then they help themselves to pizza, tossed salad, potato and macaroni salads, Greek salad, breads, puddings, cakes, cookies, and water.

CHAPTER 12

Speaking Personally

Every so often the Bible bursts from behind the scenes into the public. Maybe that surprises, startles, or even offends onlookers, strange as that would have seemed to an America once accustomed to having references to it popping up all over the place.

Steph Curry, the Golden State Warriors pro basketball sensation, joined a recent trend among top athletes by inscribing a verse from Saint Paul on the inside of the tongue of his first "signature" sneaker, "Curry One," in early 2015. It was a signal achievement that at once became a hot item in the Under Armour line of sports shoes. The inscription was Philippians 4:13: "I can do all things through him who strengthens me." It is a commonly used saying and a natural one for Curry, a committed Christian who grew up reading the Bible with his family every morning. And there is nothing particularly unusual about athletes adopting such phrases. So nonsectarian is it that Dave Dombrow, vice president of the company's shoe division, said he'd "never actually looked at it as a Bible verse" but as a capsule expression of Curry's self-confidence that "he can go beyond and do something greater, go further and silence the critics."

However valuable as a marketing tool the inscription might be, it rankles one of the country's most popular sports talk-show hosts, Chris Carton. During his early morning broadcast on March 2, 2015, the often hilarious, reflexively sharp-tongued Carton complained that he'd looked at the shoe while shopping for his son and was taken aback by what struck him as an attempt to push religion. To Carton, it crossed a line. His sentiments didn't sound to me like hostility toward religion, but part of a growing consensus that religion really should be kept separate from commerce, politics, and uninvited personal space, without the "leaks" that had been tolerated.

It is a familiar secular point of view. Many others, including a strong though decreasing religious population, tout an older tradition in which, conceptually at least, the American republic is unthinkable without its having had a substantial infusion of religion. Carton's aversion to "being preached to" in a shoe store wasn't so much a sign of conflict as an indication of how far the secular and religious outlooks have moved away from each other.

US Senator Tom Carper (D-Delaware) picked a televised congressional hearing to try his hand at biblical instruction. As the then head of the Senate's Homeland Security and Governmental Affairs committee, the senator was in charge of investigating a scurrilous incident involving the hiring of prostitutes by Secret Service agents in Cartagena, Colombia, while preparing for President Obama's visit there. On the interrogation grill was Mark Sullivan, director of the Secret Service. After dutifully chastising the accused agents, Carper said his search for guidance had led him to the story of Jesus's encounter with a woman that is told in the first eleven verses of John 8. What happened next baffled some and inspired others.

Carper paraphrased the story in considerable detail. The Pharisees, often wrongly stereotyped as grouches and worse by today's untutored Christians, claimed that they had caught this woman in the act of adultery and thus hauled her in front of Jesus for him to decide her fate. In the senator's words, the captors said, "Look, what do you think should happen to this woman?" Whereupon Jesus ignored them, bent down on the ground, and began writing something in the dirt that remains a mystery. With rocks in their hands, the Pharisees asked him again, reminding him, "The laws of Moses say she should be stoned and her life taken from her." Then Jesus delivered his renowned conversation-stopper: "Let him who is without sin cast the first stone." They were nonplussed, and they slowly dropped their stones and walked away, leaving her alone with Jesus. "That's all he said," the senator reminded them. Facing the woman by himself, Jesus said, "Your accusers have gone, and I'm not going to accuse you either." Then he said to the woman, "Go and sin no more."

Likewise, said Carper, "nobody is going to lose their life because of what they did down in Colombia. They've lost their jobs. They've lost their reputations. They've harmed the reputation of a wonderful agency." The New Testament story he quoted is among the New Testament's most powerful testimonies to God's love and compassion. But what did it mean in the setting of a congressional hearing? And to whom was it addressed? Sullivan? The offenders? The public? This was a situation that cried out for biblical interpretation; unfortunately, Carper had none. Or he hadn't been able to choose among the various interpretations that were possible. Was he comparing the Secret Service "johns" to the woman in the story, thus absolving them from further punishment? Was Mark Sullivan a stand-in for Pharisees, who might take no action against the agents after examining his own sinfulness? Taking the Bible public doesn't guarantee that its meaning will be transparent or beyond debate, though it is often treated that way when it comes to weighty moral issues.

Steve Green decided that Scripture was speaking to him loudly and clearly in his refusal to provide birth-control services to his employees at the Hobby Lobby Corporation. As president of the company, he won his case (in a Supreme Court decision) on the grounds that the religious beliefs of a family-run corporation could exempt such compliance with that feature of Obamacare. Years earlier, Green and his family had set their sights on a bigger display of Scripture's influence on American life, a project that they eventually envisioned as a Bible museum two blocks from the National Mall in Washington (after its originally proposed site in Dallas was overruled). Plans call for an eight-story building that would house Green's huge collection of biblical artifacts (including the largest collection of Torah scrolls ever assembled) at a cost of $800 million. It is scheduled to open in 2017 and has drawn much curiosity and skepticism. Whether Green will open the museum to historical-critical viewpoints or restrict it to belief in the inerrancy of Scripture, like his own worldview, is unclear, though he has vowed that its orientation will be nonsectarian. His motive chimes in with the wider anxiety concerning the Bible's decline and, by implication, America's. The nation is "in danger because of its ignorance of what God has taught," Green told the American Bible Association, referring to the Bible. "We need to know it, and if we don't know it, our future is going to be very scary." He is banking on the museum's helping to stem that tide.

The image of the "museum" as a showcase of a long-gone past could hamper Green's hopes of promoting a living tradition and dampen an already slumping interest in the Bible. But then again, anything seems possible for a man like Green, who owns Babe Ruth's Bible.

*   *   *

Lest I digress further, the focus of this chapter is the Bible's more familiar terrain, the sphere of the individuals seeking wisdom, solace, or merely good literature from it. In many ways, people from every corner of the country have found their way into its pages and have chosen, among its passages, offerings for uplift, courage, and fuel for righteous anger. It serves as an "icon" in the authentic sense, not as the term has recently been corrupted to mean simply someone or something that has become famous or influential (Einstein, Marilyn Monroe, the Beatles, Gandhi, iPhones, etc.), but channels to something higher. Originally, as developed in the Eastern Orthodox tradition, the icon has been a holy figure *through which* the light of the divine shines, not the object of worship in itself. Now it mainly signifies celebrity — without a hint of that sacredness shining through it. The Bible is thus an icon in the proper sense: being a conduit to the Almighty rather than the Almighty itself.

These are among the remarkable people who have befriended the Bible, with intriguing results.

Sharon Jackson felt tired and empty the day before we met at a diner. A normally vigorous, cheerful woman of striking accomplishment, she was off her stride, on a downward slope of dejection. As the caretaker of a family member during the preceding few months, she felt a growing concern about the treasured relative's very slow improvement and was both emotionally and physically spent. The dejection was not what she would perhaps call being "depressed." It was more like "depressive realism," a melancholy state of mind arising primarily from adverse circumstances rather than inner conflicts or body chemistry.

It was no accident that she had found balm in the Bible, because it was a frequent recourse for her in times of distress. In Matthew 11:28-30, she saw the familiar words of Jesus: "Come to me, all you that are weary and are carrying heavy burdens, and I will give you rest. Take my yoke upon you, and learn from me; for I am gentle and humble in heart, and you will find rest for your souls. For my yoke is easy and my burden is light." That mixed with copious prayer.

Panacea? No, she says. It is the awareness of being on the right path again, of easing away from false remedies and self-involvement and heading in the direction of true strength. At an earlier time in her life she craved "magical" and "total" answers from self-help books, from friends, and from the Bible. What she got were sincere surface answers, the kind that she has given to other people herself but do nothing to address her deepest needs. The transition from that to a deeper, more soulful level resulted from a stunning awareness that "God is alive." She knows that it sounds like a cliché, and it isn't happening with a heavenly brass choir playing in the background; but it has quietly emerged, she believes, from her ability to hear and see the spiritual realities behind the surfaces of her own consciousness and in the depths of the Bible. Now she thinks she understands Jesus's teaching that salvation belongs to those "with the eyes to see and the ears to hear," eluding those who never saw or heard beyond the superficialities, those who basically missed the point. It is a gift to her that needs constant nourishment. Her perception of faith has expanded in every dimension of her life. God had been a concept, an abstract picture; the turning point for her was when God became "a relationship." The Bible took on more excitement.

"Before, I felt that I was in a twenty-room mansion but confined to a closet in the garage," she says with easy precision, her voice trailing upward. "There was so much else that was out there for me by finding that relationship." Discovering God — "not just as a concept but as a person" — has taken "the blinders off my reading of the Bible. It isn't just words any longer; it is a witness to God's speaking to me then and now." For years Sharon read the Bible regularly; she'd read it cover to cover. Now she "awaits the prompting of the Spirit." It has led her in past weeks to 1 and 2 Corinthians.

The most persistent prompting was implying that "there is something God wants me to accomplish" that differed from anything she has done before. It has sounded to her like the kind of surprise call to service that others heard and responded to since Abraham left everything behind in Ur thousands of years ago to answer God's urging to establish a chosen nation in his care. Peter and the disciples likewise walked away from their occupations when Jesus asked them to join him. So she felt in good company — along with countless believers across the centuries — but she was as nervous about it as she presumed they had been.

There was a lot that Sharon would potentially have to give up. As a bright, studious young woman, she finished college and went on to earn a doctorate in epidemiology at the University of South Florida, the first ever earned by an African American woman at that institution. She'd worked at the august Centers for Disease Control in Atlanta and taught at the University of North Carolina and most recently at Wake Forest. The "call waiting" factor led her — surprisingly, she said — to recognize that her profession had fulfilled only part of the self-giving required by that otherworldly prompting. Despite the risks of losing health insurance, job security, and financial comfort, she accepted the challenge to dive into something new. She recalled Jesus's assurances in the Gospel according to Matthew that those who trusted God would have their needs met just as the birds of the air and lilies of the field did.

Also in her favor is a gentle strength and resolve that she exudes effortlessly, it seems. It might be a legacy from her father who, as a young man, went to Florida to practice general surgery and, as one of a small number of African American doctors, was denied privileges in white hospitals. Sharon described the courage with which he persevered and eventually crossed those barriers. Not only that, he'd become the mayor of the town.

One day Sharon packed her belongings and left Wake Forest to follow the prompting. It has turned into a foundation to help small, struggling churches stay afloat and enable spiritual renewal. "I feel at peace," she said, though admitting that the labyrinth of legal and economic necessities for setting up such an organization can be daunting. Her heart is in keeping the flame of faith alive in congregations closest to needy people. She is providing resources to those whose proposals offer that potential. There are times when the mystery of it all astounds her. "If this were up to Sharon," she says, "it wouldn't be done. It's 'not my will but thy will be done.'" Her reorientation is still in its early stages, but she believes that it has been in the works longer than she'd ever imagined. "I think I've known that a period like this was coming in my life, something I had to conquer," she says. "God has achieved the victory. The more I accept that, the more it becomes healing."

*   *   *

Natan Bourkoff brought Joseph, hero of the age of patriarchs, to his management job at the Disney Corporation. He'd studied the Genesis accounts of this towering biblical figure and discovered in Joseph, among other things, a keen aptitude for succeeding in business. "Joseph was in prison when he was called on to interpret the dreams of one of the pharaohs," Natan explains. "He puts on neat clothes to impress the boss, and when he hears about the dream, he says, 'Here's the problem and here's how to fix it. And I'm the person to fix it.'" It worked, and Joseph moved up several rungs on Pharaoh's organizational chart.

Natan said it with a trace of whimsy but not all that much. He reads stories from the Hebrew Bible for their deeper messages. "If you're going to be more religious," he reasons, "it's not enough to do rituals. You also have to be devoted to the text."

Natan is in his thirties, with a wife and three children — an older son and twin girls. He joined Disney after graduating from Columbia University, and he likes his job in that family-friendly climate. At the same time, like many passionate devotees of the Bible, he keeps that part of himself private, from a cautionary instinct to avoid being misunderstood. His values tend toward conservatism — both morally and politically. And as someone who thinks of his colleagues and California surroundings as decidedly liberal, he hesitates to discuss his views on matters such as homosexuality. In general he perceives America as "straying from the ideals depicted in the Bible." And he remains most at ease with those with whom he shares common ground in the synagogue.

His own devotion to the Bible began in his high school years in Berkeley, California; he'd moved there from Baltimore with his mother after his parents' divorce. He'd been raised in an orthodox Jewish home and taught in a Jewish day school, but it was unclear how much that would continue after the cross-country move. "I was in a public school, and that provided impetus for me to decide whether to connect with my upbringing or leave it," he recalls. "I became committed to it — basically more devoted to studying the Bible."

The Berkeley synagogue nearby, Beth Israel, was a big factor. Natan's feelings of being out of place in the high school were more than offset by the synagogue's warm embrace. It was there, he said, that he felt "validated." Years later, he counted the rabbi at Beth Israel among his esteemed teachers and mentors; with a few other boys, he met with the rabbi after Hebrew school classes for extra Bible study ("ten of us eating ice cream," he says). He remembers being especially enthralled by the dramatic goings-on in the books of Samuel. The sagas in Kings also caught the boys' attention, "with so much blood, sex and violence." It had pulled back a curtain on the sharp edges of human nature.

An instructor from New York arrived, further fanning the flames of Natan's desire to learn by offering to train him for competition in the 1997 National Bible Contest, sponsored by Jewish organizations as part of the international competition in Israel established by David Ben-Gurion, the nation's founder and first prime minister. That sent Natan into a swirl of daily reading of the Bible in Hebrew, which meant more memorizing and deeper learning. He met weekly for a challenging tutorial with the instructor. He entered the contest (which drew thousands of potential aspirants), which consisted mainly of multiple-choice questions on the fine points of the biblical text. Natan won the American division prize, and that earned him the right to compete with twenty-five other national winners at the international final on the date, coincidentally, of Israel's Independence Day. He came away a runner-up and profoundly impressed.

By that time, he says, the Bible had become "much more than academic. I can't isolate the Bible from my whole life and how it drives all my views." How public those views will be depends on circumstances. At work, he thinks it best to be discreet while retaining his core identity. "I represent the Bible and Jewish religious life," he said. "I'm comfortable with it, but it's not something I flaunt."

At his seven-year-old son's bedtime, Natan passes on that heritage. Together they read a chapter of the Torah and talk about it. He glows as he says, "It's great bonding."

*   *   *

Like Natan, John Campbell was psyched up by the Bible's war stories when he was a boy. It's as though those grand stories are in there just to keep young boys coming to Sunday school. "When I was in the sixth grade, six of us in a Sunday school class read about the battles in Joshua and Judges," John says. "Because it was almost all military, we were enthralled." Natan had fastened on these stories in his synagogue; Campbell's awakening came in a United Methodist church.

John is more than a regular churchgoer. He is engaged with the church on many levels, most fervently as a student of the Bible. Unlike many of his more liberal baby-boomer cohorts (he was born in 1959), who either ignore the Bible or shy away from identifying with it, he is an unabashed advocate and student of it. Sparks planted in his boyhood have become a burning search for guidance and purpose: his Bible study has yielded both, and continues to expand his consciousness. It leads him to places and people he could scarcely imagine encountering otherwise, including his recent joining of a picket line at a supermarket in support of farm workers.

We sat in a sports café in South Florida, near the office where John manages a mortgage company. He extended a glad hand but wasn't a glad-hander in any slick sense. His handshake came across as sincerely as his gaze, and his forthcoming manner and speech indicated a striking quality of openness. He credits the Methodist church that he attends, especially its invigorating pastor, Roy Terry, for fostering honesty in matters of faith and courage in displaying it. But John himself shows a lot of willingness to go in those directions. He has not turned aside at crucial junctures that might have dissuaded him from responding to spiritual urgings.

Take a turning point in his boyhood, for example. The six boys in his Sunday school class were caught up in the war stories, to be sure, but the origins and accuracy of those traditional "history" narratives of the Hebrew Bible (as well as the readings that followed) were inevitably open to question — either directly or indirectly. In his church, he recalled, "we were liberal Methodists, not literalists. In the sixties and seventies we knew something about the Bible's critical history. We knew about the Dead Sea Scrolls and how those texts could influence how we understood biblical history and theology."

Many of his neighborhood friends, however, went to Baptist and Presbyterian churches that did preach literalism. Some of them "tried to use the Bible to save me, over and over again by getting me to sign on to bottom-line beliefs." Being faced with two starkly different ways of looking at Scripture reinforced his historical-critical instincts, he says: "It gave me a place to stay."

One day as he was running clothes through cycles in a laundromat, he realized how much that outlook had crystallized. "A man from a little nondenominational church sought me out," John says. "He told me he had read the book of Hebrews. Did I know about it? For him all the answers were there in black and white. He talked and talked.

"His insistence that I agree with his word-for-word reading of it ruled me out, of course," John continues. "For me, all the mystery was there, not all the answers."

Along the way, John thought of entering the ministry; in fact, he spent time after college at a theological seminary, but he decided to leave before finishing. As he looks back on that experience, he says that its most lasting effect was the understanding that the Jesus of the New Testament is alive and active in the world around him. "It is the awareness that I can participate in what God is already doing," that is, in contrast to seeing Jesus as an alabaster statue or a rule-giver who has gone off to hide until a second coming of some sort. "He's bringing mercy and justice, redeeming me and the world, and I can participate in that."

As that understanding opened up, John said that the Bible stories about Jesus took on astonishingly new relevance. They became for him the links between the redemption Jesus was enacting and his own role in it. In order to make these links, he found it necessary to depend on allegorical readings of such texts as the parable of the sower or the miracle of loaves and fishes. The freedom that allegory allowed (compared to literalism's restraints) struck him as never before, granting him the opportunity to interpret sayings and stories with a flexibility needed to be applied to the complexities of the world in which he lived. No longer were they static, ancient narratives but daily fresh incentives. "I now take the allegorical stories with me into the world," he says. "I can see the connections, how the world really works." To keep plumbing the depths, he reads biblical scholars and commentators, from the highly regarded traditionalist and Anglican bishop N. T. Wright to Billy Graham. A few years ago he took the rigorous Disciples Bible course, a sixteen-week study of the entire Hebrew Bible followed by an equal period devoted to the New Testament. He said it helped him "see the broad patterns and frames of reference" and gave him greater depth. He has attended as many as three Bible studies each week.

One means of participating in "what God is already doing" has been to put a shoulder to the wheel of social justice. The most pressing issue for his church is the suffering of migrant workers who pick tons of tomatoes in the area for major food outlets. Their working and living conditions are deplorable, and their wages, such as they are, keep them in indentured servitude.

"They are exploited — horribly," John says. He has joined a coalition pressuring buyers such as Taco Bell and McDonald's to increase compensation a single penny for each pound workers picked. Some fast-food corporations, such as Taco Bell, have agreed to that proposal; McDonald's has not as of this writing. Neither has the large local supermarket chain Publix, which was why John walked a picket line in protest. It hadn't seemed like a big deal to John until he got there the first time and felt exposed. "In a picket line, I had to give up my white privilege," he says. "Was I willing to give up my status? To give of my heart?" He did — and he felt chastened. "It's so easy to rationalize inequality," he says.

John's journey as a Christian stems from his realization that the Bible is about the mysteries of human-divine encounters rather than instruction per se. "The Bible doesn't prove things," he reflects. "It opens things up to us. It's a tool for my life, not the god of my life. When [Scripture] talks about the kingdom of God, the thing most emphasized is being for each other in this life."

*   *   *

Burnie Jones had had just about enough of such talk not long before. She had lent her trust and support to a young man who had started a Bible study group, and she had become personally attached to him. "He said he was a strong believer," she says. Suddenly he disappeared. "We found out that he'd been leading a double life. He was not at all what he had convinced me he was. It was devastating. I was so angry at being betrayed that I wanted revenge."

Friends from the group came to her rescue, calming her with regard to those raw emotions and steering her to the Bible. Read a portion of those commonsense Proverbs every day, they advised her, and she did so, along with other servings of biblical wisdom. In Psalm 4 she came upon words that helped her get beyond the rage and the shallow consolation that "nobody gets away with anything." However tempting it was to fight back, the psalmist had something else in mind, a kind of passive resistance that sounded counterintuitive:

> When you are disturbed, do not sin;
>   ponder it on your beds, and be silent.
> Offer right sacrifices,
>   and put your trust in the Lord. (Psalm 4:4–5)

Leaning on that and other passages, she says, she slowly recovered. "I received so much peace," she declares. "If I would lie down to sleep, God would take care of it and let me sleep. Satan entered my home and I'm still safe."

Burnie was at a crossroads as she neared her fortieth birthday. After a decade in Los Angeles, her hopes of gaining a foothold as an actress were virtually exhausted, and she was sketching scenarios for moving on. She was able to count herself among the minuscule 3 percent of aspiring actors who actually land enough acting jobs over a decade to qualify for health insurance and pension benefits from the Screen Actors' Guild. She has been in episodes of television series, including *The Closer, Bones, Criminal Minds,* and *NCIS;* but, other than a few minor appearances in minor films, nothing like a breakthrough has happened. "I've often found I don't have a place out here," she says. "I came to Hollywood to make it in acting. I'm coming to understand that is not my purpose."

Burnie's eyes reflect a note of sadness and longing in a face whose smoothness and liveliness project vitality. Her lithe frame suggests that of a dancer and gymnast, and her manner tunes into the resonances of those around her. Originally from Phoenix, she attended Princeton University, where, in addition to her studies, she was the art director of the Black Arts Company. She even wrote and directed a play, entitled *Saul Lost in Babylon,* which echoes her own sense of alienation from the culture of her college surroundings. Her plumb line in life has always been the Bible: she can still see clearly the Bible storybook her family had read to her as a child, as well as the first real Bible she received, with a blue cover, after she'd accepted Jesus as her savior.

While she looked back gratefully at Princeton's benefits, she was dismayed by what she saw as its indifference to the study of Scripture and to religion in general, the cornerstones of her existence. She was "religious" without apology, and she huddled with Christian students with whom she felt a bond. "A friend once told me that another friend wouldn't date me because I was 'too religious,'" she said. "I was never part of the larger crowd to begin with."

Having grown up in what she described as a tight-knit church community circumscribed by Scripture, Burnie had a formative youth experience that continues to pull her away from her forays into the wider world.

"There was a time when I wondered what the Bible had to do with all areas of life," she explains. "How the Bible connected with the modern world and with personal issues. As I became more spiritually mature, I've been able to find answers to these things in Scripture. My reading of a verse or a passage now is completely different when I take my time. Each word makes a difference. I meditate on the word. I'm not rushing.

"I try to apply God's Word to my life. I've been at it so long I think I know most of the time what is aligned with God's Word and what isn't."

Most everything in movie land isn't, she believes. Like most bornagain Christians who have ventured into the jaws of the film industry, she has yearned to succeed in an industry whose values and behaviors are condemned by evangelicals as wicked, even demonic — infested with selfishness, greed, sexual sin and perversion, and so on. Part of Burnie's coping mechanism has been to imagine a transition to performing explicitly and exclusively in Christian films; but so far she has not been able to do so. It is a niche that some aspiring Christian actors view as worthy, but still second best. But for her, it has the resonance of that comfort zone from her background.

More and more, she thinks of herself as doing "ministry," an ambition that also bears the marks of her Phoenix past but has since been tempered by the refiner's fire. For many years that calling has strengthened her in her work with low-income high school students preparing for college, most of them Latino. Every Saturday she teaches them writing and literature in a program run by the University of Southern California. College guidance is her other function. The assignment has touched her heart and opened a possibility. One sign of her love for it is that she tutors the students on her own. "I think teenagers are my mission," she says. "God has given me a gift with them. Somehow I come into their lives, and they come into mine.

"Grace is something I understand more as I get older," she says. "In my twenties I felt that I needed to be perfect to obtain it. But I've come to see that Christ loves me as I am. Intellectually, I understand that, but I've needed to understand it at the core of myself. A big moment for me was when someone showed me grace when I expected to be criticized."

*   *   *

Al Pulaski came at it the other way around. After years of skepticism, he'd become a garden-variety believer: God and the Bible were for real. Then he was hit by dread. "Everything was great, but once I realized there was a God and he spoke through the Bible, I started to realize that I was in trouble." There's no free lunch, he remembers thinking. Becoming a believer must mean he would face a comeuppance for his iniquities.

"I looked into the mirror," he says deliberately. "I'd broken the commandments. What would a good judge do? Pass sentence, I'm guessing — judge me and not give me a pass." He read furiously through the entire Bible looking for what was missing in his faith. He came away sure that what he needed was a relationship with Jesus, the one who had died to save him. "It radically transformed my life," he said. "I no longer had a desire to do it my way."

Al was raised in a religious household, but he thought that "faith was a crutch, and I didn't feel I was that weak." People dressed up and went to church so "God would like them better," he observes. He didn't like school any better, sputtering through the grades and leaving for good at nineteen after one semester at a Christian academy. He married the next year, managed a car dealership for more than seven years, and started in the insurance business about four years ago. He has a wife and four children.

None of his aversion to "learning," Al insists, has lessened his desire to soak up the Bible. He kept looking into the Bible, among other things, and was eventually convinced it was the absolute truth. "Either it was true, or it was a worldwide conspiracy to make it seem that way," he says. "It just screamed at me, 'This is truth.' It was exactly what was written at the time." Its accuracy included the Genesis version of creation (as I have noted above, there are actually two versions), thus making Darwin's evolutionary theory impossible.

In an effort to stay on track, he read in the Bible twice a day to remind himself of his "dependence on God." He'd read through it many times, like an astronomer viewing a planet again and again, searching for reminders of what was familiar and for never-before-noticed nuances.

Al is percolating with energies running every which way, sometimes in opposite directions. As the owner of an insurance agency, he spends long days fielding phone calls and dashing in his car to answer the needs of one or more of his 3,000 clients. He has the likable personality and outgoing nature to handle it, but inevitably the stress of emergencies and complexities of paperwork can spin him far out of the Bible's orbit. Connections with the remedies of Scripture become harder to maintain.

He readily acknowledges getting out of joint in those ways. Al's candor is striking. He says that he dithers over matters involving family, business, and finances to the point where he forgets to check in with his mentors in Isaiah, Psalms, and Luke, among others, until an emergency light goes off in his mind and he takes corrective action. He tries to seek that help before losing his temper.

"When I want to be caustic and blow up at someone," he says, "the Word of God changes me." That is, when he remembers — which often means recalling one of the many passages he's memorized.

"Many times things get out of control and I want to yell, kick, and scream," he says. "But I pray for help." That includes times when he feels most tempted to run afoul of virtue, such as in his role as a parent. "When I read Scripture, I find instructions on how to be the right kind of father," he says. "Wrath will turn them into rebels; soft words will turn away anger."

His forthright admission of his lapses does not always sit well with fellow Christians, who are inclined to believe that they have put such temptation behind them and are thus uncomfortable hearing about it. But the New Testament has blessed his candor, such as in the person of the publican of Jesus's parable (Luke 18:13), who utters, "God have mercy on me, a sinner" in response to a Pharisee's boasting that he has done all the right things to deserve righteousness. Saint Augustine spoke for those who admit to being of two minds about being rescued from wrongdoing in his famous phrase, "God, make me pure, but not yet."

"There's a war between spirit and flesh," Al says. "When you see an attractive woman walking down a street, you have to ask for the power to resist."

That dilemma was the stuff of life and faith, and Al vowed he was in it for the long haul. He had a good deal in common with rambunctious souls like Augustine, who cling to faith even as their human appetites bid for their attention. It is, in its own way, a sign of life and of a healthy connection with the real world. In short, he is in good company.

*   *   *

For ordained clergy, of course, the Bible is generally considered standard equipment, but some are much more intimately involved with it than others are. Since ministry traces its origins to Scripture, it stands to reason that it would be a top priority in seminary training. While that remains the case, theological schools differ widely in the amount of Scripture study they require. Nearly all of them do more remedial education these days as students arrive with less biblical knowledge than in years past. Almost anyone contemplating becoming a pastor, however, is still expected to learn the inscrutable art of spinning a passage of Holy Writ into a sermon or homily that stirs the people.

Preaching is unlike any other kind of message. It can contain elements of a sales pitch, a lecture, a standup routine, poetry, drill instruction, bluster, and motivational speaking. But at its best it is equivalent to none of those things. A great sermonizer, such as Martin Luther King Jr. or Rev. James Forbes, formerly of New York's Riverside Church, can touch the sky, rattle the timbers, evoke tears, and rekindle hearts. To its hearers, a godly voice augments the preacher's own to provide the key ingredient that separates sermons that upend and transform souls from the many pedantic or mundane ones that fall short. That is not to say that the clergy can depend on a sudden infusion of holy inspiration to make up for a lack of preparation. Creating a sermon worthy of its name typically requires much time and effort, prayer and study. The touchstone for building it has always been the Bible, the opportunity during worship to convey how the lessons from Scripture apply to the contemporary age. A few decades ago, many liberal Protestants, in particular, believed that the sermon was outmoded and ineffective in an age when big media presentations delivered vastly more color, variety, and punch. Those factors had influence, to be sure, but nothing has replaced the extraordinary power of one preacher to open the minds and spirits of a live congregation. It is dazzlingly ineffable.

Good preachers have typically in the past bonded with the Bible early in life: it became a companion to which they owed allegiance and an ongoing relationship. The call to ordination was usually a byproduct of this interaction. For Protestants, to whom the Bible is central, that has been more common than among Catholics, who placed far less emphasis on it. For evangelical Protestants, the tie is even stronger than it is among preachers in mainline churches. But it has been an indispensable source, to one degree or other, for everyone who stands behind a pulpit to preach. Presumably, the lessening of familiarity with Scripture is now changing the shape and content of much current sermonizing.

I have been privileged to hear many splendid preachers who have kept the Bible as close as their next breath. Two come to mind as examples. One of them maintains an exceptionally high level of preaching week after week; the other delivered what was, to me, an extraordinary Easter sermon.

Rev. Roland Hammett is the senior pastor at Lehigh Valley Baptist Church in Pennsylvania, having taken over the pulpit from his father. He is youthful, dynamic, and thoroughly steeped in a very conservative evangelical principle: "The Bible is written by God" and should not be tampered with is his starting place. Rev. Hammett is tall, handsome, and lean, with short-cropped black hair and beard, and he is accustomed to wearing mostly earth-toned suits and print ties. Every Sunday he preaches for a half hour, and his sermons are timed to be carried on local television. His theme is always interesting, conventional rather than adventuresome or profound, but the product of a fine mind with serious intent.

His entire approach contributes to a smooth, unlabored delivery that he parcels out in remarkable cadences and variations of tone, marked by lifting his black leather pulpit Bible in the air and swooping down to the cross-shaped pulpit to glean a passage or two. Hammett unpacks portions of Scripture in flourishes of, alternately, storytelling or straight-ahead biblical instruction, as he paces back and forth on the rostrum, fixing his gaze on sections of worshipers. He is an evangelist who pitches conversion at full throttle — forgiveness and salvation, rescue from damnation — but whose manner is invariably kind and accepting. He just wants you to know he stands for biblical perfection, but he is not there to play judge or to condemn those whose interpretation of Scripture is worlds apart from his own. Nowhere does self-righteousness appear in his speech or behavior. In fact, he often tells stories that make fun of himself and gently remind his congregants that, since all go astray, they need to practice constant vigilance on themselves. The tyranny of television timing appears to be the only thing to restrain him. Because of that pressure, it seems as though his pacing is faster than it might otherwise be, and there is no room for such spontaneous diversions as humor. It may also have resulted — as it does for most, if not all, television preachers — in a posture of detachment. Without the television factor, the preacher speaks directly to the congregation for the sake of strengthening that real, live community; on the other hand, the television sermon becomes more oriented to an abstract audience. The intimate connection between preacher and the people he baptizes, counsels, buries, and sees regularly as pastor and friend gives way to unknown viewers. Under those conditions, Rev. Hammett comes across a good deal less personal than he is by nature, not free to quip or refer in certain ways to himself or add an impromptu aside about an issue that parishioners are familiar with as insiders.

Evangelical preachers' custom of calling the "unsaved" to conversion toward the close of every sermon (the so-called altar call) risks becoming numbing repetition. Never in my hearing has Hammett let that happen. His main message flows in and out of that appeal so easily and effectively that it never ends in a routine "commercial." He teaches the Bible from his own learning, which allows anyone to learn something and to be impressed by the degree of his discernment.

*   *   *

Rev. Patricia Coughlin also preaches out of devotion to Scripture and an abundance of gifts — but from a different window on the Bible than Hammett's. Her studies at Harvard Divinity School have deepened her commitment to the historical-critical approach, abetted by the teaching of Krister Stendahl, a world-renowned New Testament scholar. When it comes to preaching, she has retained a favorite Stendahl maxim: "He would say that we are responsible for what they hear," she says, referring to the duty of the clergy to be careful what they say and how they say it.

When I spoke with her, Pastor Coughlin was on the verge of retiring as pastor of United Church in Brookline, Massachusetts. It has been a long, fruitful tenure for herself and for the venerable old church swathed in wooden planks and beams in the heart of Boston. She was raised Catholic, and she spent several years as a Little Sister of the Assumption before getting married and being drawn to ordination as a Protestant. She was celebrating her last Easter with her beloved congregants — a lively mix of backgrounds, ethnicities, and occupations.

In the days before Easter, the makings of that last sermon had marinated within her in the usual fashion. She first fastened on the passage from Scripture that would serve as its matrix, Mark 16:1-8, which tells of Jesus's resurrection. She contemplated it, waiting for something to "jump out" of the text — "something that would surprise me" after reading it again and again. When that happened, she let it rest on her mind and heart before reading "tons" of material written about that passage by scholars, who put it into context. Then it was time simply to "sit with it," letting it speak to her as it would. At one point, she felt "overwhelmed" by the complexity and walked the dog to clear her head. Toward the end of the week, she says, she had moved from sitting with the verses to "living into them" as a sermon that she could feel good about took shape. "Somewhere along the line it assumes a structure," she says, "and I work a lot on transitions."

The culmination of that process was a marvel of applied scholarship and Christian challenge, a seamless melding of revised history and gospel force. Mark's account of Jesus's empty tomb is the oldest and shortest among the four versions in the Gospels, she said on Easter Sunday, pointing out how Matthew, Luke, and John variously include or exclude elements of the story, making each distinct. In Mark, the risen Christ never appears, and "there is no theological elaboration of the meaning of the empty tomb," just a stone rolled away from the tomb, a mysterious young man, news that Jesus has gone to Galilee, and the three women who have found the tomb empty — "so full of fear and terror that they cannot speak." Whereupon, the story suddenly ends. Drawing on sound research, Rev. Coughlin notes that a longer ending had been added later to that passage in Mark, but it didn't belong to the original. The original "stops" right there. "Surely something was meant to follow, but we don't know what."

What had jumped out at Pastor Coughlin early in the week, based on her fidelity to the Word and responsibility to sound scholarship, was that Mark's Gospel has left the story portentously open-ended:

> Friends, this story stops where you and I live. It needs us to write the ending. It needs you and it needs me to do what at that moment those women could not do — to witness in word and action to the risen Christ, who has gone on ahead of us, who is not bound to the past, but is still leading us into a future where our world is transformed and made whole.

CHAPTER 13

Song and Dance

C hristianity's mandate to spread the Word has over the centuries inevitably blurred the line between worship and theater. Preaching and
performance art depend on similar talents and mannerisms, and the result
to which they incline has fluctuated between two extremes: the primacy of
the message or the primacy of the actors.

Concentrating on the message dwells on ideas and beliefs, while centering on the actors highlights the allure of personalities; but the culture insists that both of them speak America's language — entertainment. Whatever the seriousness of the subject, getting it across successfully means
delivering it with at least a modicum of panache and special effects that
keep viewers and listeners coming back. We Americans have developed
an insatiable desire to be made happy by what we seek out to hear and
see. More than a century ago, the Chautauqua education-and-enjoyment
circuit foreshadowed this trend. Among the "dry" lecturers and didactic
preachers, an abundance of music performances, stage shows, and artists
leavened the starchy loaf. The fun side has escalated incalculably across
society since then. By now, nearly all the thinkers have to be dipped in
entertainment sauces. With all due respect to *Mary Poppins*, it takes a lot
more than a spoonful of sugar to make the medicine go down these days.
Some church services are indistinguishable from television awards shows.

Bible stories continue to excite the human imagination to all kinds of
emerging ends. The most absorbing, provocative example I came across
was an animated film featuring phastasmic woodcuts and multimedia
hybrids galore that took the Garden of Eden story as a vaguely familiar
launching pad. The *Jackleg Testament Part I: Jack and Eve* was produced
over a five-year stretch by Cincinnati artist, writer, composer, and histor-

188

ical-literary browser Jay Bolotin and was being shown at Smith College's art museum. Billed as a "postmodern" tale, it was a mélange of biblical and non-biblical elements that glimpsed Genesis even as it took off in unrelated directions.

Both the Hebrew Bible and the New Testament are inherently dramatic, of course, and lend themselves to thespian flair. David plays his lyre and sings of Israel's history, and public recitations of Scripture go back to the earliest years of the church. Hymns and liturgical music integrated art and the gospel from the beginning, advancing from Gregorian chant to Bach's masses to *Jesus Christ Superstar* and Christian rock and pop. Medieval cathedrals staged "miracle" and "mystery" plays to recall the momentous biblical tales, including the birth of Christ. The emergence of printed books made creative adaptations of those stories, such as John Bunyan's *A Pilgrim's Progress,* widely obtainable. Jumping to the threshold of the twentieth century, film became a new medium, the first example showing *Oberammergau,* the annual enactment of Christ's passion in Germany. A stream of Bible movies has followed.

Technology saturates North America with the Bible as never before at the very time that interest in it has sharply dwindled. It is a striking coincidence, though by itself it hardly proves that greater interconnectivity has anything directly to do with biblical illiteracy. However, there is the matter of fiercer competition for our eyeballs. The Internet and video industry flood Americans with programming and reading options that relegate religion in general to the margins. Distractions are everywhere, attention spans have shrunk, and the mass audience is more segmented into special interests than ever before. On the other hand, who's to say that the Bible's decline wouldn't have been worse if it weren't a click away on electronic media?

*   *   *

As I have noted above, Bible promoters, sometimes reflecting a justifiable wariness toward the latest thing, are often slow to see electronics as friendly to their cause. But as the crisis of Bible ignorance deepens, they have rushed to find whatever potential there might be for using these rapidly spreading means to win the public back to Scripture, even though there are no solid proofs that such strategies succeed.

At Billy Graham crusades, seekers responded in droves to his call to conversion by streaming down the aisles to pray at the altar and receive blessings and guidance, all televised to the wider world. But if those watching from their living rooms undergo life-changing salvation at the same time, that phenomenon attracts no attention. Do gospel stage productions, movies, iPad music, or spiritualized fiction bring their patrons to a closer walk with Scripture and/or a born-again transformation? Mel Gibson's flash-point movie *The Passion of the Christ* reached a huge audience and in doing so ignited Hollywood curiosity about the rewards of reviving the long-obscured genre of Bible movies. But has Gibson's divisive, bloody, gruesome story of Jesus's last days actually brought new and committed readers to the Bible? What lasting religious effects, if any, result from any arts and entertainment wrapped in Scripture? Nobody really knows. In terms of Marshall McLuhan's aphorism that "the medium is the message," perhaps the electronic media's message is that it is missing an elusive element of depth and persuasion that is available to those who experience it at the source.

The combined power of new media, starting with radio and film, complicated Christianity by paving the way for impressions of Jesus that became alternatives to more conventional interpretations. Jesus's nature and character have always been debated, and distinct portraits have emerged in varying sectors of the church, often fashioned to fit regional or doctrinal preferences. The image of the ethereal Christ in Eastern Orthodoxy differs markedly from the more this-worldly portraits, for example, among many Western Protestants. Theological debates over Jesus's essence have never ended since church authorities in the early centuries arrived at the definition that he was both fully God and fully human, a conclusion whose meaning and substance have been questioned ever since. Until the modern age opened the discussion to anyone with access to the latest gadgets and mass distribution, however, the debates and visual imagery were mostly confined to a limited range of debaters. Suddenly it invites anyone with even passing interest in Christian tradition to join.

When Jesus becomes subject to a greater range of interpretations, it makes viewing and imagination richer, but it also detaches him further from the Jesus of the Bible and the lived experience of Christianity. The Jesus of new media sometimes resembles the New Testament Lord and sometimes does not. The point is that the exercise of interpreting him has become an enterprise quite distant from the Bible's own terrain. While there is nothing surprising or prohibited about communicators shaping Jesus to fit their religious or political views, the greater openness and independence that come with the technology accelerate the process of creating alternative Jesuses — with no formal accountability to biblical history. Some of the producers, like Gibson, are devoted to the faith; others, like Denys Arcand, who wrote and produced *Jesus of Montreal* (1989), are acclaimed filmmakers with no religious preference (Arcand is described as a "lapsed Catholic"). Of course, one's views on religion don't predict quality or fidelity to the Bible. Gibson the believer scandalizes the Gospels in an effort to re-create the real surroundings, while Arcand the dropout captures the turning-the-tables Jesus of the New Testament with stunning authenticity as a vagabond in modern Montreal. Since viewers are less apt to know how the content of such films compares to corresponding Bible texts, however, filmmakers can and do take liberties that sometimes portray Jesus with abandon. Best-selling books have taken the trend further in that direction, *A Portrait of Jesus,* by the late Joseph Girzone, being a spectacular example. It has blended pieces of Scripture and the Christian past with a totally fanciful plot that is full of empty claims. But to a wide readership unschooled in the Bible, authenticity doesn't much matter: fabrications are often accepted on a par with Scripture or as a substitute for it. In a similar way, a recent succession of authors have chased their own half-baked theories (the popular *Left Behind* series comes to mind), which are assumed to be credible by many readers whose lack of biblical knowledge keeps them from noting troubling omissions, invented additions, and stubborn contradictions.

Drawing a distinction between flights of fancy and creative leaps that plausibly stretch conventional categories (in the portrayals of Jesus, for example) can be hard to determine. Can the rock star Jesus in *Jesus Christ Superstar* fit within a broader picture of Jesus, or not? Is the Jesus of the television series *The Bible* a fair depiction and an earnest attempt to stay true to the Word? News media bring endless possibilities for enhancing the Bible's story or fostering a cottage industry of renderings that spring largely from secular sources.

As worried Bible promoters met in Orlando to mobilize in response to growing biblical ignorance, filmmakers, dramatists, and communicators stepped up efforts to feed what appeared to be growing receptivity to art and entertainment related to Scripture. It made elemental sense that a populace that has lost touch with something so culturally significant would reach a turning point — a point where the Bible again became a subject of curiosity. The "trend" is mostly intuitive rather than hard fact, but the astonishing appeal of *The Passion of the Christ* raised hopes in film and television circles that audiences want more (two years after its 2003 release, it had earned more than $600 million). A qualifying factor suggests that something else is going on. Across the evangelical landscape there was a huge push to piggyback on the Gibson bonanza. Its success intensifies optimism that Bible films will regain a footing in Hollywood and, perhaps more significantly, that evangelicals could use inspirational films to shore up their own ranks at a time when they, too, are experiencing losses.

Gibson's screen revival of the Bible after a long absence caught the attention of a cadre of Christian filmmakers who had long accused mainstream Hollywood of shunning faith-based movies. To those who denounced the industry as a den of iniquity and a servant of the devil, the Gibson phenomenon was a rebuke to the industry and a signal that they were missing a lucrative bet by ignoring such films. It was a booster shot of encouragement to their religious film colleagues.

*   *   *

At the conservative end of that spectrum is *Movieguide,* a self-styled guardian of Christian standards founded by a confrontational minister and former lawyer named Ted Baehr. *Movieguide* has, since 1985, assigned itself the task of judging movies according to biblical content and morality — as Baehr and his editors define them. Its three main outlets — a magazine and review segments on radio and television — have become the cutting-edge voice of the Christian Right, operating in Los Angeles and keeping close tabs on the movie business. Baehr himself has not hesitated to bash the big boys as morally polluted; he has gained notice if only because no other religious group has been on such a crusade. He proclaims that his enterprise is aimed at pressuring Hollywood to turn away from perversity in favor of faith-friendly, family-healthy movies. Gibson has contributed some of his earnings to the cause.

Critics accuse Baehr of narrow-minded morality and intolerance. Among other public floggings, he has condemned Charles Darwin as a "racist bigot" (based on a movie about the evolutionary scientist). But Baehr, who formerly ran the radio/television arm of the Episcopal Church, has found a following and claims to be winning the David-Goliath battle (as he has characterized it in *Movieguide*). Thanks largely to his lobby's dedication to "redeeming the values of the movie industry, according to biblical principles," he writes, the percentage of films that his staff rated good for families has zoomed from a scant 6 percent in 1985, when *Movieguide* was founded, to 45 percent in 2008. That claim is essentially based on Baehr's personal opinions about what is or is not acceptable; unsurprisingly, his verdicts have sparked disagreements. They can be unpredictable and, to his critics, inconsistent. He warned his followers against the blockbuster movie *The Hunger Games* (2012) on grounds that it was "corrupting young children with death, humanism, and evil"; but he gave thumbs up to its sequel, *Catching Fire* (2013), for promoting a "strong moral worldview."

Criticism aside, Baehr's organization has stuck around as a pesky reminder that there is a formidable population of Christian conservatives out there who can be courted for economic gain or can be alienated by movies that they, perhaps swayed by *Movieguide*, might boycott. *Movieguide*'s influence is hard to measure, but it has at least become a professional, polished voice for a segment of Christianity that has some clout.

That subculture, as I have noted above, is a central feature of a parallel universe of evangelical lifestyle and institutional alternatives to dominant features of the nation's mainstream. Conservative Christians, like self-defined outsiders everywhere, have their own music, vacation spots, counseling services, schools, and bookstores that offer a full range of religious and everyday accessories (toys, games, digital devices, etc.) along with a plethora of published works on faith-based approaches to everything from creation to weight-watching, aimed at those who are consciously establishing a "Christian home." Steadily adding to that inventory are films with explicitly Christian themes from companies specializing in that niche. Small studios are producing DVD movies for an expanding market of Christians looking for entertainment that reflects their convictions. Faith-based filmmakers hold their own festivals and awards shows modeled after major secular attractions like Sundance and the Oscars.

Movieguide's Faith and Values Award Gala hands out hundreds of thousands of dollars for "spiritually uplifting screenplays," religiously oriented films, and Hollywood movies that meet its standards. At its 2014 ceremonies at the Universal Hilton in Los Angeles, Baehr boasted that "for the first time ever, ninety-six percent of the top movies in the U.S. were *Movieguide* award-winners, from *Iron Man* and *Despicable Me 2* to *Frozen*, *Gravity*, and *Man of Steel*." Moreover, by his calculations, commercial films with "strong Christian redemptive worldviews" made four times as many millions as those that didn't: $87.07 million to $21.64 million. Lagging way behind were those with "humanist/atheist worldviews" that, according to Baehr, scored a measly $3.66 million. The implication is that *Movieguide* is doing something right, unprovable as that is. On the other side of the ledger, however, Internet pornography is also spreading like wildfire.

*   *   *

Naturally, some producers hope to traverse the line between overtly religious and marginally religious Hollywood productions. If a script is heavy-handedly Christian, obviously plotted as a barely concealed attempt to convert viewers, it has little chance of crossing over to a general audience. The question is whether creative freedom can successfully pair with even vaguely evangelistic purposes. Freedom implies that all avenues are open; evangelism, at its heart, insists that everything depends on steering the viewer in the single right decision. Can a film with direct religious ends appeal on its merits as a film? Can a film be good enough on its own that skeptics and doubters will give it a chance?

John David Ware is trying his hand at it. In 2003, inspired by Gibson's success, he founded the 168 Film Project with a statement of purpose aimed at producing films that "uplift and inform the human condition, showing real consequences for actions and reflecting traditional, conservative Biblical values." Ware's devotion to promoting the gospel has led him in another direction that isn't typical of conservatives. He welcomes entrants who have no religion and approves secular content as a means of keeping subjects real. He prefers the organic weaving of the Bible into a story over any kind of hard sell, he says, and is content to let those biblical messages work their own magic in the custody of the nonreligious as well as the religious. "I'm not proselytizing," he says as if he were in the midst of such unbelievers, "but here it is."

Ware has the courage and determination to back up his pipe dreams. A wavy-haired dynamo with a lean frame and quick reflexes, he has recently turned forty and wears a genial, puckish expression that has won him friends and gained him entry to sources of financial and professional support that have allowed him to survive the perilous movie climate. Taut as a banjo string, he dashes, whippet-like, from one brushfire to another. But his hyperactivity at work does not come with a short or snappish attention span in personal conversation. He can simmer down to calmness and attentiveness, receptive to a variety of ideas and beliefs, responding with notable intelligence and insight. Except for his physical build, he is in no way narrow.

Ware's origins helped condition an open mind. Raised in Ohio by parents who taught school, Ware studied film at Miami University of Ohio, graduating in 1995. The Hollywood itch led him to Los Angeles, where he did movie production work. He says that, religiously, he was nowhere until a busload of missionaries returning from Mexico stopped to help him after he had been rear-ended on the highway. The missionaries were from a church close to his Ohio home; one thing led to another, and he reentered the sanctuary of salvation. Out of that rebirth has emerged the 168 Film Project.

The Project's reputation for testing that middle ground has set it apart in its field, helping to keep "breakthrough" hopes alive. Ware vowed at the start that the Project would be "an incubator for writers and filmmakers to explore Scripture and practice their craft," and there is general agreement that he has lived up to it. With rare exceptions, competitors heed Ware's plea to avoid scripts that are stereotypically biblical. But it took a while for his caution against using any plot material to mold into "preachy" sermonettes to be heeded. As recently as 2011, the twenty entries that made the final cut were grim moral object lessons. Plots fell into the familiar formula: the protagonist has sinned mightily but has found redemption; the leading subjects are nearly all male, and their sins are confined largely to sexual sins and dishonesty. One had chosen "evil" rock music over Christian rock; another has heeded satanic forces; yet another represents a more subtle variety by showing a man's love for a woman who, he has discovered, is blind.

The ten-minute format imposes a straitjacket that tempts filmmakers to fall prey to such weaknesses. By the time the movie's premise is set up and roles are introduced, there isn't much opportunity to expand character or elaborate verbal complexities. The urgency to move on to resolution leaves virtually no room for symbolic asides, nuance, or humor. Pretty much every minute is directly tied to the end result. It is mostly straightforward action that lends itself to didactic, or "preachy," endings. But some submissions do better than others in making art out of the stringent limits of the 168 Film Project. At best, they rise to a higher level than seems possible under the demanding conditions. At worst, they collapse into themselves as turgid morality plays. Under stress, it seems that the reflex action is to resort to simplistic religion.

In its spare, cluttered offices on the second floor of a former industrial building in Glendale, California, on a spring evening in 2013, Ware and his small, avid staff scurry about finishing details before being inundated by contestants. The most intense, meaningful year of 168's life — when the "stones" would be handed out — was about to begin.

Other film contests put limits on how much time entrants can take to complete their films; Ware chose the exact measure of a week — 168 hours from start to finish. The competitors have to incorporate the meaning of a Bible verse, as they interpret it, into a film that doesn't exceed ten minutes — by even a second. At the end of the film, the verse assigned to the filmmaker is shown, and judges evaluate if it has been reflected in the film-maker's work. Content can and does include profane topics, but the rules strictly outlaw graphic sex and violence, foul language, drug use, "overly revealing wardrobe," and material that is "blasphemous or disrespectful."

The contest routine begins with the ritual of handing out randomly chosen verses to contestants on a designated evening in May in a Glendale church. The verses have been kept secret and have been picked because the staff feels they relate to the overall theme, which is "atonement" this year. The contestants have a couple of days to ponder their verses before the scramble to write, direct, act, and edit the film begins. Actors have to be recruited, settings decided on, read-throughs and rehearsals scheduled, disputes settled, scripts revised or scrapped, film crews and equipment found, and, yes, money put up to produce it if none had yet been secured — all within a week. Ware estimates the bottom-line cost to be about $2,000, but depending on the scope and ambition the total could reach $15,000 or higher. Ware and his associates will screen every entry and pass them on to a panel of judges, mostly from the movie business, to choose the win-ners. The winners will be honored at the annual 168 Film Project festival in August.

Hours before the verse handout, Ware is slithering through Los An-geles traffic in his fourteen-year-old Jaguar, a thing of vintage beauty, on his way to pick up the poster for this year's contest. It is a bird's-eye view of the San Francisco Bay Bridge, tinted in blue, symbolizing a "crossing over" such as occurs when sinners find their way to the forgiveness and grace of atonement. The printer is late, and Ware asks his staff to join him to pray that the job will be done before time runs out. He screeches to a halt at the door, leaves the motor of the Jaguar running, and darts inside, reappearing minutes later gleefully hoisting the poster aloft.

Before leaving for the church, Ware leads the staff in prayer, beseech-ing God to protect the filmmakers from fear of failure and financial ruin. Arriving at the scene, he puts on a dressier dark shirt and pulls on his black cowboy boots to greet incoming contestants and enact the role of impre-sario. Like a procession of pilgrims waiting their turn to be blessed, they circle halfway around the church, starting from the front, near the central platform, and curl up the side aisle and along the rear pew to the entryway. By type and style, they run a wide gamut. Veteran filmmakers are cheek-by-jowl with relative newcomers; teams of three or four mingle with solo artists and couples; parents inch forward with children; blacks, whites,

Latinos, and Asians are in ample supply. Graybeards are interspersed with fresh-faced students.

It is a Fellini-like scene, a "for-real" costume party. Toward the front is a tall woman with long blond hair, wearing a broad-brimmed black hat and a black-and-gold jacket with crosses affixed to it. Nearby a solitary man with a goatee sports a green shirt bearing the words "How Ya Doin' Productions." An African American woman stands proud in Sunday church fashion in a crisp designer blouse and black pants, not far behind a sinewy man with a salt-and-pepper beard and a black-and-silver head wrap.

A sensational hike in prize offerings has made competition even tougher this year. In previous years the top award was about $12,000 — respectful recognition but hardly life-changing. This year, thanks to a special promotion, that potential reward has catapulted to as much as $1 million. Unsurprisingly, the lure of that kind of money has doubled every previous year's entries: there were a total of 152 completed films. EcoLight, a major producer of faith films located in Dallas, had put up the money in search of a ten-minute acorn from which a full-grown movie oak might grow. EcoLight had to agree that the top-rated 168 Project film, to win the full amount, was potentially worth the resources and funds necessary to turn it into a feature-length film, that is, that it was likely to be strong enough pull at the box office to recoup company investments.

As of late, EcoLight was buzzing with new energy, resolved to raise its output of quality Christian films to combat what it saw as Hollywood's moral depravity. To that end, the company raised its profile by naming former US Senator Rick Santorum as its CEO in June and raising $20 million in new capital. For Santorum, a warrior of the Christian Right, it was a platform from which he could enhance his standing among evangelicals by leading an attention-getting charge against purported immorality that would coincidentally help keep his political aspirations alive. In a show of command and new direction, Santorum fired the two principal founders of EcoLight for being at odds with his vision and inaugurated his mission with his dukes up. The devil had, "for a long, long time," dominated "[movie] screens for his playground," Santorum declared in an appearance on the Trinity Broadcasting Network (*Guardian,* October 25, 2013). "And he isn't going to give up easily." Hollywood was "the devil's playground," he told Kevin McDermott of the *St. Louis Dispatch.* Too many self-consciously Christian films were "hokey" and "cheesy," he added, promising to "produce movies that rival any good Hollywood films," free of Hollywood iniquity. He had played a big role in raising the $20 million to fuel that cause.

Dallas, he boasted, could become the "new Hollywood of the faith-and-family movie market."

About a third of the competitors, mostly from Southern California, made it to the kickoff event; the others received their passages from Scripture over the Internet. Those in Burbank came forward to receive a flat stone on which the biblical verse was inscribed. The stones came from Home Depot and Wal-Mart, as well as the beach. Volunteers had painstakingly inscribed the passages from the Hebrew Bible and the New Testament. The staff had found verses relevant to the atonement theme in sections written centuries apart in a stupendous diversity of settings: from Exodus, Job, and Ezekiel to Matthew, Romans, and Revelation. These minuscule capsules contained guiding directions; their obscurity and wording often needed decoding to make sense. At any rate, these were the messages from afar whose meaning competitors were expected implicitly to unfold in a ten-minute film. On the following Thursday morning they went into action; at the deadline, a week later, nearly all turned in a finished product.

The winning entry, *ReMoved,* is a visual tone poem about a young girl caught in the undertow of parental divorce and foster homes, a film created by Nathanael and Christina Matanick of Carpinteria, California. The film begins with domestic chaos — parents yelling and physically fighting — leading the police to drag away the girl's father and protective services to whisk away the girl and her baby brother, eventually getting them to foster care (though the exact reason for this isn't clear: the father's violence obviously renders him unfit to have custody, but the mother is depicted only as a victim). Angry and confused, the displaced girl rebels at attempts to place her successfully, until an unusually resilient and compassionate woman wins her trust, and adjustment seems possible. The subject matter is evangelical boilerplate: marital relations and their effects on children. The mood is somber as the sad-faced girl narrates her story in voice-over fashion while the scenes unfold. Her duress is real; her script is not. The sentiments and language sound more like those of a mature woman looking back with the benefit of insights uncovered in therapy. The film ends on a note of optimism when the girl, looking from an upstairs room, sees her toddler brother being unloaded from a van and brought into the house, where it's assumed he'll stay. Gleeful at that prospect, she whispers "hope."

The film ends there, and the credits roll, followed by a "168 Film Project" acknowledgment. The screen fades to black, and a few seconds later the words from the verse from Hebrews 12:2 that was on their stone appears: ". . . who for the joy that was set before him, endured the cross, despising the shame, and is set down at the right hand of the throne of God" (KJV).

The display of Scripture in the very last frame fulfills the contest's key requirement: the verses given to filmmakers on "verse assignment night" in Burbank become the film's tag line and chief clue to its meaning. How well had the Matanicks ferreted out the meaning of their verse and built their film around it, either directly or subtly? Perhaps the girl's glimmer of hope after suffering was intended to mirror Jesus's glory after his agony on the cross: suffering as redemptive. If the 168 Film Project's aim is to raise biblical consciousness, has this short film done so, or is the attempt either too subtle or too indirect to allow (particularly) secular viewers to make that connection on their own? Tacking on the Bible verse at the very end might tie everything together for some, but it might seem extraneous to most. Ware is willing to take that chance for the sake of commending the Bible. In the contest's early years, entrants were required to post their Scripture verses at the very beginning of the film; but it was switched to the end of the film when filmmakers complained. Some thought the up-front option seemed too preachy or risked giving away too much of the story. But the other possibility was that the filmmakers felt uncomfortable sidling up too closely to the Bible publicly, lest it become a source of embarrassment, a sentiment increasingly evident within the wider society. For whatever reasons, artistic or religious, the Matanicks placed it at the very end.

At the August awards gala, the Matanicks and their film were duly celebrated; but the next step in landing the total $1 million production money didn't go well. *ReMoved* failed to convince EcoLight's executives that it had the right stuff to be expanded into a full-length feature (not high enough box office appeal to recoup production costs), and thus it was denied the biggest cash prize. However, it became a highly sought-after YouTube selection, and the undaunted Matanicks are planning a sequel.

Ware and others are receptive to films that are either clearly biblical or reflect the Bible's themes by inference or stretch of imagination. Films that soft-pedal explicit Bible material often err by expecting viewers to recognize indirect allusions to Scripture or allegorical interpretations of it. They might be on the "spiritual" side of the now-popular divide between "spiritual" and "religious" sensibilities; but for those most intent on improving biblical literacy (or conversions to Christianity), such films miss the mark. Few viewers have sufficient knowledge of the Bible to grasp symbolic or extrapolated references to it. Results might be only marginally better than prompting competition with pieces of Polynesian mythology.

Making that connection with viewers seems similarly remote. Likewise, using straightforward Bible stories as subject matter risks playing into a widespread aversion to stick-figure moralism and pious stereotypes.

*   *   *

The crux of the matter is whether movies sway viewers' beliefs and practices to any degree at all. Cinema is, of course, principally a festival of emotions and experiences rather than reason and logic. That makes it more likely to have an impact at the deepest personal levels; but the long-term impact of effects is largely unknown. There is also a profound difference between being in a live setting surrounded by believers and tactile persuaders and watching a movie essentially alone with none of those communal motivators.

At best, it is hit or miss, according to scholars. One of the foremost, Melanie Wright of Cambridge University, cautions in her book *Religion and Film: An Introduction* that "we cannot assume that the meanings viewers take from what they see in the cinema are encoded in the film's textual organization"; she dismisses the distinction between "popular" and "art" films that had such goals. Another scholar, Margaret Miles, former dean of the Graduate Theological Union in Berkeley, California, compares the influence of movies to the tragic drama of the ancient Greeks, which she details in her book *Seeing and Believing: Values and Religion in Movies.* In Greek tragedies, the players and audience together exercise self-examination, she concludes, whereas movies are entertainments that stimulate passing sensations rather than mutual introspection or rational thought. Paraphrasing further, it strikes Miles that tragedy is presupposed to bring about change, but entertainment is something to be consumed — like a tasty snack.

A Barna poll confirms modest expectations. Nationally, it found that just 1 percent of Americans claimed that they had seen a movie that had changed their beliefs over the past year; a slice more, 11 percent, said they'd been led to think "more seriously about religion, spirituality and faith over the same year." The survey report offered a sobering assessment:

> Much has been made about how Hollywood influences the values and spirituality of Americans. And movies do affect how people think about faith and spirituality, but in smaller numbers than religious leaders might expect. . . . At the very least, people don't think Hollywood is influencing their values and beliefs.

It matters which values are being targeted. As we have discussed in previous chapters, Americans are increasingly of two minds. One constitutes the private beliefs and values they hold from their upbringing and religious experience; they represent a set of sentiments and ideals that occupy a special place in their minds. But these don't easily transfer to the outer life of daily routines, work, and play. Those are the province of pragmatic values that allow them to get by in the world. It isn't clear which set of values and beliefs the moviegoers were referring to in responding to the polls.

Christian-faith films have shown no ability to do otherwise, though the studies of changes in belief or behavior were far from adequate to be conclusive. Meanwhile, the urge to find ways to evangelize through the latest visual and digital technology naturally remains powerful.

Mel Gibson's triumph revived optimism that the Bible's own stories could generate massive appeal after a long dry spell between "hits." The contents of *The Passion* took liberties with the biblical text, which dyed-in-the-wool inerrantists tended to overlook in their enthusiasm for the movie; but it was biblical in a generic sense. The variation between the accounts of the Passion Week in the four Gospels and how the movie script depicts them is a shining example of the fragility of texts: how they are susceptible to change as they travel from one interpreter to the next. If Gibson altered the biblical account from which he developed the screenplay, then how much more had Scripture been recast — either on purpose or not — over the centuries during which it took the form that we have inherited? The process of literary editing illustrated by Gibson might have been an object lesson that could have shaken notions of biblical infallibility; but to my knowledge, that criticism never got traction.

Though *The Passion* collected a whopping $370.2 million in box office receipts in its first six months, becoming the second biggest movie of 2003 (behind *Shrek 2*), that huge return alone left unanswered the question whether it had crossed over significantly to the coveted nonreligious audience. Breaking into the secular market is crucial to reaching potential converts. As more Americans have grown more distant from religion, the middle ground — where "undecideds" might be open to evangelistic approaches — is apparently shrinking. As I have observed above, Christians have produced their own line of entertainment choices, but success in the mainstream, on that narrowing middle ground and beyond, remains an elusive goal. The hopes of some church leaders were riding on Gibson.

The Passion immediately became the test case when it was released on Ash Wednesday, 2003. Leading pollsters quickly moved in to test the movie's effects on personal belief in addition to registering opinions around the topics of alleged anti-Semitism and gratuitous violence. Matt Nisbet reviewed the assortment of findings from Pew, Gallup, and Barna in *The Skeptical Inquirer,* a publication of the Center for Inquiry. Early data from Pew and Barna indicated that about 55 percent of the theatergoers were black and white evangelicals, proportionally much higher than are found in the general population (upwards of 40 percent). The percentage might have been higher depending on what portion of the 28 percent of Hispanics (reported by Pew) had been identified by that preference. The consensus was that vigorous promotions by evangelical churches (renting out halls to show the movie, etc.) had been a major factor in delivering the "born-again" believers. Three months after the film opened, nearly a third of the population said they had seen the movie.

For the tremendous push it had from religious groups and the movie's producer, and the millions of people it attracted, the movie had virtually no dramatic effect on viewers' beliefs or commitments, according to the polls. While Gallup's inclination to look on the bright side did report that three-quarters of attendees said the movie had bolstered their faith, disconcerting news came from Barna. Its data said that only one-tenth of 1 percent reported becoming Christians as a result of seeing the movie. Only one-half of 1 percent of moviegoers said the movie had fueled their desire to win others to Christ.

Nisbet's summary was no more encouraging to the general run of those who looked to film to deliver new life. He wrote: "Among adults, the available data show that attitudes and beliefs were not likely to have been created anew by the film, nor did *The Passion* serve as a conversion tool. Rather, the movie likely helped amplify and strengthen preexisting beliefs among evangelical viewers." In other words, its reach basically didn't exceed that of a niche Christian film.

Critics were almost equally divided between those who opined that its artistic merit outweighed its savagery and those who flatly disdained it. The website "Rotten Tomatoes" found that 80 percent of audiences applauded it, perhaps reflecting the enthusiasm of a surfeit of evangelicals. But given the firestorm of criticism aroused by the film, it is also conceivable that some went to see it to cheer and left jeering, or they came to gather evidence to buttress their jeering.

Polling is at best a clumsy measure of a movie's effect on inner thoughts and feelings, however, and quite possibly *The Passion* acted as leaven on the hearts and souls of both believers and nonbelievers in the days and weeks after they'd seen it. The Bible's imprint could take a while, eluding the quick verbal exchanges typical of polls. Life-changing awakenings could lie dormant for years before bursting through to consciousness. Lacking evidence of much incursion into non-niche and secular territory, some Christian filmmakers took reasonable comfort in that gradualist explanation. At the same time, *Movieguide* continued to claim victories in nudging Hollywood toward family-friendly films on the grounds that the "clean" ones in general made more money.

Accusations of antireligious bias against faith films have been hardwired in Christian movie circles, though every so often something like *The Passion* has been cited as an exception. Looking through hundreds of reviews of religiously themed movies, one can see that some critics do appear too prone to negative stereotyping of biblical stories; but the greater tendency is to rate them as lousy films by fair aesthetic standards. Movie reviewers rip bad movies; and, unfortunately, the preponderance of religious movies are bad, often so stilted and amateurish that they play into the hands of ridicule.

Despite the lift Gibson's sensation prophesied, it took another ten years before a Bible film to rival it would appear. That film was *Noah*, which appeared to great fanfare in March 2014, directed by the adventurous Darren Aronofsky and starring Russell Crowe as Noah, a hairy borderline madman. As usual, the moviemaker manipulated the original story from Genesis to suit his fancies, with the assistance of special effects such as giant robots in place of angels and the elimination of the scenes involving Ham's incident with his drunk, celebratory father. The flood, depicted with drenching realism, suffices to symbolize the current threat to the earth's existence, and Crowe's Noah is larger than life as the one chosen to assemble the ark and ride out the storm. It is an action-adventure picture for younger audiences and enough of a morality play to engage oldsters. During its initial run at the box office, it brought in $101.2 million and won favor from 166 of the 216 critics in the "Rotten Tomatoes" rundown.

The rudiments of the short Bible episode were there to mull over (where did Noah find that pair of giraffes?). Unlike most New Testament film scripts that incline toward asking viewers to make up their minds about Jesus as the source of salvation, the Hebrew Bible character portrayed in *Noah* carries no agenda beyond relating the story as a dramatic turn in God's dealings with earthlings (though God never talks in this one). To be sure, viewers might do well to keep in mind that God was irritated enough with human sinfulness to drown the whole business except for Noah and his kinfolk — something that could happen again if the creatures themselves continue to destroy the planet — but it doesn't exactly come down to each person making a choice for or against eternal life. Aronofsky is an apostle for environmentalism, but the Hebrew Bible isn't about evangelism. Neither is he, as he hastens to add: *Noah,* he declares, is "the least biblical biblical [*sic*] film ever made."

Christian niche films continue to proliferate and play their part in efforts to keep the secular tide from sweeping away more of the faithful, an erosion taking place among conservative Christians as well — only to a lesser degree. So much for the axiom that you don't really need to preach to the choir. Take nothing for granted; preach to reinforce their convictions as often as possible, for the choir may be among those who need it most. Faith films are important in-house means of undergirding belief among the believers, similar to the way companies like Apple show their own videos to employees to boost product enthusiasm. Most of the faith films are off the radar of major media (with the exceptions of Christmas and Easter seasons), but religious publicity and television promotions keep them circulating. Despite strenuous efforts, some flop anyway, but the market is reasonably solid and sometimes lucrative.

*   *   *

Television is still the best showcase for stirring up interest. It isn't good at examining ideas, but at its best it packs a visceral punch. It also works for subjects that are familiar and relatively uncomplicated — like many Bible stories. Therefore, an extravagant miniseries that we touched on earlier, which debuted on March 3, 2013, was wisely titled simply *The Bible.* For its host, the History Channel, the ten-part program was a risky venture, given the erosion of apparent interest in the Bible, but the astonishing size of the first night's audience, 13.1 million viewers, calmed jitters. The show topped all cable competitors not only that night but for the year to date. Numbers averaged 11.7 million over the entire series, an impressive mark that alerted television executives to the size and potential of religious watchers.

The series hurtled through centuries of Hebrew Bible and the New Testament lore by eliminating some parts, condensing others, and improvising connecting tissue. It was produced by Mark Burnett, the creator of television hits including *Survivor,* and actress Roma Downey, a faith-based married couple with the dead-on intention of winning America back to the Bible. "One of the things that we've learned making this is that there is massive Biblical illiteracy in this country — like embarrassing," he told *The New Yorker* magazine (March 18, 2013). "I'm not kidding. We've come across people who thought Joan of Arc was Noah's wife, that Sodom and Gomorrah were married."

Evangelical churches vigorously mobilized their people to see the film and, as with other productions of special interest to them, made up a disproportionally large proportion of viewers. Screenings filled church halls, living rooms, and student centers, among other places. It was another dose of tonic and communal solidarity for believers, proof that the story of the faith to which they were so dedicated could land a prime spot in America's viewing habits.

What they saw took a page from the conventional bushy-beard-and-bathrobe depictions of Bible stories. So far as I know, the look and the garb are historically correct, and there's nothing wrong with accuracy in detail; but if these episodes are designed for the Bible illiterates and nonbelievers, it seems disastrous to me. Nothing in memory turns off or amuses the "Bible outsider" crowd like that costuming. One glance at flowing robes and scruffy loincloths sends curiosity seekers to *Jeopardy* and *Showtime* — or almost anything but the Bible movie. Placing the story in that habitual visual package may comfort the "insiders," but it makes the show easily dismissible for much of the rest of the public. One glance at the sheep and donkeys flashes the message: "I know what's coming — it's from another planet and I want no part of it." Whatever exotic charm shepherd regalia might once have had, it now signals boredom and induces deafness. Expecting twenty-first-century seekers to believe that ancient figures spoke truth to them in such remote, disconnected settings seems to be a stretch. It is as if they aren't *supposed* to get it. How could such cliché packaging save new souls?

With a different, more contemporary setting, that obstacle could be removed. Not if the real purpose was to comfort the insiders, of course, but only if talk about lighting fires among the outsiders is actually serious. One example of how Jesus in jeans might speak louder than Jesus in white folds of linen is the critically acclaimed 1989 movie *Jesus of Montreal*. Its reenactment of Bible episodes in present-day Montreal, featuring actors in the throes of twentieth-century life, exposes the power of those scriptural messages rather than smothering them in stereotypical surroundings. This is true for me and apparently for large numbers of people who wouldn't have watched *The Passion* on a dare. *Godspell* and *Jesus Christ Superstar* similarly roused those who would likely have drifted off in the middle of an earlier textbook extravaganza like *King of Kings.* The History Channel's *The Bible* was sincere and serviceable enough for those who were disposed to like it anyway, but it lacked sufficient imagination or pizazz to have much impact outside the revival tent. Despite showing signs of life and being "handsome and expensive-looking," wrote Robert Lloyd in the *Los Angeles Times,* the script was "pedestrian and functional — sometimes it has the flavor of having been made up on the spot." Neil Genzlinger, in *The New York Times,* says that the series didn't "register emotionally"; the "great biblical moments" in it weren't convincingly "great." Other voices either praised its quality or ranked it high on the strength of its exceptional ratings. Among its largely unspoken achievements was that the series etched the origins of Christian faith — at least the Burnett/Downey version of it — in the minds of younger cohorts, who know little about Bible history.

Sections of *The Bible* were excerpted and spliced into a movie called *The Son of Man,* which became a reprise for believers ($26 million box office earnings in its first weeks) but flopped with most critics and the general public. There may be only so much potential in faith films, but the initial bump of that film added heft to the claim that the market is relatively untapped.

*   *   *

As Athenians and Elizabethans well knew, nothing can exceed live theater's power to reshape minds and sensibilities. Those who experienced a first-rate *Godspell* performance stood a good chance of being swept up in a cleansing, transporting wave. Over the centuries, countless lovers of Shakespeare's plays have left theaters with shuffled thoughts and feelings. Though electronics have re-created visual arts, onstage drama still occupies a slice of Bible entertainment in intimate settings. It is carrying on the church's twin dramatic pillars of liturgy and preaching.

For twenty-five years Wayne Turney has been performing the Bible word for word: he recites the entire Gospel of Mark from memory while dashing around makeshift stages to play the role of every character in the Gospel's sixteen chapters in front of audiences across the country. It is exhausting, but it leaves him exhilarated. On one particular late afternoon he hustled down the center aisle of a large Presbyterian church to make his patented grand entrance. His cloak of red, black, blue, and gray stripes rustled as he moved, as did a red robe beneath it. His salt-and-pepper full beard and shoulder-length white hair anchored an angular face with a ruddy complexion, flashing eyes, and an authoritative nose. He sprang onto the altar in full command, his posture fixed, his rich baritone voice set to bring the Word of God to life in a marathon that would run more than ninety minutes, including a brief intermission. Its derring-do was part of the attraction, like the acrobat attempting what audiences considered nearly impossible; and it was, of course, subject to missteps.

Turney, a theater professor, has thrived in a climate that allowed him to lift Mark off the page while teasing out its suspense.

"The beginning of the Gospel of Jesus Christ, the Son of God," he intones with firmness tempered by hope. "As it is written in the prophets, 'Behold, I send my messenger before thy face, which shall prepare thy way before thee.'" And with that prelude in Mark's first chapter, he is off and running.

Mark is believed by most scholars to be the oldest written Gospel. It is shorter, terser, and more prosaic than the others (for one thing, no Christmas story), but it is also action-oriented, unlike the mystical nature of John or the pedagogical nature of Matthew. So much the better for an actor like Turney to sink his teeth into. And he fervently did, recasting himself instantly from evocative narration to the overarching figure of Jesus, to walk-on characters such as the free-spirited Peter, the peevish Pharisees, the patronizing King Herod, the disingenuous Sadducees, coy chief priests and scribes, the wary Pontius Pilate, the pleading Bartimaeus, the opportunistic disciples James and John — and even the outcries of the crowd.

Mark's Gospel is a storyteller's dream, filled with vivid healings of the blind, the deaf, the physically impaired, the demon-possessed, and the dying; miraculous provision of food for thousands of the hungry; the introduction of parables like the one about the mustard seed. Turney climbs into each incident along Jesus's trail, animating and coloring their particular textures. He punctuates scenes by strutting to and fro in the church's chancel, unfurling distinct vocal imprints. He affects Jesus's acute anger at being criticized by religious officials for healing a man's withered hand on the Sabbath. His riposte is scathing: How can Sabbath rules outweigh an act of mercy? In equal measure his Jesus is calm, soothing, and assuring as he speaks to the little girl he has brought back from the edge of death. Turney's snickering tone brings the Sadducees to life as they taunt Jesus for his tolerance of the woman at the well, who had been married seven times. He acts out Jesus's eternally touching welcome of children into his midst with surpassing gentleness. His Pilate resonates with timidity and cowardice, and, as narrator, Turney's recitation of the mustard seed parable makes crystal clear what otherwise might have been hidden.

Turney holds the audience's rapt attention, notwithstanding those who pay their own kind of homage by following his monologue every verse of the way in their Bibles. For the most part, they are transfixed by "seeing" passages that previously they had only read or were read to them. Over the years he had become convinced that hearing the whole Gospel at once ties themes and meanings together in ways that many listeners had never before experienced. He lives for moments when audience members tell him they heard "things they'd never noticed before" in Mark. It matters a great deal to him as a Christian. Before a performance, Turney says, he prays for two hours "to get it right," which in part means to him being a worthy vessel. "What in an actor's training prepares that person to play God?" he muses one day at his office at the university where he teaches theater. To do it right, he thinks, means being true to the parallels between his own human experience and that of Jesus. When the text says that Jesus "looked upon them with anger," Turney says he has no problem identifying with that. "That I can understand," he says. "God has taken on our humanity."

Turney's plunge into this avocation was nudged by a financial problem. Decades ago he and his wife (now an Episcopal priest) belonged to a church in Ohio that had announced big plans to expand its education wing. As active members of the church, they had pledged a goodly amount to the building fund. Days later Turney lost his main source of income; without it, fulfilling the pledge looked impossible. Then Turney hit on an idea. He had once seen the legendary British actor Alec McCowen do a spellbinding rendition of Mark's Gospel at Chattauqua in upstate New York. McCowen had created the piece in the late 1970s, partly on a whim as a non-churchgoer with a love of the King James Bible. To McCowen's surprise, his performances of it were lavishly praised in London, New York, the White House, and elsewhere for several years. Turney wondered if he could revive it as a means of raising the pledge money. He took up the challenge, clearing off his desk and consigning himself to a regimen that the Marine Corps might have saluted: eight solid hours of memorizing passages every day for ten weeks straight ("I'm a fast study," he said). The text is full of oddities; verb tenses suddenly change, stylistic differences crop up where material has been spliced together, the "imported" sixteenth chapter, which had been patched on to the original version, had to be smoothed in. "A Gospel has to have a resurrection," he reasoned in typical good-natured fashion. The intuition panned out for the Turneys and the church. His first performance was so wildly hailed that more were immediately scheduled. The building fund received its pledged contribution from the Turneys, and Wayne had a new mission in life.

Turney masterfully makes his way through every incident, lesson, and miracle — right up to that last chapter (16), which attaches the resurrection. "So then after the Lord had spoken unto them," he says with steadfast assurance, "he was received up into heaven, and sat on the right hand of God. And they went forth, and preached everywhere, the Lord working with them, and confirming the word with signs following. Amen." The sanctuary rings with applause.

$*$ $*$ $*$

Peter Toscano's specialty is making Bible holograms that suggest that there is more to the text than ordinarily meets the eye. He is a smart and serious student of the Bible, with an impish streak, who highlights gender-bending terms and meanings that are ordinarily hidden or at best subliminal. He had spent his early life almost literally bound to a medieval rack, subjected to years of arduous treatment designed to switch him from an innate homosexual to a genuine heterosexual — under the auspices of the Bible-believing church he grew up in. Nothing worked, and he set out to live with his understanding of sexual integrity. Fortunately — for the sake of theater lovers — he is a gifted thespian and comic with the talent for translating his passion for the LBGT cause into a funny, enlightening short course on biblical gender intrigues.

His signature piece in that regard is "Transfigurations — Transgressing Gender in the Bible," a swift procession of stories, from Esther to Acts, in which eunuchs or persons of indeterminate sexuality have played vital roles but haven't generally been recognized for who they really are. His evidence is scholarly, not partisan. It involves removing figures from the psychic invisibility in which they've been regarded, raising them to a dignified status that locates them at the center of Bible societies rather than at the periphery. Word usage sometimes leaves tantalizing ambiguities. What does it mean that the term used for the "coat of many colors" worn by Joseph could be translated "princess dress," used only one other time, a fuzzy attempt to describe a man or woman carrying a water jar on the eve of the Last Supper? Or that the Ethiopian eunuch was a high government official who read the Book of Isaiah and was baptized with great honor into the church? Toscano, a man with a playful demeanor and a luminous face brimming with empathy, approaches the Bible not as a cynic or destroyer but as a committed Quaker who seeks to expand its horizons legitimately by excavating nuances embedded in it.

Toscano staged his creation one night at Haverford College, where he had been spending a semester as a visiting professor. Students, faculty, townspeople, and visitors of many religious and nonreligious persuasions filled Stokes Hall. Toscano had them laughing, crying, and oohing and aahing as his portrayals of Bible scenes unfolded, peppered with his clever, speculative quips and counterintuitive commentary that sparked audience curiosity. Did you know that the Book of Esther, which gave rise to the celebration of the Jewish holiday Purim, features a dozen eunuchs at the heart of the action, at least one in every chapter? And what about Joseph's gender? Just saying, not answering. Though the newly unearthed Gospel of Thomas, a so-called Gnostic text, wasn't officially added between the canonical covers of the Bible, it has received much respect and credibility from many Christians. In it, a case can be made that Mary was transformed into a male. Jesus says that he took Mary and made her so, Toscano explains, perhaps to disguise her identity and thereby protect her from harm. Toscano wasn't posing as the Decider, but he did want them to think about it and draw their own conclusions.

A Bryn Mawr student audibly whispered to her friend that she'd never read the Bible. "Have you?" she asked.

"I've read the New Testament," her friend replied, "not all of the Old." Why did she read it, the first woman asked — for advice, for favorite portions?

"When I was in Lutheran Sunday school we dealt with literal meaning," came the reply. "But now I know it's definitely not historical or cultural in an accurate way. It's mostly allegorical and full of possible meanings. Just like he's saying."

"Maybe it's worth a look," said the other.

CHAPTER 14

The Story of the Greatest Story Ever Told
Awaits a New Chapter

This book emerged within a bubble of reverie. In the small towns where I grew up during and after World War II, the Bible was still a strong enough ghost in the public consciousness to be a watchdog and caretaker even as it became steadily less of a factor in our daily lives. It was like the cloud of relatives whom we didn't see very often but whose presence in a general way guided how we conducted ourselves. Members of the so-called Greatest Generation, just before mine, relied on their understanding of its moral and spiritual coordinates, however unwittingly, and paid at least tacit homage to it, though the connection was attenuating.

In those days the Bible's image appeared in boldface at the center of America's mental map. As my discussion in this book has hoped to demonstrate, while it is still on that map, it appears far less boldly, and the spectrum has widened between subgroups of ardent Biblicists and those who pay it no attention whatever. It has slid to the periphery in muted gray, still there but receding from consciousness.

As I have further noted, paradoxes have surrounded that shift at every turn. Bibles keep piling up in homes and on smart phones and iPads at phenomenal rates, so the desire to own them hasn't notably subsided, but collectively we don't feel much need to read them or consider their prescriptions more binding than those from the multitude of other self-help sources. Americans still want to be friends with the Bible, honor its background, teach things about it, and even put it on a modest pedestal — but they don't want to partner up with it.

But the Bible has still proven irresistible to minds and hearts both within religious traditions and outside of them, who have found within its dazzling array of texts stores of profound guidance and purpose, practical instruction, lessons in metaphor, poetic sublimity, and allusions to our common human past. To the celebrated novelist and essayist Frederick Buechner, an ordained Presbyterian minister, among the Bible's marvels is that it conveys the mystery of human bondedness. In his book *The Clown in the Belfry* he says that the Bible is "a book about you and me whom [God] also made and lost and continually seeks so you might say that what holds us together more than anything else also is us. You might add to that, of course, that of all the books that humanity has produced, it is the one which more than any other — and in more senses than one — also holds us together."

William Vollmann, a stellar writer of novels and arresting nonfiction, does not fit a conventional religious mold but finds riches of insight especially in the Bible's timeless stories. Asked by *The New York Times* for its "By the Book" feature on July 26, 2015, to cite the book he seeks out the most, he named the Bible. He referred to Jesus's parables as "haunting in the fashion of certain Zen koans" and the narrative of patriarch Joseph's struggles as "of gripping psychological interest."

Vollmann recalls telling his young daughter the story of how Joseph's coat of many colors sparks envious rage among his brothers, which leads to their attempt to sell him into captivity. "She would say: 'But why, Daddy? Why did they [his brothers] throw Joseph underground?'" Vollmann said he answered, "Because they were jealous," which prompted another "Why?" from her. He continued: "'Because his father loved him more than the others.' She and I would follow the story backward and forward; its elegance was so perfect that my little child could understand it."

Predicting its future in American culture inevitably largely depends on how younger generations decide to treat it. Signals are mixed. While surveys show sharp drops in the reading of and interest in Scripture among young people, Bobby Gruenewald's YouVersion Bible app lights up their electronic devices in profusion. Within the broad mainstream of Americans of all ages, the Bible now rests on the bookshelf as one among several standard resources and, like Roget's Thesaurus, *The Pill Book,* and Audubon's birds, stands by to answer curiosity seekers' occasional questions on such matters as exactly how Jacob undermined Esau or why Jesus was arrested. On another front, the argument for injecting the Bible into the public schools is making limited headway, spurred mostly by the Bible Literacy Project (BLP).

The BLP was founded by Chuck Stetson in 2001 after the Supreme Court approved teaching the Bible as an academic subject so long as the teaching steered clear of promoting religion and did not use the Bible for any kind of devotional purposes (it was to be "presented objectively or as part of a secular program of education," the Court said). So long as it stuck to its historical, literary, artistic, musical, and cultural contents, it was perfectly acceptable. By 2005, Stetson teamed up with Cullen Schippe to publish a textbook, *The Bible and Its Influence,* a cooperative effort by dozens of scholars from a broad spectrum of faiths. With that remarkable consensus, the Project felt it had the means to overcome resistance from parents and school officials who remained doubtful that "objective" Bible subjects could be taught in their schools.

It is still, however, a tough sell. Though it isn't hard to convince most people that learning basic Bible facts — including key people, events, and writings — gives students an advantage in understanding biblical terms and references they will encounter in historical accounts and English literature, there is still a residue of suspicion that such classes might become exercises in favoring one religion over another. Bible classes, by definition, are electives, and electives have a fragile existence, becoming particularly expendable or unthinkable under tough budget mandates. Furthermore, qualified teachers have to be found who are willing to take on the challenge. They are in short supply. "Sometimes we can provide the text," says Sarah Jenislawski, former executive director of the BLP, "but securing a teacher can be too much." Offering materials from remote Ancient Near Eastern cultures to students unfamiliar with any of it can prove taxing. Plus, Jenislawski says, "as an elective course, when schools are trying to keep the lights on, something has to go."

Biblical literacy does get a boost when and where prominent citizens, school board members, or school administrators take the lead in achieving consensus for such classes. After ten years of promoting the cause, the Project claims to have reached more than 100,000 students at nearly six hundred schools across the country (roughly .02 percent of the 49.8 million public school enrollees in 2014). Eight states passed laws to encourage Bible education — all but one of them in the Deep South — and twenty of the one hundred largest school systems reportedly have provided at least some Bible classes. Most of the electives are attached to English or social studies departments.

Texas vowed to show others how to do it with a 2007 law that allegedly set stricter standards for teaching the subject and approved English courses in Hebrew Scriptures, New Testament, and a combination of the two, and three other topics related to social studies. Fifty-seven of Texas's 1,265 school districts chose to teach one or more. It was a task fraught with potential hazards. In particular, it was difficult to find teachers who could treat the Bible objectively. The problem is that those most interested in teaching such classes in the heart of evangelical America are fairly certain to be committed Christians who might very well have a hard time maintaining religious neutrality. No matter how fair they want to be, it is difficult to hold personal convictions in check, to avoid letting "objective" lessons become occasions for proselytizing.

Sure enough, a major review of the Texas program five years later showed that the temptation to cross over the line had proved too much for most teachers hired to do the job. With notable exceptions here and there, most classes were riddled with bias in favor of conservative Protestant interpretations. Some had imposed the fundamentalist notion that the world was created 6,000 years ago, others that the Bible was written directly by God. From the same pool of sectarian speculation were claims about the "end times," when God would gather up those who had attained Christian salvation. The review's conductor, Dr. Mark Chancey, of Southern Methodist University, scrutinized the fifty-seven districts and three charter schools that taught the Bible during the 2011–2012 school year and found rampant violations of the state's mandate. Among the most vexing was that many of the Bible teachers didn't measure up to state requirements and chose materials for the class that pushed their own religious views.

In a statement issued with his report for the Texas Freedom Network Education Fund, Chancey said his results showed that "Texas isn't giving study of the Bible the respect it deserves. . . . Academically, many of these classes lack rigor and substance, and some seem less interested in cultivating religious literacy than in promoting religious beliefs. Their approach puts their school districts in legal jeopardy and their taxpayers in financial jeopardy."

So far, these and the other campaigns to restore the Bible to the reading diet of America have had little to show for their efforts, except perhaps for the spectacular spread of Bible apps. Hundreds of millions have been downloaded on electronic devices, with no end in sight; yet little is known about their effects on Bible-reading habits compared to their appeal as a novelty to add to an app collection. Some research indicates that most apps are seldom called up after the newness has worn off. Adding the Bible might primarily provide another quick reference source rather than a gateway to deeper involvement. To Bible lovers, that might be a defeat, but in the broader view it isn't as if all has been lost. The Bible hasn't left the territory; it hasn't been exactly rejected or rebuked; at worst, it has been dropped from the starting lineup and sent to the bench, where it can be rediscovered. The pattern of usage suggests that, for a growing portion of the population, the Bible itself is, symbolically speaking, an app instead of a central focus.

Wherever my search has taken me in writing this book, it is clear that the older systems of conveying Bible lore to younger generations of Americans are collapsing or gone altogether. For cultural and religious reasons, the chief teaching instruments — parents and church schools — have been ceasing to function with the same confidence or scope. The weakening of otherworldly faith and the hectic scramble of daily life, among other things, have reduced the urgency of conveying ultimate scriptural truths. The consequences of Charles Taylor's secular age are beyond the capacity of most individuals to avoid; therefore, people of good character and faith are unavoidably affected by the ambivalences of the Zeitgeist. It is a struggle.

The breakdown in transmission has left most young people on their own to discover the Bible or not. Mostly not, as it is turning out, but there are some who do. Emerson Hamsa and Lawrence Waters are seminary students who have found their own paths to the Bible without the institutional props that earlier generations might have had. They are more typical of the hit-or-miss personal odyssey that has become more the rule than the exception — the idiosyncratic journey of the individual rather than that of a nurturing system. At one time, their promptings would have won the support and admiration of society; these days their decisions aren't readily understood or applauded. They are far more alone than their seminary forebears were.

From the first, Emerson impressed me as a young woman of hard-won strength and courage. Those qualities only grew more striking over time. She is forthright, discerning, and boldly engaged in life, a student at Wesley Theological Seminary who arrived there by a circuitous route. Before and during Wesley, she had become engrossed in and enamored of the Hebrew Bible largely on her own. Raised in Christian surroundings, she had a passion for the Hebrew Bible that gradually eased her away from a traditionally Christ-centered view of faith. Rather than reading the Hebrew Bible principally as a foreshadowing of the coming of Christ, she viewed its text "without the imposition of any kind of Christology" that would in any way devalue the "psychology of the Jewish text" by presupposing the future arrival "of a savior." Her sojourn had led her to the open-mindedness of the Unitarian-Universalist Church, in which she prepared for ordination.

Growing up in Poughkeepsie, New York, the oldest of three children of parents who had not long before labored in apple orchards, Emerson was reading at age three and soon after that got hold of a book of Bible stories published by Jehovah's Witnesses (soon after her discovery of the *Dick and Jane* story series). She remembers the catchy illustrations. Her grandmother also read to her from Scripture, and she became aware that the Bible "was the governing text of the family, whether they performed biblical morality or not."

Home life was hard, but she found refuge in a nearby African Methodist Episcopal church, where she said she felt able to be herself. As a lonesome girl who "always read the Bible" by herself, she was asked to teach a Sunday school class of five-year-olds when she was just ten herself. Left largely to her own devices, she saw no need to doubt that Bible stories described real events. Her spiritual imagination got her by. When "troubled" by the question of how Jonah could possibly live in the stomach of a whale, for example, she reasoned that God was "so lovable that even when Jonah was trapped God would make that belly a comfortable place." As she grew into adulthood, she became increasingly aware that modern Biblicists separate fact and fiction throughout the texts. She likewise saw how Scripture's meaning is not fixed but shaped by a particular interpreter. A friend played recordings of sermons by an astute Maryland pastor, and she recognized that he was "doing Biblical interpretation in the sermon."

By her own definition she was a strait-laced teenager who didn't socialize much with her peers. She didn't drink, smoke, or become sexually active. Having been enchanted by Jehovah's Witness literature, she made a bid to become part of that movement, but didn't in the end follow through. Her college years at Marymount were for the most part a respite from the Bible. A major reason was that she was struggling with her sexual identity. Acknowledging her preference for women in her sophomore year of college both confirmed her deepest sensibilities and caused further alienation from some family members.

After graduating with a major in English literature, she taught in public schools for several years, during which her love of the Bible lay relatively dormant. When the opportunity arose to enroll at Wesley to restart that vocational engine, she took it and ran with it. Biblical studies intersected with so much that she ardently cared about, she said, including gender studies, philosophy, and sociology. The Unitarian Universalist climate welcomed Emerson and her same-sex marriage partner and offered her a setting where her dissent from traditional Christianity could have a home. She was assembling a vocation that was unmistakably hers.

*   *   *

The road taken by Lawrence Waters, whose roots are in Boston, to a love of the Bible and enrollment in divinity school was similarly unprogrammed. His first Bible was a child's version with a picture of Noah's ark on the cover, he recalled, but other than the colorful images, it spurred no particular interest. Incentives were present but muted. His mother "read the Bible quietly by herself," he said, but by nature she wasn't inclined to press others to do likewise. His father had been drawn toward the military chaplaincy in the National Guard, but he settled on forming gospel quartets that included himself. Lawrence said he "never saw his father read the Bible," though he went to church now and again, and gospel music was, after all, the Bible lore put to music. Though Lawrence had become an American Baptist, he spent much time among Pentecostal congregations because the religious affections appealed to him, he cherished the Bible, and he rested easy with plain and simple interpretations of it. The kind of Bible scholarship that raised doubts about its origins and meanings was a world apart. Lawrence accepted the way Pentecostals embraced the Bible as a feature of a spiritual home that nurtured him.

Now, in his early thirties, he is a poised second-year student at Emory University's Candler School of Theology, still dealing with a measure of biblical culture shock. It is understandable. He is new to the South and its relatively genteel seminary climate — among other things. He is getting used to it and likes it. Over time, he has come to see greater continuity between his past and his new life at Emory.

In college at the University of Massachusetts, Lawrence was heading for a degree in business until he enrolled in a New Testament course about Jesus taught by Richard Horsley, a highly esteemed professor of the Bible (now retired). The class "awakened" surprising energies in him, he said. By comparison, business school now seemed boring. During roughly the same period, he had become adept at assisting young people to imagine themselves going to college and helping them achieve the grades and pass the tests to make that happen. At UMass he did it through the admissions; in Boston he served a wider community, mostly minority students typically left off the academic escalator. It was in some respects an extension of his church youth work. He made prime use of his own experience. A lack of funds had required him to take eight years to finish college. To earn money to return to school, he'd done a stint in data entry for Blue Cross/ Blue Shield. It gave him extra motivation, he says, to go back to college.

After he graduated and resumed his academic counseling, a friend urged him to try a class related to the Bible at nearby Gordon-Conwell Theological Seminary. He did, and he felt a stronger spark. Next thing, a professor nudged him to apply to a few seminaries, including Duke Divinity School, Harvard Divinity School, Andover Newton, and the school where he ended up, Candler School of Theology. That raised the ante to a whimsical realization: "I just couldn't avoid seminary."

Candler's academic distinction and congeniality were among the reasons he chose to go there. Biblically speaking, the seminary is in the forefront of historical-literary research, which means looking at the texts in vastly more complex patterns of formation and authorship than Lawrence had witnessed before. It gave him a new and, for the most part, welcome approach to Scripture, he thinks. "Nowadays I read the text as flawed," he says. "Let me look at its cultural background and the environment where it was written. At the end of the day it doesn't change my belief that God is real." Some old church friends wondered how that was possible, he continues pointedly. "They think I'm crazy for trying to use reason."

As much as the Bible serves his academic side, it fulfills an even more personal search. It has given him a homeland where he can explore who he is. He has long been aware that, as an African-American man, he has to surrender aspects of himself when seeking to better himself within predominantly white institutions such as college and seminary. It is not surprising that he, like others, has agonized over how much to adapt to a different climate and when, or if, to pull back to his roots after achieving his ends. The Bible belongs to everyone, but in common use the understanding of its teachings naturally skews toward white Christian interpretation. To what extent, Lawrence wondered, would he need to meld with the white establishment to achieve his aims, adopting its thinking and mannerisms without losing his authentic personhood — black and male? How far would he be able to venture out before drowning? Once he had gone so far, was it even possible to remain true to his roots? He came upon such dilemmas from a tradition shared by minority and subordinate people probably from the beginning of time: How do we fit in enough without losing our distinctness?

One of the many levels on which Lawrence has explored these questions involves his emerging relationship with the Bible. Scripture is loaded with examples of the "self" who assumes different poses and identities. Moses was raised by Egyptians, but then returned to his people to lead them; Jacob *became* Israel; Joseph was the classic "outsider" who became a consummate "insider"; Saul, the enemy of Christians, then became one of them — shockingly — on the Damascus Road, thereby acquiring the name Paul; Peter proclaimed himself to be one of Jesus's disciples, but later denied knowing Jesus; Ruth lived among foreigners, having adopted the faith of her beloved mother-in-law, Naomi; Gentiles found themselves to be strangers among the majority of Jews in the earliest churches, perplexed by how much they needed to give up in order to fully belong. And so on. There was much in Scripture about living in two worlds, as Lawrence sometimes feels he does.

He encapsulated that uneasiness in a term paper in which he compares African Americans to Jews who lived under Persian jurisdiction following the Babylonian exile. King Nebuchadnezzar drove the Jews into captivity in Babylon, where they remained until the Persians conquered Babylon and released the captives. The story, told in the Book of Esther, centers on Esther's heroism in rescuing her Jewish kinsfolk from destruction. The Persian king, Ahasuerus, chooses her to be his queen without doing a background check, which would have uncovered her Jewish identity (though that may not have mattered to him). Esther has been raised and looked after by her adoptive father, Mordecai, a devout Jew who served as an attendant to the king. One day Mordecai thwarts a plot by two conspirators to kill the king. The plotters are hanged (though Mordecai is never publicly acknowledged as the crime stopper). In the aftermath, the king appoints a man named Haman as his number one commander. Haman proves to be a power-mad conniver who demands a submissive bow from everyone approaching the gate to the palace. Mordecai, being an unflinching monotheist who refuses to bend to anyone but God, doesn't bend. Haman is furious at Mordecai's noncompliance and vows to kill not only him but all Jews whom he falsely accuses of lawlessness against the king. Mordecai protests this vile scheme by draping himself in sackcloth and sitting at the king's gate. Queen Esther, aware of Haman's evil design against her people, risks her own security by intervening with the king to expose Haman's treachery, identifying herself as belonging to the unjustly treated Jews. An angry King Ahasuerus, now aware that Mordecai has been framed as a prelude to doing away with all Jews, orders Haman to the very gallows that Haman had prepared for Mordecai. The Jews are spared.

Lawrence uses that story as a springboard to compare "dissimulation," by which an outsider participates in the prevailing culture (taking on its language, style, and logic) only enough to gain benefits such as social power, and "assimilation," which results in entering entirely into the dominant culture. To dissimulate can be justified, he reasons, in order to fulfill black potential; assimilation was, for him, an unacceptable rejection of his black heritage. Esther, at a time and circumstance far removed, nonetheless is an example of someone who has adopted the persona of a Persian but proves, via an act of great courage, that she has not left her Jewish identity behind. Lawrence sees useful lessons in that, but he also hears the alarms of friends who warn that the best intentions to remain true to one's origins can easily crumble before the lure of ambition.

Lawrence's paper presents a forum with no rigid conclusions; but it gave him a crack at wrestling with a live issue. In crossing cultural, ethnic, and racial lines, what does count for gain and what for loss? That is a challenge that confronts everyone who wonders what it is like to "live biblically," to let the mind and voice of Scripture mold the ordinary course of daily routines: not just to extract a few rules to live by or to clutch a fistful of sayings as quick fixes, as one might take two Tylenol for a headache, but to figuratively crawl inside of it and allow its summonses to become guiding lights in all of life, not just the private part reserved for "religion." That possibility assumes that clear commonalities do exist, of both effable and ineffable varieties, in a canon-like pattern of meaning that, to modern scholarship, appears to lack any basis in empirical fact. Only the nonrational wings of mysticism deliver that result, and society shows no rush to embrace that.

*   *   *

I have been enough of a woolgatherer in the midst of Bible warriors to believe that such common ground is available if seekers of it show a fair degree of willingness to suspend ironclad commitments to the extremes of hardened literalism or smug pedantry. This would normally be a group effort. It would require a meeting of open minds, free inquiry, and, most of all, relinquishing egoism and its militant dogma to have any chance at all. But I think it could happen — and does happen — when all the "absolutes" of interpretation and all the non-negotiable demands can be set aside enough to allow a subliminal voice to speak out of all those quarrels and the fragmented collection of sixty-six books of Scripture. I don't want to underestimate how difficult it is to drop evangelistic (both religious and academic) and personal agendas, but I have come away from my wanderings with a healthier respect for the value of "plain reading" absent fundamentalism. Which is how it is generally practiced. People look for how the voice of Scripture speaks rather than focusing primarily on whether the facts are true beyond the shadow of a doubt. Whether Jesus actually cured the blind man seems insignificant compared to its expression of compassion.

Perhaps, then, vital consensus on what it means to find light and hope — and to live biblically in that mode of simple piety — is possible. Gleaning the Bible's essence, naïve as that may sound, could coalesce a "mind" that would, as in the early days of the church, challenge the prevailing culture with its own inherent wisdom instead of continuing to mimic and parrot that culture for lack of understanding its own tradition. The secular society has many advantages over those chained by tyranny, but it makes no claim to grasp that particular voice that belongs to Christians through the Bible.

Not so long ago it was commonly assumed that living in America *was* living biblically, but fewer see it that way these days. Both religious pluralism and the tide of secularist thinking have accented differences. On the Christian side, much of what makes America tick — including its cult of personal and material success, economy, and sense of right and wrong — no longer seems to flow naturally from the Bible but seems in conflict with it. Evangelicals, mainline Protestants, and Catholics all have their own laundry lists of society's "evils," and the split between their *professed* values and those in secular society has presumably widened. But, in fact, the two largely share the lifestyle dictated by the profit motive.

Confusion sometimes arises concerning which side exhibits more biblical qualities. Under secular auspices, for example, equality of opportunity and protection of human rights have often led the way for religion. Love of money and possessions is no stranger to the churches; the strongest critiques of the rich-poor gap are apt to come from nonbelievers. Therefore, attuning one's life to the Bible involves perceiving where its consciousness has taken hold, whether in religious or secular life. A rigorous yet open study of the Bible would, in my view, tap an underlying consciousness that is discernible above and beyond endless spats about details and authorship. I realize many regard that as wishful thinking, but I think I've seen it take place on a catch-as-catch-can basis, where something like a deeper spirit has overridden the debates.

Recall the position of Saint Augustine of Hippo. He believed that the Bible's depths are, ultimately, unfathomable, but seeking them is essential. Most questions about Scripture can be answered by simply reading it, he argued. He read it mostly allegorically and recognized multiple interpretations of its text, though he did caution against getting attached to any particular one. "Some people read them [Scriptures] and neglect them," he wrote in *On Christian Doctrine*. "By their reading they profit in knowledge, by their neglect they forfeit understanding."

The reimagining of Bible study in a more holistic direction is part of what the recent "engagement" revival aims to do as a means of reversing biblical illiteracy. The idea is to get beyond its mere trappings, surface meanings, moral abstractions, and rigid formulations to the living heart of it beneath. That movement seems right, but it hasn't yet gained much of a foothold. The stumbling block so often is letting go of those nonnegotiable barriers to fresh thinking that inevitably occupy the human psyche.

I have met many people along the way who are seeking by their own instincts to conform their everyday lives more closely to the Bible, short of aiming for perfection. They want to bring consciousness of Scripture more intentionally to the wear and tear of their demanding routines rather than having it reduced it to a few moral laws. Their striving resembles Lawrence's dilemma: To what extent is it feasible to alter one's core self in order to meet the expectations of another culture without selling out the core self? Being "in" the world but not "of" it? Lawrence sees himself as a prototypical outsider entering a "Eurocentric" world to equip himself to return to his origins. What was that ever-so-subtle point of no return that could pass by without obvious notice? For Bible "livers" in general, when does a rightful pursuit of family well-being become an idolatry of consumerism or the passion for national security become love of war? Once over those lines, is it possible to return? By the same token, when do the churches adopt attitudes and policies that mock the Bible's judgments against bias, privilege, intolerance, or any kind of injustice? How may Lawrence's concept of dissimulation be practiced legitimately — and how not? Or are the independent secular megaforces so powerful that it is impossible to sustain a viable subculture? Deciding how to assess the gains and losses of crossing that border has become increasingly perplexing, but perhaps healthy in terms of building Christian character. It is no longer easy to imagine natural reciprocity between what the Bible teaches and what the American way of life promotes.

Such a dialectic can exist only among those who are biblically literate and open to further study. For the great majority who know little to nothing about it, living biblically either has no meaning or consists of a few detached commandments. The inescapable fact is that individualism, that recurring theme, is shaping every aspect of human behavior, including, of course, treatment of the Bible. Its origins are attributed to a complex web of historical causes, including Protestantism's emphasis on personal salvation, and its effects are both scorned for inculcating a cult of self and celebrated as liberation from collectivist repression of personal gifts and identity. For every complaint that individualism has fractured concern for the common good and fueled a societal zero-sum game, there is gladness for a climate that nurtures individual gifts and allows a wide spectrum of diversity. The term increasingly used to denote the difference between one version and the other is "transformation," a clear indication of growth in spiritual maturity by way of the Bible's beckoning. By their transformation are they known, to paraphrase Scripture.

The main objection is not to individualism that is somehow balanced by spiritual depth and social responsibility, but to strains of it that have gone viral, beyond restraint, the likes of which run afoul of religious standards of humility and compassion. In reality, the constructive forms of individualism have become indistinguishable from the allegedly destructive aspects of it within an economic and political environment where, in effect, there are few limits on self-aggrandizement.

Expecting the Bible to be studied and cultivated within communal settings, which some — like Stanley Hauerwas — believe to be the only way of tapping its fuller meaning, is becoming less and less conceivable on a broad level. It is still happening, but the cultural gravitation is pushing mightily against it. That could be construed as bad news for collective uses of the Bible; or it is potentially good news for personal approaches, such as iPad downloads and programs in the development stages.

*   *   *

Young people are, as always, considered the bellwether. Their success or failure at crossing that historical bridge into a biblical reawakening guided and directed by new technology could usher in a long-range return to Scripture. As of this writing, the jury is expected to be out on that outcome for a long time. A transition is in the works — whatever that turns out to be.

Because young people from evangelical and other conservative churches are in much closer touch with the Bible than are their other religious or nonreligious peers, their relationship with Scripture is a logical place to look for clues. Nobody has better perspective on changes already under way than those who have taught young people and studied their habits. Bible professors are among the keenest observers. Some see profound shifts that have implications not only for the future use of the Bible but for the sources of basic belief.

One common perception is how that juggernaut of individualism is discombobulating the confidence that evangelical young people place in a literal view of the Bible. Several professors independently noted the same thing: that even the most ardently religious students were projecting their own views on the Bible while assuming they were being "objective" and true to the author's intent. As evangelicals, they mostly uphold the Scriptures as infallible; but they reserve to themselves considerable rights to understand it as they see fit, either unaware or unaffected by the contradictions. This paradox was nowhere in my visits seen as a self-conscious attempt to impose subjective meaning but rather as a reflex that had been instilled in their cultural nervous system. And observers hasten to point out that the young people only mirror more sharply what their elders display in varying degrees. Among the most thoughtful observers is Prof. Lynn Cohick, of the Bible faculty of the evangelical citadel Wheaton College. Her affection for students is transparent, her sense of the shifting tide cautionary. "When students say they think of how the Christian faith affects them, it becomes very personal," she told me one afternoon in her campus office. "Part of that is an extreme individualism that they take for granted. That horse is already out of the barn."

A related concern is that these young people increasingly spin their own interpretations of the Bible without feeling a need to read it. They form their own conclusions about what they think — or have been told — through personal "lenses" that filter and channel their preferences and biases. As cohorts of a generation that gives priority to personal opinion, the latest in a line of Americans inclined that way, they are like their religious and nonreligious classmates, having been reared with the mantra of self, self, and more self — without much choice.

Shane Kirkpatrick is rueful about the trends. He is a top-caliber biblical scholar who teaches at Anderson University, the flagship university of the Church of God (Anderson, Indiana). The foundation of learning and belief that has given the church its character is eroding, he thinks, without anything cohesive to replace it. Like other scholars, he is chagrined at the growing numbers of students who claim authority over texts they've rarely, if ever, read — and never studied. "There's less familiarity with the Bible and a definite reduction in biblical literacy," he says. "Even at a church-related school like ours, lots of our students know nothing about the Bible except what they're told about." The church tie can make things worse, he adds, "because their minimal awareness of the Bible and strong personal feelings about it combine to result in firmly held convictions about it." Errors are harder to correct because, unlike students starting from scratch, "they think they know the answers."

The inflated subjectivity of our time carries over into the academic study of the Bible. "Students want to make arguments about the Bible that are historically grounded and in keeping with the author's intention," Kirkpatrick continues. "But even in cases in which their interpretation of what the Bible says is clearly not what the author intended, they say, 'Yes, but this is my understanding,' and they wish to leave it at that." Left unchecked, Kirkpatrick believes, that refusal to budge from self-imposed meaning further hampers progress toward meeting the greatest challenge to the authority of the Bible, which is, according to him, the power of modernist rationality, empiricism, and materialism. These are all problems that have come into the church by way of the Enlightenment, and Kirkpatrick claims that evangelicals have avoided confronting the Enlightenment. To him, this accounts for the fact that the Bible is often being taught as a mere "artifact."

Being stuck in subjectivity further delays the search for a "workable solution" between the two explanations of reality — biblical and secular — that could embrace elements and concepts of both. Meanwhile, Kirkpatrick regretfully envisions generations of "self"-oriented students continuing to be caught up in this unresolved conflict, "trying to read the Bible themselves in this trouble-filled world in which the biblical text alone seems less and less able to handle it."

Dependency on the Bible as the means of gaining the substance of faith, therefore, appears to be evaporating even among evangelicals. It is ever more likely that those who were introduced to the breadth of Scripture in college courses, for example, already had made up their minds about it based on fragments and images of its alleged content on the Internet, film, and social media. Prof. Jennifer Knust, of Boston University, is among those who report that more students are arriving in courses on the Bible having "absorbed a lot of cultural notions about the Bible" before studying it, especially Facebook impressions of Jesus that tend to stick, no matter how unfounded they might be. The logical remedy is to compare these impressions with the Bible itself, but that requires reading the Bible, which generally is a step too large.

It is impossible to exaggerate how dramatically the bottom is falling out of the last outposts of a "high" view of the Bible, once considered the essential grounding point. The implications can be debated, but the collapse seems beyond question. In setting after setting where conservative

Christian young people gather, the picture is remarkably similar. Students are passionate about their faith, but their faith is less grounded in the source that Martin Luther called *sola Scriptura*. Members of the church, from one end of the age spectrum to the other — albeit in varying degrees — march to a different drummer, or drummers. Having received their convictions from extrabiblical sources or hearsay, they are apparently prepared to carry on what amounts to a new expression of Christianity largely without the Bible — still to be determined.

The very nemesis imputed to the Religious Left by the Religious Right — relativism and cafeteria Christianity — is riding a wave of individualism within the evangelical camp. It has the potential to recast the foundations of ordinary belief, yet it has received little attention in the churches. It remains mostly subliminal. Two seasoned Bible professors at Huntington University in Indiana, a doughty little Christian college founded by the Church of United Brethren in Christ, speak candidly and dolefully about this putative revolution from their corner of the evangelical culture. One is Prof. Mark Fairchild, the veteran chair of the Bible department and an accomplished scholar who is also recognized nationally as a top-notch judge of tennis matches. He teaches with panache and a touch of whimsy, and he has spent summers digging for religious artifacts in Turkey. The other is Prof. Kent Eilers, a relative newcomer to Huntington (with a PhD from Notre Dame) who oversees theology and adds both pastoral and scholarly depth to the campus.

Over several years they have seen decisive changes in the student body and have arrived at a general consensus about where things now stand. Churches, like other institutions, are usually slow to catch on to the "signs of the times," as Scripture puts it, and often deny the existence or influence of trends they don't want to see. Fairchild and Eilers have overcome any silver-lining fantasies they may have entertained (there is no hint that they actually have entertained them) out of a conviction that the matter compels nothing less than honesty, disrupting though that may be.

Highlights of that conversation began with Fairchild declaring that the college has become "almost part of a postbiblical culture" in which students "really don't know the Bible well at all," to the point where many church people would be "shocked by the low level of biblical literacy" on campus.

Eilers fills in details. Most of their students have grown up in Christian homes and know a little "about" the Bible, as compared with knowing what the text says, having gathered "bits and pieces in sermons, worship and songs"; but generally they have scant knowledge of how its sections fit together in a canonical pattern, as their churches officially teach. One cause of this disarray, Fairchild continues, is that young people "superimpose a modern way of thinking that touches on the nuanced American view of 'freedom,' which did not exist in the ancient world" of the Bible. They then simply assume that Jesus stood for that kind of personal choice.

Eilers relates that to how students picture their own "spirituality" and their relationship to Christ as a side effect of their "rugged individualism," meaning that they "don't need anybody" but themselves to understand what Scripture means. The reality, Eilers says, is that "looking back at the New Testament, we see that we need each other and we're connected," a lesson that tends to get lost in the idea of self-sufficiency. "The bottom line is that we can't live by ourselves as Christians," he counterclaims.

Fairchild concurs: the belief that "truth is subjective" has become commonplace. Whereas, in the past, a student was expected to back up a theory with proof from the Bible, Fairchild says that now the answer is more likely to be, "That's what the spirit tells me."

"Take a flash-point issue — homosexuality," Eilers says. "There is real confusion when it comes to looking closely at how the Bible speaks to that. So it usually boils down to passions and feelings instead." Opinions about the Bible's content, from students lacking firsthand acquaintance with it, are increasingly "nontraditional, ahistorical, and the fruit of their parents."

Fairchild thinks that young people mirror a broad-based sellout of Christian beliefs to the American culture's emphases on material growth, finances, and use of religion for personal therapy. Eilers agrees that more Christians these days consider the Bible important "predominantly as therapeutic reading," and they corral portions of it for the sake of self-help and "feel-good" uplift.

All this, of course, makes a shambles of inerrancy. Fairchild defines the conundrum as a sleight-of-hand attempt "to say it's infallible without describing it as inerrant." He offers a baseball analogy: "There's one out in the bottom of the ninth inning, instead of two," he says in reference to the discovery of a textual error. "So you say, 'It's just a small detail.'" Rightly or wrongly, teachers say, students vote for inerrancy as a salute to their heritage, but they believe that everyone sees Scripture through his or her own cultural, personal glasses, depending on the circumstances. Tolerance of everyone's own individual interpretation is among the values they share with much of the surrounding society.

*   *   *

Tragic as the crumbling of the old order may be to those who rely on it and maintain it, fairness demands another opinion. Moving the Bible to the periphery of Christian life may be foreshadowing the death of one process of faith formation in favor of the arrival of another one that befits the technological revolution. Mysterious transitions are not unknown to Christianity, and perhaps there is one aborning that will usher in a new age of vitality.

Whatever the next stage, the culture that religion partakes of is in the throes of being uprooted and reoriented to such an astonishing degree that it sets minds spinning in a way that is reminiscent of Alvin Toffler's *Future Shock*. Tom Bergler, a colleague of Fairchild and Eilers at Huntington College, has studied the recent effects of cultural forces on the church's youth culture. The title of his book on the subject is telling: *The Juvenilization of American Christianity*. After World War II, Bergler argues, both Catholic and Protestant churches, in their own ways, mimicked society's urge to indulge young people for consumer purposes and other reasons. Young people were seen as a subculture that took longer and longer to become part of adult society. Churches expected little of them as serious students or critics of the faith, and the elders refrained from challenging or nurturing their charges in theology or the Bible, helping to ease their way into "me-generation" thinking. That, in turn, lent itself to the isolating, privatizing effects of digital technology. Young people did not find role models for spiritual growth and Bible maturity among adults, and hence they were left to their own devices. Christianity has been, in effect, dumbed down for church young people, and over six decades the habit has thinned the ranks of informed or curious churchgoers. But again, it is at least possible that there was a latency factor at work, a germination of unresolved inquiry and bottled-up enthusiasm that would find an outlet in new media or some other form.

Whatever the current restiveness and gestation may lead to, it will inevitably circle back to "biblical engagement," the unifying, animating purpose that brought about the Forum of Bible Agencies summit meeting on biblical illiteracy in 2011. Among those activists was Prof. Philip Collins of Taylor University's recently established Center for Scripture Engagement, a research and training facility he codirects with Prof. Steven Bird, a sociologist. Prof. Collins says that he has read the Bible every day since he was twelve years old and has eagerly soaked up its contents. But something has been missing, he says in retrospect. "I was told to read the Bible and pray," he says, "but not how to read it as a source of spiritual formation and growth." The Center would seek understanding of what students and others think about the Bible, to be sure, but more importantly, how to encourage them to approach it to transform their lives. A formidable task, perhaps, but he thinks it lies at the heart of engaging the Bible at its deepest levels. He knows from his own experience how the buzz and whir of daily distractions keeps that from happening. Prof. Bird thinks that the time is ripe for students looking for direction in life to rediscover that ancient treasure trove of the spirit. Young people have been born into a time when practically all of the coordinates of existence are in flux. Christians have generally moved from biblical "absolutism," where "all the answers" are laid out — with little challenge — to a "postmodern" phase, where there are no reliable answers or truths, to an emerging third stage, where "young people look for something other than formulas, certainty, and nihilism. They are searching, and the Bible remains a resource."

Collins refers to the evidence that those who get under the skin of Scripture and let themselves marinate in it are found to be more spiritually mature as a result. But that is sometimes billed as an achievement rather than commended as a way of life. The evidence that when people "encounter the Bible, they sense that the Holy Spirit is with them" has stopped him in his tracks and has changed the way he talks about the Bible: he speaks of it as a living entity rather than a repository of information and prosaic conviction. While the Bible will always be the means to an end rather than the end itself, he says, "When I engage the Bible, I engage God."

Epilogue

Peggy and Andy Brimer occupy the default position on the American Bible landscape. It is the place just beyond doctrine, theology, and high and low views of Scripture. The Brimers aren't breaking new ground in Bible scholarship, treating it as a Marine Corps manual or reducing it to an instrument of moral crusading. Nor do they have the slightest desire to be poster parents for Christian family perfection. They aren't preaching, arguing, judging, or boasting. They are living the life they believe God has called them to, doing their best to be Christians in accordance with how the Bible leads them without trying to be special. In secular America, that makes them rather extraordinary. Whether or not anyone else is reading the Bible, they are reading it and getting something out of it, not so much mindful of whether it is infallible but aware of its appeal to a more real, more elusive standard that is sometimes called the "rule of faith."

Their three winsome young daughters — Stephanie, 15; Vivian, 12; and Naomi, 8 — are wholly bound up in that covenant. They collectively pray and read portions of the Bible before breakfast; Peggy oversees the children's never-far-from-Scripture home schooling during the day; Andy plies his trade as a chemist in a company that produces generic medications for nonprofits. Church activities summon them nearly every day and some evenings. On top of that, Peggy runs the regional division of the National Bible Bee, a highly competitive test of biblical knowledge that was once a staple of church summer camps. Though less prevalent now, it is no less demanding. Passing the regional test requires memorization of hundreds of verses and understanding what they mean in the setting in which they appear. The summer before, nearly one hundred young people from primary school age through high school read the assigned book of Scripture every single day, completed thoughtful exercises, and were tested every two weeks; they converged on the cozy Brimer home to do so. The rite of passage includes oral and written exams administered by adults. The results this particular year were generally impressive, but such was the formidable competition nationally that no one in the group qualified for the grand finale in Nashville, a spectacle on the level of a major television quiz show.

For all the hard work and pressure, Peggy loves the process for the priority it gives to the Bible over the common leisure activities such as music and sports (her kids *do* take piano lessons, she is proud to say) and the togetherness it fosters among parents and children over the course of nearly two months. For her and Andy, it is a meeting of parents like themselves who share a common commitment to putting the Bible in the forefront of their home lives.

They live in a modest bungalow built to house workers in the bustling industries that once were the community's economic lifeblood. It just about accommodates the needs of a family with three growing daughters. Stephanie, tall and thin, shows hints of normal teenage self-consciousness; she is a quick study who memorizes verses and grasps concepts easily. Vivian, inward and exuding warmth, has visual aptitudes that come from her artistic traits. She has, for example, picked up Power Point on her own at church. Naomi is outwardly carefree; as the youngest, she is in some ways encouraged to be carefree. Whether consciously or not, she has picked up on the freedom to be the clever, insouciant "child," drawing on her store of natural charm to delight her admirers. Each of the girls is engaging in her own way; they are also just regular kids with quirks and troubles and annoyances. Their parents, on counsel of the Bible, don't believe in indulging children in self-esteem. They believe that kids have foibles like everyone else does, and they are in equal need of reform and redemption.

Peggy and Andy met at Houghton College, a church-related school that Peggy chose for its spiritual character over nearby Hamilton College. They were smart, genial, and dedicated to becoming Christian, though they weren't always sure what that entailed. Peggy, short and with her dark hair pulled back in a ponytail, has happy eyes that mirror her intelligence and an animated, outgoing demeanor. In choosing a college, she had wanted spiritual grounding that was more solid than what her family's faith provided. Andy, whose shy expression partly disguises his confident and upbeat nature, says his religious upbringing likewise consisted of a nominal church-going home without much substance, leaving him, as a college student, also searching for deeper meaning. They married before they had found answers. For years after college, Peggy taught mathematics; Andy, with a master's degree in chemistry, found his way toward work that entailed service.

As they continued to plumb the Bible's depths, their deepening faith strengthened their resolve to build their entire individual and collective lives around their newfound spiritual beliefs and practices. They see the opposite all around them: fragmentation of existence into private and public, work and leisure, business and religion, everyday pragmatism and scriptural ethics. They feel it incumbent upon themselves to strive for integration, integrity, and thoroughness. Aspiring to their vision of unity to them means saying no to the lures of egotism and the cultural gods of success and materialism. During one stretch, they led a middle-school ministry at their conservative, evangelical church and were shocked at how little the children in their care knew about the Bible. They had stored up some "sayings and big stories," Peggy said, "but none of the understanding of who God is, which comes only through really knowing his word."

In yearning to avoid that hazard, they stake out higher expectations for themselves and their daughters, not from wanting to be "better than" or "right," they hasten to say, but to be true to their calling. Rather than being known in church circles as "the couple that's got it together," Andy says with a note of self-deprecation, "We want to live for God by learning his will for us in the Bible — so that we can praise him in everything we do."

In some church settings, that would indicate an insular mentality of "us" against "them." Not so with the Brimer family that I experienced. Theirs is a joyful household, leavened with humor, warmly open to the world rather than wary of it, firm in their convictions but generous in spirit. They have sheltered their girls from much of the world's harshness while endeavoring to prepare them to be part of it, raising them, as Andy says, "to be able to ride the rapids later in life." Humility is big, the steady reminder that they can only do it with the help of God. In a society of ego inflation, where "self-esteem" is a fetish that disguises the sinful side of life, they feel a huge challenge.

The Brimers have chosen to live by unconventional beliefs in a way that appears decidedly conventional, without pretense or grand predictions. If they don't somehow manifest those beliefs in day-to-day interactions with others, they assume that their faith will be for naught. To portray them as model Christians would be unfair to them; I'm quite sure it would make them shudder. Yet they do represent a real company of Americans who demonstrate the devotion and grit to take the Bible seriously in a society that rarely does that anymore, however one might agree or disagree with how they interpret it. More liberal Christians might object to their views on gender, creationism, sexual morality, and gay marriage, but they might be taken by the Brimers' example of what the gospel means on the grandest level. Some might call it grace that transcends the tensions and rifts that divide Bible interpreters. They exemplify Saint Augustine's observation that there is no substitute for reading and digesting the Book.

They foresee the persecution of believers sometime up ahead, but they aren't engulfed in apocalyptic thinking. On the contrary, they are full of hope and trust in the present. "What matters to us," Andy muses, "is our relationship to the Lord, so that no matter what the crisis — job loss, sickness, or whatever — we don't make it the most important thing. The Lord will take care of us."

Selected Sources

Ahlstrom, Sidney. *A Religious History of the American People*. 2nd ed. New Haven: Yale University Press, 2004.

Baden, Joel. *The Historical David: The Real Life of an Invented Hero*. New York: HarperCollins, 2013.

Bell, Rob. *Love Wins: A Book about Heaven, Hell, and the Fate of Every Person Who Ever Lived*. New York: HarperOne, 2012.

Bergler, Thomas E. *The Juvenilization of American Christianity*. Grand Rapids: Eerdmans, 2012.

Berlinerblau, Jacques. "What's Wrong with the Society of Biblical Literature?" *Chronicle of Higher Education* (2006).

Borg, Marcus. *Convictions: How I Learned What Matters Most*. New York: HarperCollins, 2014.

———. *Jesus: A New Vision; Spirit, Culture, and the Life of Discipleship*. New York: HarperCollins, 1991.

Buechner, Frederick. *The Clown in the Belfry*. San Francisco: HarperSanFrancisco, 1992.

Capon, Robert Farrar. *Between Noon and Three: Romance, Law and the Outreach of Grace*. Grand Rapids: Eerdmans, 1997.

Cox, Harvey. *The Secular City: Secularization and Urbanization in Theological Perspective*. New York: Macmillan, 1965.

Curtis, Finbarr. "Speaking of the Nation: William Jennings Bryan, Al Smith, and the Idioms of American Populism." PhD dissertation, Vanderbilt University, 2000.

Ehrman, Bart. *Forged: Writing in the Name of God — Why the Bible's Authors Are Not Who We Think They Are*. New York: HarperCollins, 2011.

———. *Misquoting Jesus: The Story Behind Who Changed the Bible and Why*. New York: HarperCollins, 2007.

Enns, Peter. *The Bible Tells Me So*. New York: HarperCollins, 2014.

———. *Inspiration and Incarnation*. Grand Rapids: Baker, 2005.

Evans, Rachel Held. *Evolving in Monkeytown: How a Girl Who Knew All the Answers Learned to Ask the Questions.* Grand Rapids: Zondervan, 2010.

Gould, Stephen Jay. *Rocks of Ages: Science and Religion in the Fullness of Life.* New York: Ballantine, 1999.

Hadaway, Kirk, and Penny Long Marler. "Did You Really Go to Church This Week? Behind the Polling Data." *Christian Century,* May 6, 1998.

Hadaway, Kirk, Penny Long Marler, and Mark Chaves. "What the Polls Don't Show: A Closer Look at U.S. Church Attendance." *American Sociological Review* 58 (December 1993): 6.

Hauerwas, Stanley. *Unleashing the Scripture.* Nashville: Abingdon, 1993.

Hendel, Ronald. "Farewell to SBL: Faith the Reason in Biblical Studies." *Biblical Archaeological Review* (July/August 2010).

Johnson, Luke Timothy. "The Jesus Seminar's Misguided Quest for the Historical Jesus." *The Christian Century* 113 (January 3, 1996).

Kroll, Woodrow. *Taking Back the Good Book: How America Forgot the Bible and Why It Matters to You.* New York: Crossway, 2007.

Legaspi, Michael C. *The Death of Scripture and the Rise of Biblical Studies.* Oxford: Oxford University Press, 2011.

Lindsell, Harold. *The Battle for the Bible.* Grand Rapids: Zondervan, 1975.

Mantel, Hilary. *Wolf Hall.* London: Fourth Estate, 2009.

McDonald, Lee M., and James M. Sanders, eds. *The Canon Debate.* Peabody, MA: Hendrickson, 2002.

Miles, Margaret. *Seeing and Believing: Values and Religion in Movies.* Boston: Beacon, 1996.

Noll, Mark, and Nathan Hatch. *The Bible in America.* Oxford: Oxford University Press, 1982.

Pascal, Blaise. *Pensées.* New York: Penguin, 1995.

Schutte, Flip. Review of Lee M. McDonald and James M. Sanders, eds., *The Canon Debate. HTS Teologiese Studies / Theological Studies* 60, no. 4 (2004): 1513-23.

Smith, Christian. *The Bible Made Impossible: Why Biblicism Is Not a Truly Evangelical Reading of Scripture.* Grand Rapids: Brazos, 2011.

Smith, James K. A. *How (Not) to Be Secular: Reading Charles Taylor.* Grand Rapids: Eerdmans, 2014.

Stafford, Tim. "A Tale of Two Scientists: What Really Happened 'In the Beginning.'" *Christianity Today* 56 (July-August 2012).

Stetson, Chuck, and Cullen Schippe. *The Bible and Its Influence.* BLP Publishing, 2005.

Taylor, Charles. *A Secular Age.* Cambridge, MA: Harvard University Press, 2007.

Village, Andrew. *The Bible and Lay People.* Burlington, VT: Ashgate, 2007.

Wilkins, Michael J., and J. P. Moreland, eds. *Jesus Under Fire.* Grand Rapids: Zondervan, 1996.

Wright, Melanie. *Religion and Film: An Introduction.* New York: I. B. Tauris, 2007.

Wuthnow, Robert. *Inventing American Religion.* New York: Oxford University Press, 2015.

Index